# Public-Private Partnerships: Improving Urban Life

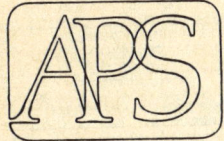

Proceedings of
The Academy of
Political Science

Volume 36
Number 2

ISSN 0065-0684

Edited by Perry Davis

The Academy of Political Science
*In conjunction with the*
New York City Partnership

New York, 1986

Copyright © 1986 by The Academy of Political Science

*All rights reserved*

Library of Congress Catalog Card Number 86-73103

Cover design by Cynthia Brady

Printed by Capital City Press, Montpelier, Vermont

# Dedication

While planning this volume, a number of us realized that our work together and much of our professional association with one another was the result of the influence of Professor Robert H. Connery, president of the Academy of Political Science and professor emeritus of public law and government in Columbia University. It is Bob Connery who as a professor and a colleague encouraged us in many ways—he sparked our interest in local government and urban affairs, and he connected many of us to the "real" world. Bob Connery is a wise man, adviser, colleague, and friend; our admiration and respect for him and his good work has continued to grow. He brought many of us together once again in the Partnership conference and in these essays that resulted from the conference. For these reasons, and for many more, we dedicate this volume to Professor Robert H. Connery.

FRANK J. MACCHIAROLA
*President and Chief Executive Officer*
*New York City Partnership*

# Contents

Preface ix

Contributors xi

Why Partnerships? Why Now? 1
    *Perry Davis*

## A POLITICAL PERSPECTIVE ON RECENT TRENDS

Public-Private Partnerships in the Carter Years 4
    *Katharine C. Lyall*

Private-Sector Initiatives in the Reagan Administration 14
    *Renée A. Berger*

## VIEWS FROM DIFFERENT SECTORS, DIFFERENT FUNCTIONS

A Panel Discussion 31
    *Ellen Sulzberger Straus, Fletcher Byrom,*
    *Neal R. Peirce, Charles Hughes, and Federico Peña*

The Role of the University in Public-Private Partnerships 47
    *Ronald C. Kysiak*

Partnerships and Schools 60
    *Susan D. Otterbourg and Michael Timpane*

Partnerships and Public Policy Advocacy 74
    *James P. Gifford*

Partners for Downtown Development: Creating a New Central
Business District in Brooklyn                                           87
    *Perry Davis*

Partnership New South Style: Central Atlanta Progress                  100
    *Clarence N. Stone*

Partnerships for Housing                                               111
    *Kathryn Wylde*

## PARTNERSHIP DOS AND DON'TS

Ingredients for Successful Partnerships: The New York City Case        122
    *David Rockefeller*

Managing Partnerships: A CEO's Perspective                             127
    *Frank J. Macchiarola*

Partnerships Redefined: Chicago's New Opportunities                    137
    *Donald Haider*

The Future of Public-Private Partnerships                              150
    *William S. Woodside*

Index                                                                  155

# Preface

This volume deals with innovative methods of meeting social and economic needs—public-private partnerships. Leaders in many communities have responded to opportunities for cooperation between the public and private sectors in various ways. From one city to another, specific conditions have determined the nature of particular partnerships and their operations; yet differences, as well as similarities, offer opportunities to learn from an exchange of information from various perspectives.

Most of the experience on which these essays draw was attained while the Federal government was substantially reducing its support of local government and social programs. Inevitably, these changes complicated the immediate problems and highlighted the desirability of mobilizing local talent from business, government, and nonprofit organizations. The volume thus provides invaluable information that can serve in the continuing development of partnerships throughout the country.

The Academy of Political Science undertook this project with the enthusiastic support of Dr. Frank J. Macchiarola, president and chief executive officer of the New York City Partnership, and a member of the Academy's board of directors. Dr. Perry Davis, a senior consultant to the Partnership, directed the project.

Financing was provided by the American Can Company Foundation and the Alfred P. Sloan Foundation. A conference on 13 June 1986 benefited from the cooperation of the Citizens Forum/National Municipal League, the Conference Board, the International Downtown Association, and the U.S. Conference of Mayors. The Academy wishes to express its thanks to these organizations, to the authors of essays in this volume, and to others who have participated.

The views expressed in this volume are those of the authors and not necessarily those of any organizations with which they are associated. The Academy of Political Science serves as a forum for the development and dissemination of opinion on public-policy questions, but it does not make recommendations on political and social issues.

Finally, the Academy is indebted to William Farr, Brian Keizer, Eric Banks, and Ingrid Sterner for skillfully editing the manuscripts and for supervising the production of this volume.

C. LOWELL HARRISS
*Executive Director*

# Contributors

RENÉE A. BERGER is president, TEAMWORKS, Inc., a management-consulting firm that assists organizations in creating partnerships. She served as division director, Partnerships, President's Task Force on Private Sector Initiatives. She is coeditor, with R. Scott Fosler, of *Public-Private Partnerships in American Cities*.

FLETCHER BYROM, retired chairman and chief executive officer, Koppers Company, is immediate past chairman, Committee on Economic Development, and chairman, Public Education Fund.

PERRY DAVIS is president, Perry Davis Associates, a firm specializing in economic development via public-private partnerships. He is a senior consultant, New York City Partnership, and former director, Office of Funded Programs, New York City Board of Education.

JAMES P. GIFFORD is vice president, Public Issues, New York City Partnership, and executive vice president, New York Chamber of Commerce and Industry. He is a former legislative representative, Board of Education of the City of New York.

DONALD HAIDER is professor of public management, Kellogg Graduate School of Management, Northwestern University. He has served as budget director and chief financial officer, City of Chicago. He is the author of *When Governments Come to Washington: Mayors, Governors, and Intergovernmental Lobbying*.

C. LOWELL HARRISS is professor emeritus of economics, Columbia University; executive director, the Academy of Political Science; and associate, Lincoln Institute of Land Policy. He has written extensively on government finance and on economic policy.

CHARLES HUGHES is president, Local 372, American Federation of State, County and Municipal Employees (AFSCME), and vice president, Consumer Assembly of New York. He has served on the charter commission of the Democratic National Committee and on the executive board of the Coalition of Black Trade Unionists.

RONALD C. KYSIAK is executive director, Evanston Inventure, a nonprofit, economic-development corporation formed by the City of Evanston, Illinois, Northwestern University, and the city's ten largest businesses. From 1979 through 1984, he was director of economic development, City of New Haven, Connecticut.

KATHARINE C. LYALL is executive vice president, University of Wisconsin System, and professor of economics, University of Wisconsin, Madison. She served as deputy assistant secretary for economic affairs, U.S. Department of Housing and Urban Development, from 1977 to 1979. She is the author of *Microeconomic Problems of the 70s*.

FRANK J. MACCHIAROLA, former chancellor of the New York City School system, is president and chief executive officer, New York City Partnership, Inc.

SUSAN D. OTTERBOURG is consultant and president, Delman Educational Communications. She has served as the coordinator of the First and Second National Symposiums on Partnerships in Education, sponsored by the President's Advisory Council on Private Sector Initiatives. She is the author of *School Partnerships Handbook: How to Set up and Administer Programs with Business, Government, and Your Community*.

NEAL R. PEIRCE, whose column has appeared in more than 150 newspapers, is syndicated by the Washington Post Writers Group. He is a founder and contributing editor of the *National Journal*. The most recent of his numerous books is *The Book of America: Inside 50 States Today*.

FEDERICO PEÑA is mayor of Denver, Colorado. He has served as legal counsel for the Chicano Education Project and the Mexican American Legal Defense Fund.

DAVID ROCKEFELLER is chairman, New York City Partnership; chairman, The Americas Society; and chairman, The Rockefeller Group. He is former chairman and chief executive officer, Chase Manhattan Bank. He is the author of *Creative Management in Banking* and *Unused Resources and Economic Waste*.

CLARENCE N. STONE is professor of government and politics, University of Maryland. He is the author of *Economic Growth and Neighborhood Discontent*.

ELLEN SULZBERGER STRAUS is a partner, Straus Communications, and chairperson, New York City Partnership Executive Committee. She has served as chair, Communications Commission, President's Task Force on Private Sector Initiatives.

MICHAEL TIMPANE is president, Teachers College, Columbia University. He is also chairman, Executive Council of the Center for Education and Employment.

WILLIAM S. WOODSIDE, chairman, American Can Company, is a member of the board of directors, the Academy of Political Science.

KATHRYN WYLDE is president, Housing Partnership Development Corporation at the New York City Partnership.

# Why Partnerships? Why Now?

PERRY DAVIS

Public-private partnerships are not a new phenomenon. One hundred and fifty years ago Alexis de Tocqueville, as noted elsewhere in this volume, cited extragovernmental associations as America's legacy to democracy. Donald Haider points out in his essay on partnerships in Chicago that the very look of that city reflects a plan designed by a public-private partnership in 1909. The Commercial Club of Chicago, comprising the city's most prominent business leaders, asked Daniel Burnham to draft the Chicago Plan, which guided the city's economic and physical growth for decades thereafter. In the 1940s the Allegheny Conference for Community Development was formed in Pittsburgh. It continues to function today as one of the most vibrant examples of public-private partnerships dedicated to improved education and economic development in this country. In St. Louis, Southwestern Bell has been an active supporter of school-business partnerships for more than twenty years. Then why the current flurry of interest in public-private partnerships?

Before that question is addressed, it will be useful to describe some of the elements that are inherent in partnerships and to consider the nature of the heightened interest in these institutions.

First, public-private partnerships often begin as partnerships between businesses or business leaders. Their collaboration precedes the more formal stage of partnership when the private, nonprofit, and public sectors actively engage in shared projects and programs designed to marshal maximum resources and to share risks for the benefit of the community. At the start, business leaders come together in the belief that their support of some civic need requires extraordinary action; that it is no longer sufficient for businesses to display good citizenship by merely paying taxes, employing local residents, and sometimes engaging in philanthropic behavior. An urban crisis, the near bankruptcy of New York City, the Chicago riots, the deterioration of waterfront Baltimore: these situations mobilized visionary business leaders like David Rockefeller and James Rouse to lead a private-sector collaborative for the common good of their city.

Of course, such efforts yield successes insofar as they engage the supportive resources of public agencies and political leaders and as they enlist the help of universities, nonprofit groups, and labor unions. Thus partnerships are born.

This heightened social consciousness of business leaders need not be motivated by simple altruism. Corporate America needs a vital urban environment in order to prosper. Its labor pool and its market base need well-educated, economically secure, properly housed, urban residents. A crumbling social infrastructure — just like a deteriorating physical infrastructure — makes a poor environment in which businesses and business markets can thrive. Peter Drucker took the concept of "enlightened self-interest" a step further on the economic scale. For Drucker, partnerships must and usually can make good business sense: "Only if business learns to convert the major social challenges facing developed societies today into novel and profitable business opportunities can we hope to surmount these challenges in the future."[1]

Second, as partnerships require novel business approaches to civic needs, so does government require a fresh view of its role. Traditionally, the business community sees city hall as a tax collector and semiefficient provider of municipal services. The public sector's image of itself is not much different. As a public-private partnership is launched, the government usually adopts an evolutionary view of its function. Clean streets, improved schools, and crime-free neighborhoods become a prerequisite for new economically defined concerns — such as viable redevelopment sites, and an enhanced labor pool — expressed by the business community. Additionally, city hall may find itself involved in the most direct economic-development activities — the sale and redevelopment of publicly held land, job-specific career education in the public schools, and tax abatements, business loans, and grants specifically designed to spur business and real estate development.

Thus the most significant element inherent in partnerships is an evolving sense of civic roles. Corporations exceed their common role as tax-generators and employers; they are school joiners, job-trainers, downtown revitalizers, and much more. Government becomes more than just a tax collector and service provider; it serves as a real estate developer, business lender, labor-pool enhancer, and so on. With new roles and responsibilities clear to both sectors, the ingredient of collaboration is added to the recipe, and an improved urban condition is the result.

The breadth and variety of essays and contributors in this volume vividly demonstrate why partnerships have become so topical:

- Formal partnership organizations are being formed in an increasing number of cities. While many of the essays in this volume focus on the New York City Partnership, there are also case studies and references to partnership activities in Atlanta, Chicago, Boston, Denver, New Haven, Evanston, and many other cities. The impetus for partnerships is coming from the White House and state houses throughout the country, and major cities without partnerships are now the exception rather than the rule.

- The kinds of people forming, leading, and participating in partnerships represent a wide array of sectors and interests. In this volume, the mayor of Denver, Federico Peña, is joined by a national columnist, a labor leader, and a retired corporate chief executive officer in a panel discussion focusing on partnerships from a multisector perspective. Similar coalitions of traditional urban adversaries have joined forces to form successful partnerships from coast to coast.

- The growing number of functional areas of urban life being addressed by partnerships includes housing needs, the improvement of primary and secondary education, public-policy formation, downtown commercial development, and high-technology business growth. At the same time, there are heightened expectations that partnerships will be able to solve more problems and generate success as defined by jobs, profits, downtown revitalization, and generally improved urban life.

In sum, more people from more diverse parts of society and in more cities are creating formal partnership organizations to address a vast array of urban concerns. In addition, partnerships are increasingly capturing media attention. They are spawning entrepreneurial activity in the form of associations and companies devoted exclusively to partnership support and development. On the academic level, an increasing number of books and articles are examining partnerships, and special interdisciplinary schools (at the University of Colorado at Denver and at Harvard, for example) are being created to study the phenomenon.

Thus while we can understand why partnerships are in vogue, the very reasons for increased attention raise fears that must be allayed or at least addressed. Partnerships must not be merely a fad and should never be seen as a panacea. Thoughtful people must address partnerships in thoughtful ways. Until more empirical evidence is acquired, case studies, such as those in this volume, remain the clearest way to view the topic. What these cases show again and again is that partnership options are not easily arrived at. True multisector collaboration is difficult and often faces numerous pitfalls. Much more continues to separate public and private-sector cultures than to unite them.

A consistent theme throughout the essays in this volume is the problem faced by business and government when partnerships seek to address social needs intensified by cuts in public budgets. Both David Rockefeller and William S. Woodside warn of the inherent dangers when partnerships are seen as budget gap fillers. But captains of industry and public-sector leaders share a common vision that partnerships are vital for the future of urban America, that the give and take between the public, private, and nonprofit sectors will heighten the sensitivity of all citizens to the problems and opportunities of urban civilization. Sometimes the added resources and support of business leaders can be the catalyst for real change. Sometimes the proper role of business is vociferously to demand that the public sector provide additional resources or do its job better. In either case, new roles and new opportunities abound.

NOTE

1. Peter F. Drucker, "Doing Good to Do Well: The New Opportunities for Business Enterprise," in *Public Private Partnerships: New Opportunities for Meeting Social Needs*, ed. Harvey Brooks, Lance Liebman, and Corinne S. Schelling (Cambridge, Mass.: Ballinger, 1984), 287.

# Public-Private Partnerships in the Carter Years

KATHARINE C. LYALL

The public-private partnership, developed as a policy tool during the Carter administration, was an invention born of necessity. National economic conditions that the Carter administration inherited were volatile and unsettling. The economy was growing and unemployment was at low levels; but inflation, fed by an energy crisis, was about 12 percent annually; and interest rates were rising toward a peak of 18 percent, creating investor uncertainty and nearly impossible conditions for long-term investment planning. Earners and savers soon discovered that investment in real property and other assets constituted good speculative hedges against inflation, while net borrowers and people on fixed incomes were alarmed at how quickly their incomes were eroding. Economists coined the term *stagflation* to describe this period of inflation with underlying economic stagnation.

Among the borrowers who felt the financial pinch most acutely were a number of major cities that found themselves in real danger of defaulting on their financial obligations; New York, Detroit, Cleveland, and many others struggled with "the urban fiscal crisis." Congress was asked to consider bailing out cities through various forms of Federal financial guarantees but declined. Cities dealt with the crises in different ways, but nearly all made substantial reductions in public services and deferred maintenance and replacement expenses for infrastructure, including roads, sewers, bridges, and other capital items. During these years, some states that had largely escaped the financial crises nonetheless experienced local and sometimes statewide referenda, such as Proposition 13 in California and Proposition 2½ in Massachusetts, to limit state and local taxes. In short, the times were not ripe for the introduction of a large number of new money-program initiatives at the Federal, state, or local levels. And yet the needs were manifest.

The growing problem of homelessness among the poor, the displacement of low-income families and households because of center-city renewal and soaring property values, urban decay, and fiscal crisis all threatened the continuation of basic public services in some cities. How could the administration solve these problems through policies that did not require substantial additional taxes and spending?

The solution, articulated most clearly in *National Urban Policy*—the President's Urban and Regional Group Report in 1978—was to *target* existing Federal programs more precisely to areas and individuals with the greatest need; to *leverage* Federal monies with state and local funds and, where possible, with private-sector support as well; and to *develop public-private partnerships* to advance specific economic development and downtown redevelopment revitalization projects in which business was perceived to have an essential interest. Public-private partnerships were seen not as a substitute for Federal initiatives and responsibility in such areas but as a new policy tool in the Federal portfolio for addressing domestic problems. Since most of the population, businesses, and jobs in the United States are located in metropolitan areas, the economic and physical decline of these areas was seen as a major policy problem touching all segments of American society and business. It did not seem unusual, then, to address these problems through a national urban policy.

### Origin of Partnerships as Policy

The 1978 *National Urban Policy* addressed economic problems as well as social conditions of the older central cities. It recognized that to revive central-city economies, basic transformations had to occur in the conditions for doing business, investing in facilities, and providing jobs. If government funds and programs alone were insufficient to rebuild urban areas, they could nonetheless leverage critical private investment and commitment to revitalization. As the Committee on National Urban Policy of the National Research Council later stated: "If public investment can leverage private investment and regulation policy can reduce costs to businesses and consumers, then public resources can be husbanded to deal primarily with those problems that cannot be addressed by the market economy."[1]

*National Urban Policy* emphasized targeting existing funds on distressed areas and focusing policies on particular places as well as on people:

> Our goal must first be to provide immediate assistance to the most troubled cities and communities. Beyond this, our goal must be to help all cities offer their residents decent services, adequate jobs, sound neighborhoods, good housing and healthy environments. Our efforts should be directed, to the maximum extent possible, at helping cities help themselves.[2]

> We should remember that urban problems are not only those of people, but also those of places. It is not enough to increase job options for the unemployed if high costs prevent them from securing affordable decent housing. It is not enough to provide basic income assistance to the poor if their neighborhoods and housing are decaying, and if public services remain inadequate. If meaningful improvements in the quality of urban life are to occur, urban policy cannot address the problems of people without addressing the troubles of cities. Put another way, it cannot address problems of places and ignore the hardships of people who live in those places. Dealing effectively with urban problems will require an emphasis on both people and places.[3]

The statement unabashedly argued for efficiency in Federal policy through conserving investments in existing cities and urban areas and relying on partnerships with state and local government, the private sector, and voluntary neighborhood organizations to provide both ideas and essential capital:

> We must keep in mind that the resources available for attacking the Nation's problems are scarce. We must carry out the most cost-effective policies possible to address the diverse problems facing our cities. Efficiency requires that urban policy be based primarily on saving the cities and neighborhoods that we already have rather than building new ones. Efficiency requires that the Federal government consider the possible impact of all its actions on cities, so that indirect effects from unrelated Federal efforts do not inadvertently make urban problems worse. Most importantly, we must recognize that urban problems cannot be solved by the Federal Government alone. A successful urban policy must incorporate a philosophy of partnership among the Federal Government, State and local governments, private businesses, neighborhood groups, voluntary organizations and urban residents.[4]

Another principle stressed that national urban policy must reflect a strong and affirmative partnership between the public and private sectors:

> Federal, State, and local funds, no matter how plentiful, will not be enough to solve our urban problems. The private sector must help. Only businesses and industries can provide enough permanent jobs for the poor and unemployed; only the private sector can provide the capital needed for rebuilding and growing; and only the private sector can carry out these large scale development programs necessary to provide healthy local economies. As the President has stated: "We should rely principally on the private sector to lead the economic expansion and to create new jobs for a growing labor force . . . . By emphasizing the creation of private jobs, our resources will be used more efficiently, our future capacity to produce will expand more rapidly and the standard of living for our people will rise faster."
>
> We must carefully plan the total range of Federal, State and local actions in order to secure the most effective participation of the private sector. We can no longer afford to have economic subsidy programs and tax laws working unnecessarily at cross purposes with each other. No longer can we try to encourage development in one area, while, without careful thought, we make other nearby areas more accessible or competitive.
>
> Thousands of entrepreneurs make location and investment decisions that are of crucial importance for the Nation's urban areas. Urban policy must provide incentives to influence those business decisions in the direction of development goals.
>
> Matching private sector behavior to urban needs will be possible only if the public sector understands the importance of affecting perceptions of business risk and business opportunities. Focused, coordinated and sustained public investment in distressed urban areas is required to compensate for the increased risk of private investment in these areas.[5]

The notion of "partnership" presented here is an interesting one. The private sector is expected to create jobs and provide basic business-investment capital, but it is the role of the public sector to understand how business risks are assessed and to create incentives that change those risks in favor of urban redevelopment and investment. Private partners are not expected to do the work of the public sector; rather, they are asked to help identify situations in which Federal, state, or local action can change the nature of business risks to provide an incentive for private investment. Thus the public sector is expected to change both its philosophy and its methods of assistance to accommodate more closely the established ways of guiding business investment.

### Implications for Organizational Change

To appreciate how truly revolutionary this view was, one must recall that in 1978 there were very few public-private organizations through which leaders could discuss such cooperation. Several major cities had corporate organizations with civic purposes and "save the downtown" campaigns. Among the oldest and most successful of these were the Allegheny Conference in Pittsburgh and the Greater Baltimore Committee. But the main focus of these entities had been a kind of chamber-of-commerce boosterism for business and an effort to preserve the declining commercial activities in center cities; relatively little effort had been focused on the broader needs for housing and neighborhood preservation, support for the public schools, or the maintenance of basic urban infrastructure, such as streets, sewers, and public transportation. *National Urban Policy* called for the transformation of many of the existing private-sector organizations and the creation of many new ones to include membership from both the public sector and the private sector.

To address this problem, eligibility conditions for Community Development Block Grants and other Federal programs were rewritten to make capacity-building activities supportable, including the development of a variety of community-based neighborhood organizations. In the beginning, the private sector was generally a reluctant partner, skeptical of public commitment and fearful of making "foreign alliances" with government at any level. But it quickly became apparent that the revival of the commercial centers of cities was a task beyond the grasp of even the best-funded corporate groups. A way had to be found to revive cities as balanced communities, or the private sector would have to write off billions of dollars in investment in plant, equipment, land, and headquarters facilities. The conditions for both public and private interest in partnerships had finally emerged.

In addition to partnerships and the targeting of existing Federal programs, the Carter administration explored several other new ways to stimulate urban revitalization. The first of these was the creation of "enterprise zones" in distressed areas of center cities. These zones would provide special tax incentives, land-value writedowns for businesses that invested for specified periods and even exemption from certain Federal and local regulations, such as minimum wage laws and Occupational Safety and Health Administration (OSHA) requirements for firms agreeing to provide employment in these areas. In a sense, "enterprise zones" were the embodiment of the partnership notion in which government creates attractive market conditions for private investment. But an agreement could not be reached either on the designation of enterprise zones or on politically acceptable packages of incentives to offer in them. Thus the idea was never implemented in policy.

A second idea, the concept of a National Development Bank, was also explored. Such an institution, supplied with an initial capital endowment by Congress, would be assigned the task of making long-term development loans at preferential rates to businesses located in distressed areas. It was unclear whether such a bank would also function as a venture capital lender in the conventional sense or would be confined to subsidizing risks related to location. Ultimately, a combination of opposition by the established banking community and fears that such a government-run bank might only subsidize projects with no realistic chance of economic success forced its abandonment.

## A Boost from the Private Sector

The Committee for Economic Development, a prestigious Washington- and New York-based organization of chief executive officers and academics, took an early interest in the idea of public-private partnerships. Its Research and Policy Committee began almost immediately a careful examination of partnership successes and failures in a number of United States cities, including Baltimore, Pittsburgh, Chicago, Minneapolis-St. Paul, Portland (Oregon), Dallas, and Atlanta.[6] The Committee for Economic Development also issued a policy statement, "Public-Private Partnership: An Opportunity for Urban Communities" in 1982 that drew important lessons about what makes such partnerships work and legitimized the partnership process among more conservative segments of the business community.

While recognizing that national and international conditions can sometimes swamp even the most creative local efforts, the Committee for Economic Development policy statement acknowledged that "successful experience with such partnerships spans decades and the country." The statement continued:

> To make full use of the private sector's potential, local governments will need to adopt an entrepreneurial approach that anticipates needs, seeks out opportunities, and encourages an effective coalition of public and private efforts. The private sector, in turn, needs to determine what it realistically can contribute. If it sets its goals too high, its performance will fail to match expectations. The private sector cannot assume full responsibility for meeting needs that will result from cutbacks in federal domestic programs. However, if the local private sector is unwilling to make a sufficient commitment of money and effort, its community will lose position to those that respond more energetically.[7]

The policy statement noted that successful partnership efforts have both a policy dimension and an operational dimension. The policy dimension "involves a process that produces consensus on community goals, agreement on institutional roles, and sustained support for action." The operational dimension "can take three general forms: private initiative for public benefit, government initiative to facilitate or encourage private activity in the public interest, and joint ventures by government and private organizations." Moreover, the statement identified three areas that can be legitimate arenas for partnership activities: strengthening the local economy, revitalizing neighborhoods, and bolstering key community services, such as education, transportation, safety, social services, health, solid-waste management, and water-supply and sewage treatment.

This scope of public-private partnerships is broader and more expansive than earlier efforts. It does not constrain legitimate private-sector activities to those directly related to employment and investment but recognizes the importance of sound social institutions, schools, and neighborhoods as legitimate areas of corporate concern. And it suggests that these responsibilities be incorporated into the expectations of business managers whose firms depend on the local community. As the Committee for Economic Development stated:

> Businesses should view the improvement of social and economic conditions in the communities in which they operate as a goal tied so closely to their bottom-line interests that it requires direct and effective action. This means going beyond traditional corporate philanthropy. It means more active and effective involvement by the corporation, including:
>
> - use of the full range of resources available for community purposes, including employees, facilities and services, operation and investment decisions, and leadership, as well as financial contributions
>
> - integration of the public-involvement function into the corporate management structure
>
> - establishing standards of performance and procedures for accountability in the public-involvement function akin to those applied to the traditional business functions of the corporation.[8]

As interest in public-private partnerships grew, the role of voluntary and nonprofit organizations was increasingly recognized. The National Research Council report *Critical Issues for National Urban Policy* in 1982 called nonprofit organizations "an important third sector in many urban economies." The report noted:

> Many have played an influential role as "change agents" and as a means of introducing innovations in programs, services, and processes of management, participation, and conflict resolution. Particularly at the neighborhood level, nonprofits have often been the institutions of choice for reconciling business, government, and citizen interests and legitimating programs. They can act as "mediating" institutions . . . . Government is often too inflexible and insensitive to perform [these functions] effectively through its regular bureaucracy . . . . Few such activities are attractive to profit-making enterprises. Nonprofit agencies can mix public and private resources and engage the people of a community in working on their own problems.[9]

### Evolution of the Idea—Some Examples of Success

Since 1978, public-private partnerships have been increasingly seen as legitimate and effective tools for achieving a number of public purposes. Virtually every major United States city has had redevelopment programs mounted, at least in part, through successful and increasingly sophisticated partnerships. Baltimore's Charles Center/Inner Harbor, Toledo's Sea Gate project, St. Paul's Galleria, San Antonio's RiverWalk, Boston's Quincy Market, Milwaukee's Grand Avenue and Theatre District projects, Denver's Larimer Square, and many more display the results of effective partnerships for commercial redevelopment that have, in turn, spurred spillover investment in housing and adjacent neighborhood areas.

Since the emergence of the public-private partnership as a legitimate public-policy tool, the concept has taken on a life of its own. Both long-established and newly established nonprofit organizations have found corporate partners to mount local and sometimes nationwide initiatives in housing renovation, youth apprenticeship and employment programs, urban homesteading, Adopt-A-School and other programs to strengthen public education, energy conservation, economic-development projects, job training for the hard-to-employ, and a host of other areas. Three examples will illustrate the vigor of the concept.

*Jubilee Housing* is about three miles from the White House in a neighborhood of old brownstone apartments that has been kept from becoming slums or being gentrified by Federal housing assistance, a loan of private venture capital arranged by James Rouse (the developer of Baltimore's Harborplace and Boston's Quincy Market), and the efforts of a church-based tenant management organization. Jubilee Housing was acquired with capital contributed by the private sector and renovated through "sweat equity" of the tenants, who helped repair their own units. As a nonprofit organization, Jubilee Housing, Inc., is exempt from local property taxes, and financial contributions to the organization are tax deductible. An Urban Development Action Grant (UDAG) of $1.8 million provided funds for materials for reconstruction and renovation.

A tenant management organization defines the tenants' responsibilities to keep up their units and to contribute to the maintenance of public spaces and also sets certain behavioral standards for occupants. Nonconformists are subject to eviction. Long-term plans call for the project to encompass housing in a fifteen-block area; ownership of housing units will be gradually transferred to tenants through the purchase of shares in Jubilee Housing. The result of this partnership approach to providing low-income housing is certainly far different and more satisfying than it would have been if the government alone had undertaken the project or if the private market had been allowed to displace the current tenants.

*Public/Private Ventures, Inc. (P/PV)*, a Philadelphia-based nonprofit organization, works with state and local governments across the country to address the problems of at-risk youth through employment training programs. Using a combination of private-foundation and Federal-government support, P/PV sets up and manages a variety of programs designed to give minority and disadvantaged youths work experience, training, and basic education that will enable them to complete high school and enter the regular work force. Basic apprenticeship programs in repair, maintenance, and weatherization of low-income housing and summer youth conservation corps programs for urban youths are in operation. These programs, among others, instill proper work habits, provide training in particular skills like carpentry and stress basic educational skills, including instruction in career and family planning. Controlled evaluations of each project determine what works most effectively and how it might be adapted by others contemplating similar programs. Private employers support these projects financially and provide jobs for participants and graduates of the programs. States and localities are encouraged to keep successful projects going beyond the pilot period by arranging for continuing support from public and private funds.

*Baltimore's Charles Center/Inner Harbor* redevelopment is one of the oldest and most successful public-private partnerships in the United States. Physical redevelopment projects totaling more than $400 million have transformed what was once a dirty, dangerous, commercial waterfront into the focal point for widespread commercial and residential revitalization. Those who fled to the suburbs in the 1950s and 1960s return regularly for leisure and recreational opportunities unimagined a decade ago. And many are opting for city living in the city's renovated neighborhoods. A more complete description of the Baltimore process emphasizes the importance of people who learned a partnership working style from their early experiences in civic organizations like the Citizens Planning and Housing Association that serve as "incubators for civic entrepreneurs."[10]

The earlier Charles Center development project was undertaken largely at the initiative of the private sector, which provided the plans, the developer, and 70 percent of the capital cost of the project. The public sector provided the necessary infrastructure investments and guided the process through the political and bureaucratic shoals. But key actors in the public sector also saw the potential for leveraging the Charles Center success with larger- and higher-risk public investment in the Inner Harbor project. Charles Center consisted entirely of office towers and commercial redevelopment space, but the Inner Harbor projects included a world trade center, a market house called Harborplace (containing food kiosks, craft shops, and a variety of other attractions for strolling and relaxing), an aquarium, a new Hyatt hotel, and a science museum. The Inner Harbor project reversed the financial ratios of Charles Center, with 88 percent of the total investment coming from the public sector, including UDAG and other Federal grants as well as funds provided by the city. Moreover, the partnership mechanism evolved from one of simple financial arrangements and separate investments by public and private partners to a far more sophisticated mechanism coordinated through a quasi-public corporation, the Charles Center/Inner Harbor Management Corporation, which can comingle funds from a variety of sources and which must devise and oversee complex financial deals that reconcile Federal guidelines with private financial guarantees. In a real sense, public-private partnership for urban development has been professionalized and has now come into its own as a legitimate and effective form of entrepreneurship in the public interest.

These experiences and many others teach some lessons about success in public-private partnerships. Among these are:

- The personal commitment of individuals is essential to overcome the natural inertia of governmental and corporate bureaucracies. In every successful partnership project, the individuals responsible for its success can be named and are conspicuous public advocates for the partnership and its projects.
- Public partners bring the capacity to employ tax increment financing, industrial revenue bonding, UDAG funding, and the positive commitment of public regulation and planning tools to achieve project goals. Private partners bring private capital and the ability to move quickly to execute plans. Over time, the assets of both partners are being blended in increasingly sophisticated ways to achieve project goals.

- The development and use of new kinds of quasi-public organizations with delegated powers and responsibilities from both sectors is growing. Such vehicles for partnership help to insulate projects from political instabilities and at the same time assure lenders, developers, and the public that private-sector commitments will be sustained.
- The capacity for sustained long-term partnerships depends on having a vehicle that serves as an incubator for teaching civic awareness and entrepreneurship. The most successful of these appear to be organizations in which people participate as individuals, not as representatives of their companies or agencies. These organizations serve to focus attention on the definition of the problem and to gain consensus about its importance to the community outside of a partisan political atmosphere. They help to legitimate the issues to which corporate and public partners can then turn their professional skills and attention.
- Public-private partnership is a continuous process, requiring a stable network of interpersonal relationships developed over a long period, a fairly even balance of capacities in the two sectors, and the ability to bring about institutional innovation when needed.

## Conclusion

The successes attributable to public-private partnerships across the country are impressive. While partnerships as policy tools have been more conspicuously successful in urban redevelopment than in addressing more elusive social needs, they continue to be used experimentally in a wide variety of public-interest areas. These partnerships have become substantially more sophisticated over the last decade both in their organizational form and in their legal capacity to formulate financial deals, oversee performance, and manage projects. Their purposes and justification have broadened to include not only economic development and job creation but longer-term social and quality-of-life projects as well. Partnerships have developed new mechanisms for citizen participation in project planning and sometimes operation, and more imaginative use has been made of voluntary organizations of all kinds.

Since its first appearance in the 1978 *National Urban Policy*, the idea of the public-private partnership as a policy tool has changed substantially. Originally conceived as a means to supplement scarce public resources in meeting pressing national needs, the concept has evolved into the idea of substituting private for public efforts in a wide range of areas. The Carter administration thought of partnerships as joint efforts in which government created improved market conditions for private investment, but the Reagan administration has advanced the idea of privatizing public services so that Federal support can be cut back in these areas. In this latter view, partnerships are less a tool for meeting certain needs and more a means of realigning various social responsibilities between government and the private sector.

The history of successes, apparent in one city after another, demonstrates that private involvement in public-private partnerships cannot exclude a Federal commitment if these partnerships are to be successful.

## Notes

1. National Research Council, *Critical Issues for National Urban Policy* (Washington, D.C.: National Academy Press, 1982), 69.
2. President's Urban and Regional Group Report, *A New Partnership to Conserve America's Communities: National Urban Policy*, March 1978, 4.
3. Ibid., 5.
4. Ibid., 6-7.
5. Ibid., II-8-9.
6. The results are published in *Public Private Partnerships in American Cities: Seven Case Studies* (Lexington, Mass.: Lexington Books, 1982), ed. R. Scott Fosler and Renée Berger.
7. Special Summary, "Public-Private Partnership: An Opportunity for Urban Communities," Committee on Economic Development, 1982.
8. Ibid., 4.
9. National Research Council, *Critical Issues for National Urban Policy* (Washington, D.C., 1982), 83.
10. Katharine Lyall, "A Bicycle Built for Two: Public Private Partnership in Baltimore, in *Public Private Partnerships in American Cities*, 17-57.

# Private-Sector Initiatives in the Reagan Administration

RENÉE A. BERGER

On 5 October 1981, President Ronald Reagan announced his private-sector initiatives strategy. In a speech before the National Alliance of Business (NAB) — a group that had been created during the Johnson administration to increase private-sector involvement in government efforts to reduce unemployment — Reagan outlined a two-part program to establish a special presidential task force and to initiate a comprehensive effort to be undertaken by the cabinet. The President's Task Force on Private Sector Initiatives (hereinafter the Task Force) was to be a blue-ribbon panel composed of thirty-five civic leaders (later increased to forty-four). Its purpose, the president explained, would be "to promote private sector leadership and responsibility for solving public needs, and to recommend ways of fostering greater public-private partnerships."[1] The directive for the cabinet stipulated that it was to "review agency procedures and regulations and identify barriers to private sector involvement . . . [and] develop pump-priming and seed money programs that offer incentives for private sector investment." Furthermore, the cabinet was to "provide technical knowledge to develop private initiatives" and was to examine "existing programs . . . to determine which could be more productively carried out by the private sector."[2]

The concept of private-sector initiatives has a long history predating the Reagan program. Over time, the concept has grown more expansive — both in terms of the groups participating (initiatives now encompass youth, senior citizens, and business executives) and the constituencies affected (these now include the poor, the elderly, children, the unemployed, cities in distress, and even new businesses in need of technical assistance). All of Reagan's recent predecessors used conventional policy tools — budget, legislation, organizational structure, and leadership —

---

Adapted, with permission, from Renée A. Berger, "Private-Sector Initiatives in the Reagan Era: New Actors Rework an Old Theme," in *The Reagan Presidency and the Governing of America*, ed. Lester M. Salamon and Michael S. Lund. Copyright 1984 by the Urban Institute.

to assert their priorities in this area. Reagan's private-sector initiative is not only more expansive but includes innovative dimensions not present in earlier efforts. For one thing, Reagan has maximized the symbolism of presidential leadership, using the presidency to highlight leaders as role models and to persuade them to encourage their constituencies to engage in private-sector initiative. In a sense, President Johnson's appeal to create the NAB had the same basis. However, with Reagan the scale is broader — calling on business, labor, religious groups, and so forth. In addition, an organizational structure has been created to give the concept White House status as well as to blend the initiative with other administration actions.

The motivation for private-sector initiative was to soften the impact of the budget cuts by demonstrating that the private sector — the business community — could help solve community needs. The initiative can be viewed as a cousin both of Reagan's economic policy and of his New Federalism, although the program's administrative handling never clearly placed it within a policy context.

It is problematic to determine whether the Reagan private-sector effort should be regarded as a policy. On the one hand, the program was not placed in a policy-making office, its staff did not have policy backgrounds, opportunities for utilizing legislative clout were steadfastly avoided, and a proscription was placed on accessing public funding. On the other hand, a special White House office was established, a presidential task force was created, an advisory board is now in place, the president routinely speaks on private-sector initiatives, and a private-sector initiatives structure has been established across agencies. Since 1983 strictures on using public funds have been relaxed, but the legislative docket is still largely moribund. Over time the private-sector effort has taken on features associated with policy, but it has never been comprehensively organized as such.

Overall, the private-sector initiatives effort has suffered from a lack of clarity as to what it was expected to accomplish and how it was to proceed. Furthermore, the range of policy tools at the White House's disposal was applied slowly and unevenly. On matters of budget and legislation, in particular, the private-sector initiatives effort has fallen silent in the face of philosophical restraints and political sensitivities.

*Phase One: Planning*

One concept shared by the original architects of Reagan's private-sector initiatives strategy was that the budget cuts were facing a hostile public and that there would be a need to mitigate the impact of these cuts. Given Reagan's private-sector orientation, it is logical that the administration would look to the private sector for assistance in "selling" the budget. A key element in the planning stage began with a memorandum from Robert Mosbacher, Jr., to James Baker in January 1981 suggesting that the expertise of the business community be tapped in solving community problems.

The Reagan private-sector initiative program could logically have been a part of the administration's New Federalism proposal. In fact, Mosbacher's appeal to

James Baker was initially referred to Richard Williamson, the White House official in charge of the New Federalism effort. New Federalism suggested a realignment in the delivery of services, and private-sector initiative implies that there is a role for the private sector — specifically, the for-profit firm — in service delivery. Beyond an initial meeting of Mosbacher with Williamson, however, the administration did not capitalize on this logical link.

After the initial meeting with Richard Williamson, Mosbacher's proposal was referred to Elizabeth Dole, then director of the White House Office of Public Liaison, who was in charge of a "business coalition" strategy designed to recruit the business community's support of the president's economic package. This was the first of several critical junctures that shaped the private-sector initiative. It suggested that this was intended to be a public-relations strategy more than a policy-oriented effort.

Many business executives were wary of Reagan and of the untested theory of supply-side economics. To calm their anxieties, Elizabeth Dole had orchestrated gatherings of corporate and trade association executives in order to develop a network and to facilitate lobbying on behalf of the administration. The respective responsibilities for organizing a private-sector program effort and a business-coalition strategy were given to two aides in Dole's office.

Mosbacher and Dole's aide assigned to the private-sector initiative met with members of the business community and with executives from business associations, such as the Business Roundtable, the National Federation of Independent Businesses, and the National Association of Manufacturers. These meetings were designed both to obtain input from the business community and to stem a growing concern that the corporate sector would be caught in an untenable position of high expectations that they could not meet.

In another memorandum to James Baker dated 28 May 1981, Mosbacher offered a proposal for "a modest, realistic private-sector program in the area of employment, which we believe has a high probability of success and a relatively low risk of exposure or embarrassment to the Administration." Mosbacher outlined an organizational strategy of forming a "steering committee of approximately 15 to 25 top representatives of small, medium, and large businesses" who would implement a specific goal "to employ as many of the 325,000 displaced CETA workers as possible."[3]

Mosbacher asked Senator Howard Baker to urge the White House to move ahead with planning a program. Mosbacher reported that the senator sent a letter to Michael Deaver, deputy chief of staff, emphasizing the "priority" of a private-sector program. The senator was successful in reactivating the effort, and Michael Deaver was put in charge.

This was the second critical juncture. Under Reagan, policy responsibilities fell largely to Presidential Counselor Edwin Meese III and to James Baker, whereas Deaver dealt principally with the president's image. White House aides contended that had the proposal been placed in the policy area, it would have risked becoming a peripheral aspect of the economic program. Deaver, they noted, guaranteed proximity to the president and ensured that the initiative would be on Reagan's calendar.

Deaver in fact proved successful in keeping private-sector initiatives high on President Reagan's agenda. In midsummer 1981 James Rosebush, the director of business liaison at the Department of Commerce and former manager of contributions at Standard Oil of Ohio, was loaned to the White House to work under Deaver on the private-sector initiative. Deaver, Rosebush, and Mosbacher agreed that business should take the lead and that action should take precedence over conducting a study.[4]

By late August 1981 Rosebush had completed an "action plan" for the president and his senior staff, outlining the organizational arrangements and proposed schedule for implementing a private-sector initiatives program. The approach was approved, and Rosebush officially became the president's assistant for private-sector initiatives. Although the appointment demonstrated the president's high regard for the effort, Rosebush was given no staff or budget, under the rationale that Federal funds should not be used to support the initiative. Philosophy and politics thus may well have initially undermined the development of a viable program.

In sum, this first phase of action planning reflected the business backgrounds and promotional orientation of its primary architects. There was unanimity that the effort would be action oriented and that it would be promotional. But it would be ingenuous to believe that the administration was solely interested in public relations. Mosbacher's May memorandum described a specific program to alleviate unemployment. The issue the Task Force would confront was: If the effort was to be more than public relations, what else should it be? Further, although action was to be the modus operandi, what did action dictate? The Task Force was to find itself explaining what it was not—that is, it was not to be a way of "filling the budget gap"—rather than what it was. *Action* became defined as not producing a report with policy recommendations.

*Phase Two: Operations*

The centerpiece of the second phase of the administration's private-sector initiative strategy was the President's Task Force on Private Sector Initiatives. Four dimensions of the Task Force are reviewed here: the mandate, management culture, organizational structure, and products.

*Mandate.* In his October 1981 announcement of the creation of a Task Force on Private Sector Initiatives, President Reagan stated that he was instructing his cabinet to review impediments and to develop seed programs and incentives for private-sector investment. C. William Verity, Jr., chairman of the executive committee of Armco Steel, was named to the post of Task Force chairperson. The Task Force's key missions were stated as follows:

1. To identify existing examples of successful or promising private initiatives and public-private partnerships and to give these models national recognition in order to promote their broader use.

2. To encourage increased and more effective use of the human and financial-contribution resources of religious groups, businesses, unions, foundations, and philanthropic organizations, including more creative use of leadership, management expertise, training, and volunteer work.

3. To encourage the formation and continuation of community partnerships — private-sector organizations working with local government — to identify and prioritize community needs and then marshal the appropriate human and financial resources.

4. To identify government obstacles to private initiatives and make recommendations for their removal, and to formulate new incentives to inspire and incite the private sector to undertake new initiatives.

5. To contribute to the development of public policy in areas of concern to the Task Force.

On 3 December the *New York Times* reported, "President Reagan established a Task Force on Private Sector Initiatives today to seek ways to help take up the slack left by the deep cuts he has made in Federal spending."[5] This perception is exactly what the president, his advisers, and Verity were laboring to prevent. The White House had been particularly concerned not to raise expectations that business — financially or otherwise — would be expected to fill the gap from the budget cuts. In addition to being a political liability, such a perception was philosophically and pragmatically unacceptable.

Philosophically, the president and his aides had argued that the cuts in nondefense areas were both to be a part of the economic-recovery package and to eliminate programs they regarded as wasteful. Pragmatically, the aides were aware (from their early meetings with the business community) that corporate giving averaged $3 billion annually and that, with profits declining, growth in this area could not be expected. Furthermore, even if the administration had sought a dollar-for-dollar replacement — and it would be naive to believe this were the case — contributions would have had to increase tenfold. Nevertheless, Verity and the Task Force were confronted from the outset by a press corps demanding to know specific goals. The sweeping mission statement, the president's smorgasbord of case examples cast within the rubric of voluntarism/private-sector initiative/public-private partnership, and the timing of the Task Force's creation unfortunately fed this perception.

In its attempt to be broad and to encompass the full range of potential activity and constituencies affected, the mission statement avoided delineating particular problems — for example, unemployment, child care, illiteracy, and hunger. The only specific project proposed was to create a data bank of examples of private-sector initiatives. The mission statement, it should be underscored, was developed with bipartisan input and may well have been a reflection of a mutual desire to find common ground while leaving the specifics to the Task Force members.

Task Force committees, too, were not project specific but were broader in orientation. For example, committees were created on the topics of community partnerships, contributions, liaison with government and national organizations, the marshaling of human resources, communications, impediments, incentives, and governors. Only the models committee had a project—the data bank. Although several Task Force members argued for a focused and project-specific approach, they were unable to get such a proposal on the agenda for discussion by the entire Task Force. This was owing to an early decision by Verity to let the Task Force committees operate independently of the whole, thereby granting them freedom to act but preventing group consensus.

The following example illustrates the problems that arose from this lack of specificity in operating procedures. In February 1982 the contributions committee passed a recommendation urging businesses, within four years, to double the level of cash contributions for public-service programs. A goal of tax-deductible contributions totaling at least 2 percent of pretax net income was established. (The law provided for special tax considerations up to 5 percent of pretax profits, but 1981 legislation increased the ceiling to 10 percent.) The Task Force also asked corporations to double their involvement in community-service activities through employee volunteer programs. Given no clearly specified rules, the committee faced the problem of how this recommendation could be a policy statement of the Task Force.

Moreover, the subject of the recommendation—corporate philanthropy— reopened the debate over whether the Task Force mandate was to "fill the budget gap" with private-sector dollars. It is ironic that in what appears to be an attempt to keep everyone happy and to avoid controversy by not picking a specific project, Verity found himself confronting conflict. Externally, the statement magnified the administration's political sensitivities. Internally, it highlighted the indistinctness of the mandate and the chairperson's reluctance to establish a clear decision-making process for policy statements.

Five months had passed since the NAB speech, but a clear mandate and a decision-making process to achieve full consensus had yet to be outlined. As the clock ticked away, the ambiguity would heighten, ultimately affecting the products of the Task Force.

*Management culture.* As the ethos of the Task Force took shape, two sources of confusion perpetuated the original ambiguity concerning what the Task Force was expected to accomplish. The first source of confusion had to do with whether this president-appointed body was supposed to produce a report. The Task Force members got mixed signals. In January 1982, President Reagan stated: "I told Bill Verity 6 weeks ago, I don't want a committee report. Give me action and results. Get the private sector in the driver's seat so we can start using market incentives and philanthropy to find lasting solutions to community problems."[6] But presidential commissions are typically designed to produce a report based on considerable study and hearings, which offers a legislative package to affect public policy. Numerous members of the Task Force had formerly served on commissions, and several were simultaneously serving on other commissions; indeed, Task Force member John Filer had headed a private commission to study voluntary giving. Thus, it can be assumed that Task Force members who had served on presidential commissions would expect to focus their attention on producing a report and that precedence might have led other members to such an assumption. Both the executive order and the mission statement, moreover, had expressly asked for "recommendations," which, it would seem, required study and a report. Thus, when the chairperson explained that the Task Force was to be action oriented and that the president did not want a report, his appeal was not understood by the members.

The second source of confusion arose out of the differing backgrounds and organizational experiences of the Task Force members. The Task Force was composed of representatives of three types of institutions: for-profit, nonprofit, and public sector. Apparently, the Task Force never fully understood or addressed the different values that underlie these three spheres. Although it is not the purpose of this essay to expound on management culture, a brief comparison of public-sector and corporate styles is pertinent to an understanding of the group dynamics of the Task Force and to its influence on the final products. Whereas public-sector style emphasizes dialogue and allows for open challenges to leadership, corporate style avoids conflict in the boardroom, and rarely is the leadership of the corporate chief executive openly called into question. In the public sector, the leader seeks to appeal to multiple constituencies; in corporations the leader is primarily concerned about the bottom-line interests of the investors. The corporate sector is risk rewarding, while the public sector is risk averse.

Meetings of the Task Force on Private Sector Initiatives utilized a corporate style of management. The chairperson's authority was not publicly questioned; meeting time was consumed with committee reports, leaving minimal time for dialogue; and decisions were made by the chairperson (as would be his prerogative in the corporate setting, even when consultation had been sought), without appealing for clear consensus. The most dramatic evidence of the exclusivity of authority was demonstrated by Verity's decision that consensus would not be sought for the final document to be submitted to the president. This was a logical extension of corporate decision making, in which authority is clear and the operating rule is to optimize, not to compromise.

The stylistic differences were also manifested in another Task Force product: the data bank of case examples of private-sector initiatives. The data bank, initially designed by the head of a national nonprofit organization, was established in the beginning of the Task Force. But it was managed by corporate executives. The decision at the outset was to keep the information brief and simple, another reflection of a style difference. Corporate executives prefer their information in a terse format and rely on simple, straightforward case examples to highlight a point; public-sector style, on the other hand, often prefers lengthy justification and backup information. Moreover, there was no systematic process for validating the data. For public-sector people, valid information is essential; for the private sector, validation was assumed to be the user's responsibility—that is, the market would determine whether or not the information was satisfying consumers. These managerial conflicts were never resolved.

*Organizational structure.* Organizationally, the Task Force administration, personnel, and budget lacked a clear definition of roles, lines of authority, total budget, and spending priorities. On the one hand, the internal administrative structure for the Task Force members was established early and appeared tidy, despite the vagueness both of the mandate and of members' roles. On the other hand, creating the structure for the external relationship to the White House consumed the entire first quarter of Task Force operations. Although the White House sought the benefits of its association with the Task Force, it also labored to establish a structure independent in financing and administration in order to permit the Task Force to receive private funds. Instead of creating a new nonprofit organization to achieve legal and financial separation, the Task Force made arrangements to utilize an existing organization—VOLUNTEER: the National Center for Citizen Involvement. (George Romney, a Task Force member, was also the chairperson of the board of VOLUNTEER.) Essentially this was a bookkeeping arrangement. It was an innovative approach, but the first three months of operating time had already been lost.

Strategically, the White House Office of Private Sector Initiatives thus positioned itself as structurally independent from the Task Force, but this was more illusion than reality. The White House and Task Force were in fact interdependent, requiring each other's resources to achieve their goals. For instance, the White House Office of Private Sector Initiatives staff worked with the Task Force staff in organizing White House meetings with leaders from national associations, such as religious groups and trade associations. These meetings were conceived by Task Force members and held at the White House. They were typically attended by about 150 people and showcased private-sector projects. In addition, the White House used the data bank to identify possible sites for presidential visits to highlight private-sector initiatives. For the Task Force, the White House affiliation helped to open doors, though at times the assumed political affiliation sparked resistance.

Although the Task Force office was located across the street from the Office of Private Sector Initiatives and staff in the two offices routinely worked together, in actuality the White House senior aides for private-sector initiatives generally did not attempt to influence daily operations of the Task Force. Indeed, none of the Task Force staff were political appointees.

On matters of personnel, both the White House Office of Private Sector Initiatives and the Task Force were undergoing change. In February 1982, James Rosebush became Nancy Reagan's chief of staff, a job transfer that critics cite as further evidence of the public relations origins of the private-sector initiatives. The appointment of Jay Moorhead as Rosebush's successor (Moorhead, a thirty-year-old political appointee, had formerly worked in the White House personnel office and as an organizer for the Republican party) raised further questions among critics as to the administration's understanding of the effort and of its commitment to it. Neither Deaver nor Moorhead was policy oriented. Moorhead had other sizable barriers to overcome: an office without a budget, only one other professional staff member, a task force of illustrious American leaders with an unclear mandate, and an increasingly impatient and suspicious public.

The ability of the staff to carry out their responsibilities was severely hampered by the ambiguity of what they were to accomplish, the lack of staff assistance, and the lack of funds. Eventually, the staff did define their functions and attempted to raise funds to implement programs, but the designated termination date of early December 1982 restricted their ability to accomplish proposed activities.

Thus the personnel situation was riddled with uncertainty and obstacles. Critics argue that philosophical biases and political sensitivities could have been overcome, that other presidential commissions have been given an adequate complement of staff and funds. Furthermore, had the planners thought more about how "action" could be carried out, the loss of the first quarter of the year's time might not have occurred.

Finally, the budget presented problems. Public funds had been set aside to support basic office needs, such as space, postage, and copying. No public money, however, was available for staffing needs or for programs, and funds had to be raised for these purposes from the private sector. Total contributions were $506,000. Despite the prevailing belief that all staff were loaned, $355,000 was expended for consultants and payroll. Therefore, the Task Force tacitly recognized that expertise needed to be purchased, despite its operating thesis that volunteers and loaned executives would be both available and capable of efficiently performing tasks otherwise done by hired experts. The remaining expenditures were for travel, printing, and meetings.

Although the idea of a private-sector-funded effort was politically and philosophically attractive, it ultimately created a range of practical problems. If a conference, publication, or other project was to be more than just an idea, funds needed to be raised and adequate time had to be allotted to do this.

In addition, corporations as well as foundations were inundated with requests for funding, which they claimed were coming both from organizations that had lost their Federal funds and from other groups that were trying to avoid government dependence. The strategy of using private-sector funds for the Task Force may have sounded safe, but it pitted the Task Force against groups that in theory it was supposed to be assisting. In sum, the issue arises of why there was a lack of sound financial planning in a task force that was purported to be a presidential commitment of the highest priority.

*Products.* There were, to be sure, innovative dimensions to the Task Force. Philosophically, it was to be a model of its mission: there were loaned personnel from corporations and government, funds were raised from the private sector to support its operations, and equipment was loaned by corporations and government. Strategically, the action orientation generated considerable activity—though it is difficult directly to correlate these efforts with Task Force impacts. The action focused on process. Had a thesis of change been articulated—and one was not—it appears that the White House and Task Force leadership would have contended that change could result from exhibiting leaders as role models and that persuasion was preferable to getting bogged down in traditional approaches to bringing about change through regular policy channels.

By summer 1981, it was clear that the Task Force would be action oriented.

Action translated into serving as an information broker, engendering networks, and promoting new approaches, particularly at the state and local levels of government for solving community problems. The emphasis throughout was on using leaders to exhort other leaders, providing recognition and endorsing efforts, and promoting self-reliance — especially at the state and local levels. This was a new model of operations for a presidential task force.

The Task Force coordinated meetings of leaders of religious organizations, trade associations, community-based organizations, and community colleges, as well as meetings of governors' aides, corporate chief executives, congressional aides, and numerous other groups. In addition, the press was aggressively cultivated, resulting in a flood of articles and television spots. A monthly newsletter was produced as well as three other publications: a brochure on volunteering, a booklet on corporate community involvement, and a book on alternative investing in community and economic development entitled *Investing in America*.[7]

As an information broker, the Task Force operated a data bank. Despite the data bank's technical weaknesses (depth of information, accessibility, and questions of validity), the concept remains useful. Unfortunately, records providing an accounting of the bank's use were not maintained. It is important to note, too, that the information brokering placed the responsibility for action back in the hands of the users; this was not a mechanism to provide technical assistance.

The Task Force was in a unique position to utilize the White House as well as the high profiles of its members as a magnet for events. Thus the network effort focused on hosting meetings of institutional groups, of youth volunteers, and of corporate chief executives together with community-based organization leaders. The meetings ranged from the traditional White House one-hour "walk-through," in which the president would make a brief appearance and several Task Force members would make speeches, to a day-and-a-half conference on corporate social investing. In each case the thrust was that it takes leaders to make a difference — and that those assembled were the leaders. This was the role-modeling and persuasion approach. Again, no technical assistance was offered attendees; follow-up was to be their own responsibility.

Finally, Task Force members were urged to speak out in favor of private-sector initiatives and, where feasible, to promote the formation of task forces locally. This strategy resulted in the creation of a few local task forces (San Francisco's and Houston's are notable examples that were started by Task Force members and are still flourishing), as well as of corporate executive partnerships devoted to civic problems.

Unfortunately, no systematic effort has been made to monitor initiatives that have emerged throughout the nation. Some groups evaporated as quickly as they were formed; others still survive. The president's Task Force provided a context of legitimacy for these groups and an opportunity for presidential endorsement. Beyond such encouragement, however, the attitude was that local groups are best at solving their own problems. The opportunity still remains to identify those efforts that took root and to determine what made them successful.

How "action" displaced policy is also seen in the preparation of the Task Force's final report. Despite the president's call for action instead of a report, the idea of producing a report surfaced repeatedly. Reasons for this include White House ambiguity about how the Task Force should proceed; the fact that "recommendations" had been requested in the executive order and the mission statement; the subculture of commission expectations for a report; and the influence of Task Force members who saw an opportunity to affect policy. However, aides in the Office of Private Sector Initiatives did not perceive themselves as policy initiators. Rather, policy-related issues were routinely referred to the Office of Management and Budget for analysis. At the Task Force, the senior staff who were experienced in policy had their time diverted to "action" projects.

Nevertheless, a policy-development expert was hired. This nonpolitical appointment was approved by the chairperson and a bipartisan group of Task Force members. The White House could not technically prevent the appointment, but it could have pressured the chairperson not to allow it. Jay Moorhead, however, chose not to interfere. During the summer of 1982 the Task Force policy expert conducted meetings on an individual basis with Task Force members. A draft of a conceptual policy framework was submitted to Task Force committee chairpersons in early September, their approval being critical for the Task Force meeting later that month (the last formal meeting before the closing ceremonial session in December). The framework was approved by the chairpersons.

At the September meeting, however, Task Force members John Gardner and Richard Lyman queried why a report was being written when the chairperson had repeatedly asserted that the president did not want one. These members were expressing the feelings of others that the time remaining between September to December was inadequate for dialogue and for meaningful consensus on a policy framework. Conceivably, the confusion over a policy report might have been avoided had Verity better communicated the role of the policy-development expert to the Task Force members. Also, evidently the members had not been notified that the chairpersons had approved the conceptual framework. Thus, an opportunity for consensus over a policy structure evolved but quickly dissipated because it was not seen as an opportunity.

It was subsequently decided that a summary of the Task Force's activities would be written and presented to the president but that there would be no policy statement. It was decided, moreover, that if committees chose to make recommendations, they could include them in the committee summaries; however, they would not be Task-Force-approved recommendations.

It was further agreed that Verity would write a letter to the president about the Task Force's efforts. This letter and the report would be reviewed by the communications committee in the name of the entire membership.

The assignment to write a summary of activities fell to the public-relations staff, with input from senior staff. Ambiguity therefore ultimately undermined the opportunity for the Task Force to be more than an information broker, a networker, and a promoter of local initiative. Furthermore, the chairperson would assert his corporate prerogative of making his own decisions regarding the letter and its contents. As such, the chairperson recommended that the data bank be continued;

that the president continue to articulate the need for private-sector initiatives; that an interagency committee chaired by a cabinet officer be established to "encourage increased sensitivity in policy making to impact on initiative, voluntarism, and private sector involvement" and to "encourage cabinet initiatives which increase agency reliance on the private sector and public/private partnerships, in program development and implementation"; that the Office of Private Sector Initiatives be strengthened and become a "focal point for federal government initiatives"; and that a new bipartisan advisory council be established.[8]

The Task Force terminated in December 1982. Two weeks later, Newsweek's year-end feature was titled, "The Hard-Luck Christmas of '82: With 12 million unemployed and 2 million homeless, private charity cannot make up for federal cutbacks." The article described the activities of the Task Force, quoting Verity as saying "the last thing in the world we could try and do was fill the gap. The gap remains. We're up against the wall."[9] Thus, despite the Task Force's attempt to overcome the shadow of the budget cuts, the public's image of the Task Force and expectations for it appear to have remained the same.

One month later, Reagan lauded the Task Force's activities in his State of the Union message. He said that the Task Force had "successfully forged a working partnership involving leaders of business, labor, education, and government to address the training needs of American workers," and he credited the Task Force with helping "thousands of working people . . . [make] the shift from dead-end jobs and low-demand skills to the growth areas of high technology and the service economy." The Task Force had certainly tried to accomplish the former, though it did not focus on training. However, the latter goal had been pushed off the agenda from the start.

Senior aides in the Office of Private Sector Initiatives were pleased that the president had chosen to praise the program, viewing it as a writ of importance within the White House. Inaccuracies were excused as an error of "tense." With numerous White House offices vying for the president's attention, it was perceived as more important that the program received air time than that the coverage was exaggerated.

*Phase Three: Implementation*

In January 1983 the Office of Private Sector Initiatives underwent another personnel change when Jay Moorhead left government and was succeeded by James Coyne, a former congressman. The third phase of the private-sector initiatives strategy, which began after the Task Force ended and is still evolving, is marked by some organizational and programmatic activity.

Over time, the private-sector initiative strategy appears to have spread throughout the administration. Whereas the Office of Private Sector Initiatives had been the focal point especially during the time of the Task Force, several agencies have now developed their own interpretations of private-sector initiatives. In some cases these initiatives are loosely associated with the White House through routine, required reports that are submitted to the Office of Private Sector Initiatives. However, contact with the White House is minimal and infrequent, and the agencies generally function with relative freedom. The Office of Private Sector Initiatives' priorities have been asserted in the agencies' organizational structure and programmatically. The organizational structure operates through cabinet secretaries, who are given the authority to delegate staff and who typically set their own priorities. The following provides a sample of the efforts of the Office of Private Sector Initiatives during this evolving third phase of the private-sector initiative program.

*Office of Private Sector Initiatives.* The White House wasted no time in January 1983 in establishing an internal working group under Michael Deaver. However, after the Task Force was dissolved, the White House did not announce creation of the new Advisory Council on Private Sector Initiatives until 28 June 1983. Explanations for this lack of haste included James Coyne's newness in the position of presidential assistant, as well as the desire to exert more caution as a result of the lessons from the Task Force difficulties.

The Advisory Council's makeup differed from that of the Task Force. Of the council's thirty-nine members, nine were from the public sector—including seven cabinet secretaries, the director of ACTION, and Deaver. The remaining members were from the private sector, but they were not the Fortune-500 names that were a big part of the Task Force's identity. Seven committees were established: communications/marketing, education, family/community, impediments/incentives, international, networking, and work place. Committee assignments were not formalized until October 1983, but during the following year, the committees met an average of five times each. They appear, moreover, to be operating in an environment that is more permissive—as manifested by the willingness to employ government funds to leverage some of their programs and the willingness to initiate new projects.

A key change is that the White House has overcome its philosophical rigidity and political sensitivity regarding the use of Federal funds to encourage private-sector initiatives. The administration appears to have recognized that to initiate efforts realistically, Federal funds have to be accessed. Although the White House Office of Private Sector Initiatives has no funds for grants, it can—and has—sought to influence Federal departments. Thus some grants awarded by the Department of Health and Human Services, as well as other departments, may be traced to White House influence. But it is important to understand that this clout does not guarantee releasing department funds or ensure White House control over recipients.

The Office of Private Sector Initiatives has utilized its access to the president principally for recognition and promotional endeavors. Most notably, an awards program for recognizing outstanding volunteer service was launched early in Reagan's first term with the assistance of VOLUNTEER (the National Center for Citizen Involvement) and has continued. The role modeling approach was followed again in 1984 in the creation by the Advisory Council of a "Presidential Citation for Private Sector Initiatives." The president also proclaimed 1984 as the Year of Adopt-A-School and advocated an adult literacy campaign. A challenge program convening forums through local Chambers of Commerce to develop business-education programs has been conducted in three cities. The role of the Office of Private Sector Initiatives in promoting partnerships in education is thus largely confined to informal networking and holding meetings and conferences. In addition, forums informing employers of day-care options have been held in over twenty cities. International initiatives include efforts to promote economic development in Grenada and a fellowship exchange program with Japan. While all these efforts have been effective in stimulating significant press and television attention, it is difficult to ascertain their precise impact on the development of local programs.

In sum, during phase three the role of the Office of Private Sector Initiatives has been to put into place an organizational structure within the Federal bureaucracy, to undertake selected program initiatives, and to continue promotional efforts. The office has not sought to influence budget priorities within the Office of Management and Budget, nor has it offered legislation that might affect private-sector initiatives. Its strategy appears to go further than did the Task Force, but it has yet to tackle its mission by utilizing the full array of tools available to policymakers.

*Private-sector initiatives in the agencies.* Some private-sector initiatives by the Reagan administration were given inspiration by the efforts of the Task Force and White House Office of Private Sector Initiatives but did not operate under their guidance. Several agencies established private-sector initiative liaisons or created a separate office for such activities. The liaison idea was originally a Task Force strategy. Many of these liaisons were principally political appointees with a minimal knowledge of the private-sector initiatives concept, but the agencies nonetheless endeavored to develop programs.

Some of these agency efforts predate the Reagan administration. The Department of Housing and Urban Development had established an office for public-private partnerships during the Carter administration. Although this office focused on neighborhood issues, another division was implementing the Urban Development Action Grant (UDAG) program, which the Reagan administration has continued. Described simply, the UDAG combines public- and private-sector funds for urban economic development. HUD also serves as the lead agency for an interagency agreement with Partnerships Data Net to develop and provide for public and private groups case examples of a wide range of partnership initiatives.

Both the Economic Development Administration (EDA) and the Small Business Administration (SBA) have a history similar to HUD in the private-sector initiatives area. During the Carter administration these agencies played a key role in funding a range of development efforts. Their interest in promoting public- and private-sector collaborative activities has continued during the Reagan administration. The EDA has funded projects to help network public- and private-sector leaders in midsize cities. The SBA established a separate office for private-sector initiatives and staffed the effort with professionals. Its projects include working with county supervisors in California to create small-business incubators in cooperation with Chevron Oil, Crown Zellerbach, and the San Francisco Chamber of

Commerce; helping the state of Ohio develop a new pool of equity capital for the state's small companies; and working with HUD, finding ways better to utilize community block-grant funds for small business. In 1984 this SBA office launched a program to encourage the development of small-business incubators. Conferences, a newsletter, and booklets on incubators have been produced.

Unlike the first two phases of Reagan's private-sector initiative strategy, this implementation period allows for "pump priming" with Federal funds. Indeed, the period of rhetoric and promotion that dominated the initial phases of private-sector initiatives shows signs of evolving into an organizational structure with programmatic content.

## Developments in Reagan's Second Term

The start of a second presidential term provides an opportunity for reorganization. The Task Force had already gone through one transformation, into an Advisory Council — and, in January 1985, another change took place. Michael Deaver announced his planned departure, but before he left arrangements were made for Frederick Ryan, the president's appointments secretary, to succeed James Coyne.

Ryan retained his former position when he assumed responsibility for the directorship of the Office of Private Sector Initiatives. Critics asserted that both were full-time positions and that the dual appointment augured a demise of the White House private-sector program. These concerns were first assuaged by Donald Regan's decision to give Ryan the title of deputy assistant to the president (at a time when these positions were being eliminated) and further dispelled by increasing the staff assigned to the White House office.

In January 1986 a new Presidential Board of Advisors on Private Sector Initiatives was announced, succeeding the Advisory Council. Headed by John J. Phelan, Jr., chairman and chief executive officer of the New York Stock Exchange, this group contains some of the same people who served in the past, such as William Verity and Robert Mosbacher, Jr., as well as new appointees. The board is composed of thirty leaders drawn mostly from the private sector, including nonprofit agencies. As in the past, subcommittees have been established, covering areas such as communications, education, partnerships, and international issues.

Each subcommittee shapes its own agenda, primarily by conducting conferences. The education committee, for example, has held three annual national conferences; the partnerships committee is planning regional conferences hosted by the mayors of Columbus (Ohio), Houston, Stamford (Connecticut), and San Diego that will focus on organizing partnerships; and the international subcommittee is planning a meeting to be hosted by the government of France, which will include representatives from five other countries.

In sum, rather than dropping the private-sector program at the start of the second term, the Reagan administration has reorganized the office and established a third generation of the Task Force. Legislative issues affecting charitable giving, such as changes in the tax code, are handled in policy-oriented offices like the Treasury

Department and the Office of Management and Budget. As such, the Office of Private Sector Initiatives and the Advisory Board operate as a communications and educational effort, bringing attention to the subject. In addition, the conferences offer a forum for networking and information exchange. The administration now has a structure and program (there is a subcommittee on long-range planning) that is likely to continue for the remainder of the second term.

## Conclusion

As noted earlier, it is naive to believe that the Reagan administration created the private-sector initiatives effort as a dollar-for-dollar replacement of the budget cuts. On the other hand, the strategy explicitly sought both to soften the blow of the cuts and to capitalize on an attitude that was central to the administration's ideology about the private sector — namely, the local business and individual initiative could be channeled to meet community needs. The history of the private-sector initiative efforts suggests the following conclusions:

1. The effort was not initially conceived as a policy. It was not assigned to a policy office and was not under the command of individuals with policy capability. In 1983, however, it appears that the groundwork laid over the prior two years set the stage for initiatives that have now assumed the shape of policy.

2. The administration succeeded in expanding upon a concept that had its roots in President Kennedy's volunteer programs and that had grown into Carter's public-private partnerships. Reagan's program added corporate philanthropy — monetary and noncash giving of time and equipment, as well as corporate leadership — under an umbrella called private-sector initiatives (whose roots appear to start with Johnson's NAB initiative). This important conceptual advance, however, was undermined by the Reagan administration's ambiguity and apparent unfamiliarity with the subject, as well as by the poor timing of the creation of the Task Force.

3. In addition to an awareness that the administration was not attempting to fill the gap outright, it is important to recognize that despite the Task Force's "policy statement" recommending that corporate giving be doubled, it is doubtful that this ambitious goal could have been achieved. The Filer Commission had made this "2 percent" recommendation in the 1970s, and change did not result then. Corporate giving, regardless of these mandates and pressures, has stayed at 1 percent of pretax profits for well over a decade. Furthermore, corporate monetary giving has appeared not to change significantly even with modifications in the tax code. A Council on Foundations study of chief executives and corporate giving concluded that tax breaks played a relatively unimportant role in corporate decisions about philanthropy. Also, given the consistency of the 1 percent figure, changes in the overall economic climate do not seem to influence monetary giving. However, it appears that changes in the tax code regarding equipment donations have succeeded in increasing this type of giving. Data, however, suffer from collection and from methodological problems.

4. The administration's highlighting of private-sector initiative has received sig-

nificant press attention. While impossible to quantify or correlate, the resultant leadership pressures and networking have created opportunities for information exchange where few had existed before.

5. The private-sector initiative effort thus far has been an assortment of pluses and minuses. It has succeeded in encouraging public discussion on the subject, but it has taken only limited advantage of exploiting opportunities for legislative or budgetary changes. Although organizational structure and leadership have been effectively utilized, their full potential in this area has yet to be realized.

6. Presidential task forces and commissions tend to fade quickly from memory. The innovation of this Task Force (in addition to broadening the concept of private-sector initiative) was its novel structure — a quasi-nonprofit status — and its action approach, which has continued in other administration efforts. These innovations were undermined by lack of clarity, but they deserve recognition and study.

## Notes

1. *Public Papers of the Presidents of the United States: Ronald Reagan,* Remarks at the Annual Meeting of the National Alliance of Business, 5 Oct. 1981 (Washington, D.C.: Government Printing Office, 1981), 885.

2. Ibid., 885-86.

3. Robert Mosbacher, Jr., memorandum to James Baker, 28 May 1981.

4. In 1981 the Committee for Economic Development (CED) completed drafts of two publications on public-private partnerships that were the products of two and a half years of field work in eight cities. These manuscripts were eventually published as: R. Scott Fosler and Renée A. Berger, *Public-Private Partnership: An Opportunity for Urban Communities* (New York: Committee for Economic Development, 1982); and R. Scott Fosler and Renée A. Berger, eds., *Public-Private Partnership in American Cities: Seven Case Studies* (Lexington, Mass.: D.C. Heath and Company, 1982).

5. *New York Times,* 3 Dec. 1981.

6. *Public Papers of the Presidents of the United States: Ronald Reagan,* Remarks at the New York City Partnership Luncheon in New York, 14 Jan. 1982 (Washington, D.C.: Government Printing Office, 1982), 29.

7. Renée Berger et al., eds., *Investing in America: Initiatives for Community and Economic Development* (Washington, D.C.: President's Task Force on Private Sector Initiatives, 1982).

8. C. William Verity, Jr., made these recommendations in the final summary of the Task Force. "Building Partnerships: The President's Task Force on Private Sector Initiatives," Dec. 1981–Dec. 1982, 5.

9. "The Hard-Luck Christmas of '82," *Newsweek,* 27 Dec. 1982, 15.

# A Panel Discussion

ELLEN SULZBERGER STRAUS
FLETCHER BYROM
NEAL R. PEIRCE
CHARLES HUGHES
FEDERICO PEÑA

ELLEN SULZBERGER STRAUS: Before we begin our discussion, I want to mention one of the major reasons why the New York City Partnership has worked, and that is the leadership provided by David Rockefeller. I think all of us who serve with him will agree on that.

What are public-private partnerships? Are they here to stay, and if they are, what does their future look like? We've heard the terms "private-sector initiatives," "community-based partnerships," and "public-private partnerships," but they mean different things to different people. So I think we should start with a brief summary from each of you on what a public-private partnership means to you. We have a unique panel, with divergent interests—representatives from business, the unions, the public sector, and the media, which report on all of the above.

FLETCHER BYROM: In the first place, I don't think we are talking about a new phenomenon; it's just one that has been rediscovered. If you go back to how societies governed themselves before they became so complex that they needed specialization, cities and towns got together and decided as a group what they wanted to do for each other in a common purpose. Under specialization, we're starting to realize that the various constituencies, particularly in our complex cities,

---

This is an edited transcript of a panel discussion presented at "Public-Private Partnerships," a conference sponsored by the New York City Partnership, Inc., and the Academy of Political Science, New York, New York, 13 June 1986. ELLEN SULZBERGER STRAUS is chairperson, New York City Partnership Executive Committee; FLETCHER BYROM is retired chairman and chief executive officer, Koppers Co., Inc.; NEAL R. PEIRCE is a syndicated columnist for the Washington Post Writers Group; CHARLES HUGHES is president, Local 372, American Federation of State, County and Municipal Employees (AFSCME); and FEDERICO PEÑA is mayor of Denver, Colorado.

need to get together, to share their expertise, and jointly to work out their goals. Then the result would not be what somebody in a leadership position has decided the community needs but rather, something the community itself has decided it wants. To me, that's what it's all about.

STRAUS: Would you like to add to that, Mr. Hughes?

CHARLES HUGHES: My definition of "partnership" is that unions, government, and private institutions work together to solve the complex problems of society as a whole. Certainly, suspicions exist between labor unions and private industry, because we have always felt that private industry's only concern was the profit margin and the unions only wanted to take and take. But that is not necessarily true of the new groups of labor leaders and, in some cases, new groups of executives within the private sector. To me, "partnership" means that we work together on real problems — the gut issues — and we understand that we as a single entity do not have all the answers. We have to take into consideration the various ethnic groups in this country. Their thoughts about solving their problems should be placed on the table. And leaders in business, labor, and the public sector should be willing to listen to some of their recommendations without the fears and suspicions that have existed over the years.

STRAUS: Mr. Mayor.

FEDERICO PEÑA: I don't think there's a perfect definition of "partnership," but certainly the first two are characterizations that I would accept. Before I try to define "partnership" from a city perspective, let me say that partnerships in cities across America are absolutely crucial and essential tools for developing our cities. They are absolutely critical to our survival. In defining the word "partnership," I would agree generally with what has been said, and I recall the definition that I learned in law school—"bringing together various persons and stakeholders to pool their resources for a common good." For a city like Denver, the definition of "partnership" now means a return on our investment. We are looking at the notion of a partnership from an entrepreneurial perspective — what does a partnership bring? And there are all kinds of partnerships we could discuss. For example, in Denver, we have full partnerships, limited partnerships, and other kinds of partnerships. But essentially, I agree that "partnership" means bringing together all the parties — the stakeholders — pooling their resources for a common good and, we hope, for their mutual gain.

STRAUS: Neal Peirce has been covering state-city relationships for years. Neal, what would you say?

NEAL R. PEIRCE: I agree with all of the above, for once. We reporters are supposed to take a different view, but in this case they're all correct. I think I will add a little twist to your question. Partnerships have accomplished a great deal in many cities in the last few years. Now if they're going to be effective in the future, they must move beyond helping with housing, education, crime programs, and so on and determine how strategically to change the way the systems operate so that they will create fewer problems in the future. An example of that in education is the Adopt-A-School programs. The intervention of the business community into schools is very valuable. Even more valuable is when, as in

California and in Texas and in some other states, the business community says unless we make some fundamental changes in the schools we're not going to have an educated enough populace.

We do not only want to see that appropriate charity and cooperative ventures are undertaken in the neighborhoods. We want to undertake them in a way that will empower neighborhood people to act effectively on their own housing and economic-development programs so that they won't need as much charity or special assistance in the future. The heavy concentration that the New York City Partnership has had on housing is a very important breakthrough and extremely important in New York, because of the critical housing shortage here. One consideration has to be how to change the system so that intervention is possible when the flow of Federal money is inadequate. Mr. Rockefeller has referred quite appropriately to the problem of reduced Federal funds, but there is now an era of opening opportunity to tap more state funds and real estate transfer taxes—a percentage of that taken for low-income housing. My point is that a broader, strategic look at how to change systems is probably the direction that partnerships will have to take to be really effective.

STRAUS: Leading from that, then, are there some issues that belong just to the public sector and some that belong solely to the private sector? Or is it all going to meld together? If there are such issues, what are they?

PEIRCE: I think the answer is no, but I want to elaborate on that. Each issue needs to be looked at in a broad sense by those involved in partnerships operating within their city or state. They can't leave one entirely to the private sector or to the public sector and say it's going to be taken care of.

STRAUS: I mean, for instance, defense wouldn't—

PEIRCE: Well, we're dealing on the state and local basis, with partnerships.

PEÑA: Let me respond to the question of defense, because I think even a fundamental service like police protection and safety—one form of defense, locally—is now being shared in many ways with the broader community. An example is the the Crime Stoppers program in New York. We have had a similar program in Denver for a long time. In providing and ensuring safety through police work, we rely heavily on partnerships with neighborhood organizations—setting up neighborhood crime watch programs, for example. We have been vigorous in encouraging citizens to be partners with our safety department to ensure that we can effectively provide protection. I can't think of any other major traditional government service that could not, in some way, be shared with others in the community.

HUGHES: Certainly the feeding of the children in our school system is one. I think that is the responsibility of the Federal government. The program was established in the 1940s because many of the young men being inducted into the service were found to be suffering from malnutrition. And yet, over the last five or six years, the Reagan administration has cut back on that program by more than $5 billion. This not only hurts the nutritional level of the child but also hurts the economy as a whole, because every time a student drinks a carton of milk the canning and container industries profit. Everytime there is a cutback on a school lunch meal, someone loses—the people, mainly in the private sector, who transport those goods, the manufacturers, and the farming industry. I believe very strongly that the Federal government should assume responsibility for feeding our children. Hands Across America raised $28 million, but that isn't enough money to deal with the needs of the students of today. We did a survey in District 20 in Brooklyn, for example, because everybody usually says that these kinds of programs are strictly for the poor, blacks, Hispanics, and other minorities. But we took the survey in a blue-collar, middle-class neighborhood, where some students ate breakfast and others did not. Those who ate breakfast were not nearly as hyperactive in the classroom as those who did not. So there is a direct correlation between education stabilization and the socialization pace. I think the Federal government ought to be a single partner for housing and other needs.

BYROM: Frequently, I am on a platform with Michael Harrington. I am billed as the capitalist, he is the socialist, and everybody expects a fight. But on about 85 percent of what each of us says we're in agreement. Unfortunately, the 15 percent on which we are in disagreement is how to deal with the problem. I happen to be in complete agreement with Mr. Hughes as to what the problem is and that it needs to be solved. I don't think the way to do it is solely by Federal subsidy, and we've got to get away from the idea that the Federal government is the place to turn for the solution to every problem. I'm not sure how I would view the question of who has the greatest amount of responsibility for the food program in the schools. I understand the concern, but in education, in the delivery of health care, in the question of unemployment, and in the question of housing, communities can do much more about their own problems than the Federal government can do for them. I am certainly eager to see these public-private partnerships in communities beginning to work. I would like to mention one problem that we need to do something about, and we need to do it fast—the question of preschool education for minority-disadvantaged people. The country is going to suffer tremendously by the year 2000 if we don't do something now. But we cannot expect the Federal government to overcome the inertia of the system and get something done soon enough. Somehow, communities will have to deal with this question.

PEIRCE: Consider excluding breakfast and preschool education. We've learned in the last few years how vital those things are; how they lead to an educated populace, which is a competent populace, which can then make enough money, I suppose, to pay the social security for the rest of us when we become old. Without an effort to nurture a competent populace, there will be real problems. Should the Federal government do it? Let's say that we agreed it *should*. The reality remains that the Federal government is not about to pick up major new responsibilities. But there's another reality: the Federal government is spending mostly for older people; it's leaving a great deal of the expenditure responsibilities for youth to the states and the cities and, in effect, to the partnership type of organizations. The wealth exists in New York City and in New York State—probably more than in most states because it is not having the economic problems of the rural South and some other parts of the country—to take care of every social problem. In addition, the human resources exist here. I can't think of another place in the whole

United States as a community, as a state, or as a city about which one could make that statement with as much confidence. So while one waits, if one wishes, and lobbies for the Federal government to intervene, the real question is, Will this community take the steps that it needs for its own social future?

PEÑA: I agree with Neal. We in Denver accepted many years ago that the decentralization process was here. Frankly, I don't care who becomes the next president of the United States. Decentralization will continue. Which means that at the local level we are not going to get the funds that we used to receive from job training and other programs. And it really is up to all of us at the local level to pool our resources, our talents, our energies, and our ideas — as you're doing here in New York and as we hope we're doing in Denver — to deal with these challenges. That is really the answer for the self-reliance, the self-sufficiency, and the real independence of every city in this country. I think the big question is going to be, Does every city have the ability to become self-reliant? What happens when a part of the country is in such a state that it cannot, even through partnerships, provide minimum food requirements for school children. Is it the national responsibility to help to equalize where there is inequality? I don't know, but I think we're in it by ourselves at the local level.

STRAUS: I think both the mayor and the governor of New York would be thrilled to hear Neal say that we enjoy so much wealth here in the state of New York. I wonder, following up on what you were saying, is it possible that this concept of public-private partnerships is a way of letting government off the hook and then blaming the private sector for not doing enough on social issues? Is government using partnerships as a kind of gap filler? *We're getting out of the business, you get into the business.* And then when it doesn't work, it's the private sector's fault.

PEÑA: From our perspective, I don't think that's the attitude. We are at a point where if partnerships are not formed to address these problems they will not be addressed. Many of us in city government are having our own financial difficulties, and we are unable to pick up many of these programs. It's not a question of abdication of responsibility; it is a question of sheer physical and financial ability. Voters across America are refusing to increase taxes to continue some of these programs. So, as a mayor, I have a question to face. If we do not form a partnership with the business community, neighborhood groups, and others to address some of these issues, they will not be addressed.

BYROM: A lot of you are aware that in the mid-1940s Greater Pittsburgh formed the Allegheny Conference for Community Development, which was one of the forerunners, if not *the* forerunner, of public-private partnerships. It accomplished a lot, and everything went fine until we got a mayor by the name of Pete Flaherty, who chose to believe that his political interests were best served by removing himself from contact with the business community — and in fact with practically every other constituency. Mr. Flaherty found that people don't vote for people on the basis of what the candidates are for but what they are against. So he chose to be against everything. He was an extremely popular mayor in that he could get reelected, essentially without opposition, but he damned nearly ruined the city, because the public-private partnership was dissolved during his term of office. When we got a new mayor, he immediately brought the public-private partnership back. And the difference is fantastic. You would assume that because of the demise of the smokestack industries the city would be in the depths of despair, but despite some severe problems it is doing very well. It is the existence of that public-private partnership that makes it work. At the risk of sounding as though I'm picking on an individual, I thank the Lord that Pete Flaherty wasn't mayor when the steel industry declined.

PEIRCE: There are times when it's very helpful, though, to have a negative figure from the point of view of the business community. The best thing that ever happened to Cleveland was a mayor named Dennis J. Kucinich. He alarmed the business community, which had ignored the city for years. So when George Voinovich came in as mayor in 1979, they were ready to do anything that he asked, and Voinovich has been a good enough mayor to mobilize the civic resources of that community. He has revitalized Cleveland in the last few years. Only a financial crisis akin to the 1975 one in New York could awaken the complacent business community in Cleveland. The question now, during less obvious crises, is how does one get the active participation of a broad-enough band of the business community and of all the other groups in society when some mutual sacrifice is perhaps necessary.

BYROM: I think Neal Peirce has put his finger on something that is very important. Years ago Sydney Harris, the columnist, said that human beings don't accomplish anything important because of positive constructive motivation. They react to crisis with heroics. And I think one of the reasons that public-private partnerships are doing so well is that many of us are perceiving near crisis or crisis in our communities. As we start to correct some of the problems, I am fearful that we will go back into a euphoric state and fail to continue to do the good things that we are now doing.

HUGHES: I think partnerships have to do more than just start a forum. We need to think about partnerships in our schools, particularly in our business colleges, because there are two attitudes. Business deals strictly with the business world and has no concern about some of the social needs. The labor unions are concerned about some social needs but basically about the priorities of their members, as they should be, as the private sector should be concerned about profit margins. But we must work together if we are going to have a successful partnership. There are real suspicions of each other. I was happy to hear what Mr. Peirce said about the 1975 fiscal crisis in the city of New York. The labor unions played a very important role in keeping this city from going into default. But when we see in the trade magazines the story about what happened, the unions usually get only about two or three lines. Many employees, including minorities, had to give up one hour of work a day, which represented $20 a week per worker. There was a difficulty then, across the board. People should be given credit for their sacrifices and they will be encouraged to work closer with those in the business arena. I believe we have to start at an earlier age, in prekindergarten perhaps, to develop the attitude that business, government, and unions can work together to help society turn itself around.

PEIRCE: New York is swimming in resources, but it is not using them well. The human resources in New York City are staggering. When you think of the talent in the marketing sector, in the communications center, in publishing, in Wall Street, in finance, you have within this city the greatest reservoir of human talent. It seems to me a strategic question for the partnership is how to mobilize that talent to work cooperatively and creatively with people who are living in neighborhoods that have major problems and to work with the school system that has major problems. Looking at all of your assets is a good strategic plan, if you will. It is the kind of broad thinking that a partnership needs to bring into the game.

BYROM: I'd like to agree and add to what Neal Peirce said. In addition to human resources, the actual material resources are available. I don't want to sound like a college economics lecturer, but in *Capitalism, Socialism and Democracy*, published in 1942, Schumpeter discussed poverty and what can be done about it. He pointed out that between 1878 and 1928 per capita income in the United States doubled on a real basis. It would be wonderful, he said, if it could double again between 1928 and 1978, because we would have probably eliminated poverty. But he said of course it wouldn't happen, because there had just been a depression, and per capita income was down; and he said by 1978 we would have 160 million people in the United States, so the divisor would be much greater. Per capita income in 1928 was $600, and to be doubled on a real basis it would have to be $1,300 in 1978. It was actually about $1,800 in 1978, which was close to tripling it, and the population was 222 million. His point was that poverty need not exist, and I agree. Our problem is not the availability of material and human resources; it's a distributive problem. We do not know yet how to distribute wealth on an equitable basis in all senses of wealth in this society.

HUGHES: I sit on the mayor's Commission of Black New Yorkers, and to my chagrin I find that colleges like the City University of New York do not have a cooperation network so that their students can get into the real world. It ought to have one. Another aspect of the problem is capitalism. I believe in capitalism, but I also believe that when you deal with the divisor factor you ought to understand where the money turns over and where it does not. In most of the minority communities, the money turns over only once or twice, and then it goes into the larger community. I think it is the responsibility of the private business sector to review that and find ways to keep that money in the community for at least two more turnovers so that it can finance itself and become self-sustaining. At the same time, through those profit margins, we could help the larger community. I think we ought to look at that.

STRAUS: Let me ask a question here. How many people in this room—please put up your hand—own one share of stock or more? Now, I assume, when you bought that stock you hoped that it would increase in value, and that was your primary reason for buying it. Which brings us to the question we have to ask:

Isn't the primary interest of business to increase the bottom line? If so, why should it take its eyes off the bottom line and get into a social issue like the partnerships that we're talking about?

BYROM: I may surprise a few of you. I start with the premise that the institutions by which a society accomplishes its purpose must be perceived over a period of time as making a positive contribution to the well-being of society. Admittedly a corporation like Koppers Co., which I chaired, is an economic entity, and to a major degree decisions are made on the basis of economic criteria. But we must operate in accordance with socially accepted ground rules. We have to consider other stakeholders besides the stockholders. You must understand that profit per se is not what a lot of people think it is; it's not some Adam Smithian predatory result. Profit is the means by which a corporation is able to maintain itself and thus fulfill its purpose. The profits are used for two purposes — for dividends and for investing in plant and equipment. One increases the industrial base of the nation so that it can increase its capability for creating wealth. The other is interest paid for the use of other people's savings. Profit, therefore, is a fundamental requirement, but it is not a result of greed; it is an economic reality. On the other hand, if in order to show a reasonable return on investment, a decent profit, it is necessary to ignore the fact that you are polluting society, that you are running an unsafe plant, and that you are not providing employment opportunities for people who need upward mobility in our society — if you shortchange society in all of those respects in order to get a bottom-line result, that is not an acceptable way to run a corporation. The institution must be perceived as being an appropriately viable operation within the guidelines of contemporary society.

STRAUS: I wish Mr. Byrom were twins! And I wonder, Mayor, as a prominent Democrat about to be reelected, how does it feel to jump into bed with the business community?

PEÑA: I didn't know those were inconsistent concepts. My Democratic father, who's a businessman, would be shocked to hear you ask that question. How a city like Denver becomes economically stable, diversified, and strong is not a Democratic or a Republican question. It is not a partisan issue. The question that we're addressing is how partnerships can be used to achieve important objectives in a community.

STRAUS: How is Denver different, since it has had a partnership?

PEÑA: I want to give one example. In city government we have taken the approach that we must work in partnership with the business community, with labor, with neighborhood organizations, with everybody in the community to move our city forward. We talked earlier about what happens if we do not do these things. We questioned, for example, whether the bottom-line concern is inconsistent with involving oneself in the community projects. I would argue strongly that it's not, if you look at both long-term and short-term gains. Let me be very specific. We recognized in Denver that our downtown, like so many others across America, was plagued with some difficulties. We knew that it was important to our city that the downtown be revitalized. The community understood that the downtown was important to the entire economy — to neighborhood residents, to the unemployed, and to business people. We also knew that the city government alone could not develop a downtown plan, a blueprint for the future, and so we formed a partnership — the Downtown Denver Partnership. After the business community spent more than a million dollars, and twenty-eight diverse citizens with diverse concerns gave of their time, we produced a document that serves as a blueprint for redeveloping downtowns. This is one way that the investment of the business community is going to pay off in the long term — not just for the business people downtown but for the entire city and for the neighborhood people who live around the downtown and want it to be successful. I think we have to work. I don't think the question is whether I as a Democrat am nervous about working with the business community. We're all in this together, and we had better use all of our resources.

BYROM: Just last night I was rereading John Gardner's last official letter when he retired from the chairmanship of the Carnegie Foundation in 1965. The essay is titled "The Antileadership Vaccine." John Gardner in his inimitable and profound way was examining the manner in which the United States tries to destroy the potential for leadership in our society. Barbara Tuchman some time ago referred to "elitism" as a nonpejorative term, something that we really need. I happen to be a believer in that. I think we have to understand that when we talk about a public-private partnership we aren't really talking about institutional arrangements that operate per se in a bureaucratic sense. These partnerships work because there are true leaders of the various constituencies in the community. They recognize, as Robert Greenleaf suggested, that fundamentally a leader is an enabler whose presence allows things to happen that would not otherwise happen if he weren't around in his position as servant leader. Mayor Peña doesn't know that when I retired from Pittsburgh I moved to Colorado, and I was a citizen of that state for about four years. I happen to know that he inherited a mess, because the prior mayor wasn't worth a damn. Maybe he had been at some point, but the city was in a mess. What Mr. Peña has accomplished in a very short time is outstanding, but it's a function of his leadership capability. I mentioned Pete Flaherty's disastrous leadership in Pittsburgh, and I think that we must understand that public-private partnerships are not inanimate objects but dynamic organisms made up of people who in fact are great. Absent that, a public-private partnership won't accomplish anything.

STRAUS: Let me say that I'm delighted we're not on the air at this moment, because if we were subject to the Fairness Doctrine I would have to invite quite a few people to respond. We've talked a lot about the business involvement, but I get a sense that unions are not as involved across the country in partnerships. Can anyone tell me whether that's because they're not invited or because they choose not to join?

HUGHES: I've been president of Local 372 since 1968. Before that the circumstances were different, and the attitude and atmosphere in which we had to fight for workers were a little different. Again, during the 1975 fiscal crisis in New York

City the unions were there when they were needed. When unions get an opportunity to sit on some of these boards and have a say in the decision-making process, I think you will find that the cooperation from labor will improve. If you've been burned a few times on either side, you are reluctant to be involved. For example, because of my local and my being the chairman of the 150,000 school employees of AFSCME throughout the United States, it was my job to develop alliances. I developed an alliance with the American School Food Service Association, which is basically a management-type institution. They were reluctant for me—a minority and a labor leader—to come in and make recommendations as to where we were going in this industry. But we found that we had a lot in common, whether in Mississippi, Alabama, Georgia, Tennessee, New York, or California—we all had a common problem. That was particularly so when I began to work with the milk industry. Of course, the milk industry had nothing in common with our philosophy as a union, but it needed to survive, and we needed to survive. We therefore formed a partnership.

Unions in many instances have been the backbone of this society. It was the labor movement that said we ought to have a free education. Today business should be involved in the education curriculum. You who are in business set the jobs, the pace, and the standards, and you are going to absorb those students in your industry. If there is no contact, then we have a problem. Sometimes we use some terrible language, and that frightens everybody. But I'm sure it's no worse than that being used in the stockholders' room when profits are down. Labor leaders are afraid to be too close to business, because their membership may perceive them as being in bed with management, and they could therefore lose an election. And the executive chairmen of private institutions are concerned when the profit margin goes down if it's perceived that they are involved in a declining industry.

STRAUS: Neal, how come no one except you is writing about partnerships? Do you think that the lack of public attention threatens their future?

PEIRCE: I think it's a sad commentary that no one wants to compete with me. Being the only national columnist who ever chose to concentrate on state and local affairs, it's a lonely field. I don't see the pack of journalists very close to me. Does it imperil partnerships? It might. There is a basic problem with the media, which have not had a happy relationship with local government, business, or utilities over the last few years. Some of it is the Watergate mentality—the idea that they're all a bunch of crooks, so if you look far enough you'll find something wrong with what they're doing that you can expose. That has always sold newspapers, and I assume it sells television viewership. You also have a lot of educated young reporters who are out to make their mark, and it seems easier to find the crooks than to find those who are doing constructive things. So, the question then turns, how do you encourage a culture to look more at creative types of partnerships that may not make as many flashy headlines but do explain a lot more of the substance of what's happening in the community? The business community and its labor and other allies must speak frequently with those who control the media—from reporter up to publisher and owner—and talk about these issues, saying we do have a community here that is going to sink or swim together. It's necessary to balance your coverage of what is wrong within the community. But let me stress that an independent press is necessary when you have corruption like that in New York City and other cities around the country this year. You need to have the media there asking hard questions, but the leaders of the media need to be told that it is their responsibility to show how the society is pulling together and that they are a part of the system and need to view their responsibility that way too.

STRAUS: Now I'd like to open this up for questions from the audience and then let the panel tell us where they think partnerships will be in the year 2000. Are there any questions?

GRAHAM FINNEY: I'm an outlander from Philadelphia. Partnerships assume in many ways a necessary and close working relationship between the sectors. My question is, What should the stance be of the privately led partnership at a time in a city's or state's life when a divisive issue takes form—like the resolution of solid waste or a change in the charter? It might be the Pittsburgh situation that Mr. Byrom described. How far should a partnership go in becoming an advocate of fundamental change which may be necessary in that city's future? Do partnerships in any way put a cap on reform?

PEIRCE: Whether you do it as the New York City Partnership or as some other organization or whether the individuals who are leaders within that group go out and make a public position and conduct a fight on a major public issue—that is really the difference. If you make it the partnership that is going to get into things that are highly emotionally charged, taking one side, it may make it difficult for the organization to gather everyone under the fold to move ahead. Certainly, its individual members have as much responsibility as everyone else to take a position when there is a major charter change or what have you.

BYROM: I think it's very interesting, since I've been a resident of various states. I was born in Ohio and spent most of my time in Pennsylvania. Then I went to Colorado, and now I'm in Arizona and spend most of my time in New York. Anyhow, it's interesting that you asked the question, because it's hard for Philadelphians to admit it, but they have a real problem down there. Part of the reason is that the state of Pennsylvania shouldn't even exist. I knew Dick Thornburgh very well. Before he decided to run for governor, he came to me—giving me the great privilege of asking my opinion—and said, "What do you think?" I told him he was crazy. I said nobody in his right mind would want to be governor of Pennsylvania. He asked why and I said the state shouldn't exist. There is no way that Philadelphia and Pittsburgh can be in the same state and assume a decent form of governance. There's no way a senator can represent both Philadelphia and Pittsburgh. Philadelphia ought to be in a state called Philjerdel—southern Jersey, Delaware, and metropolitan Philadelphia. The interesting thing about it is that the partnership in Philadelphia is in effect operating on that basis. Despite state boundaries, there is a separate private Philjerdel committee that recognizes what the true boundaries of the state should be. Despite the failure of the political system to deal properly with it, the private and public people are working together to overcome the obstructions of the state lines.

In Pittsburgh we needed a metropolitan government, and the basic reason we couldn't get one was the volunteer fire department. There are about 139 of them in Greater Pittsburgh. As you all know, it is through membership in these fire departments that a lot of people achieve dignity in their lives. The political pressure that can be generated within a small community by the volunteers in the fire brigade is tremendous. If a metropolitan government is perceived as dangerous to the continuance of the volunteer system, a referendum opposed by the volunteers will fail. Richard Lugar, when he was mayor of Indianapolis, got one of the first metropolitan governments by forming a pact with the volunteer fire department so that for fifteen years they wouldn't change their charters. By that time, all the present volunteer firemen would be retired, so they didn't care about the future. There have to be those kinds of understandings and arrangements. The partnership supposedly represents most, or all, the constituencies of a particular society, and they must decide what's best for a particular community in the long term and do something about it.

STRAUS: Other than the political role of volunteer fire departments, I wonder if the panel would care to say anything about how they see the role of voluntary nonprofit organizations in these partnerships, particularly since they have historically been dependent both on government and on business for support.

PEÑA: In Denver they are playing a very active role in many of the partnerships. For example, there are many nonprofit organizations that are involved in development projects in their neighborhoods. The city has formed partnerships with them to help with some of these projects, which range from affordable housing projects to retail projects to small-business projects. They are also very much involved in many other efforts. Recently, for example, we signed an agreement with the neighborhood organizations in Denver, which will clean up a certain part of the city where the city owns property. The city was not doing a good job keeping it clean, and now neighborhood organizations are going to do it for us. So there is clearly a specific, positive role that they can play in these partnerships.

HUGHES: From labor's point of view, though we believe in volunteerism, I think we ought to be very careful about private industry taking over public responsibilities and jobs in many instances. It's great to talk about volunteerism, but what happens to the livelihood of the workers? The sanitation department workers would be very sensitive about volunteers cleaning up the streets, unless they felt that there had been enough discussion surrounding the quality and lack of service. So we ought to be very careful. I was a little surprised to hear Mr. Rockefeller say that the Reagan administration ought to understand that the private sector can't absorb all of the social responsibilities. That's a big statement, and I agree with it. This attitude that government has to get out of business makes a lot of us nervous. I think there are enough resources, if they are distributed fairly, and we can provide people with adequate incomes and incentives to move up in their jobs. We ought to sit down and work those differences out without making a general across-the-board statement about volunteerism.

DON SHARP: I'm from Chemical Bank. How can the resources available through public-private partnerships be communicated effectively to banks, for example, and to small- and moderate-sized businesses? There are many resources available, but so few people know they are really there.

PEIRCE: I don't think there is an easy answer to that. The rest of the panel may have answers about reaching the smaller-business sector and the resources that are there. But, since I made the statement that all the resources are there, I should try to answer the question. You would indicate in your strategic plan for a partnership how to make those links, the forms of inducement, and the professional peer pressure that can create interest and involvement by those other groups within the society. The tactics have to be laid out to reach that goal.

HUGHES: One of the things that the banks have to recognize is that there was a point in their history when they were redlining a lot of neighborhoods and wouldn't loan money to those neighborhoods so they could get started. Although I believe in capitalism, we have to find a mechanism to roll the money over more than twice in certain neighborhoods. Right now, if you are a minority business person getting into the construction industry, for example, you can't even buy a bond. The banks won't lend you any money unless you are bonded, and it's difficult to get a bond. So, when we're talking about all these zones we ought to be aware of what's happening right now. The problem with society is that you have to take care of a certain group of people because there is a basic need for it. Then there is another level that needs a little push, a little guidance, so that it can become self-sustaining. For every private job, every amount of money that is invested in private industry, one or two jobs are created. So those who can be self-sustaining will eventually show a profit margin. What is happening in the boardroom does not speak to this (and I'm not criticizing the business people), because everybody seems to be frightened at the loss of a dollar. I think a partnership through its networking of communication can satisfy the fears of these two entities. If we do it with the educational material available for the community, you will find more respect for the private sector, more respect for the public sector, and certainly more respect for the unions that are going to be involved in that area.

DICK FLEMING: I'm with the Denver Partnership. I'd like to go back to a point that Mr. Byrom touched on — the role of the enabling leader. A critical ingredient in public-private partnerships seems to be a leader who can share power and in some cases give up power. That flies in the face of traditional expectations and some traditional models, whether you are a union leader or an elected official or an officer reporting to a board of directors of a private corporation. I would be interested in the panel's thoughts on how that kind of leadership style can be reconciled with some of the traditional expectations that individual sectors have for their leaders.

PEÑA: Let me try to answer that, since we're from the same community. We come from a city that has a strong mayoral form of government, where decisions have traditionally been made by a few individuals. My philosophy is one of inclusiveness, trying to bring in all of the actors, the stakeholders who were involved in any one issue. That is a high-risk proposition. By sharing and giving up some power and authority that you have traditionally had either by virtue of the office or because of the people in that office you take a risk—that somehow the project may go in a direction that you may not fully support. And you are criticized for that, as I was when I put together a number of committees. For example, when I selected my cabinet, I brought in the labor and business communities and neighborhood groups, put a committee together, and asked for its advice. It took two months. The media said that was not leadership, that a leader would pick his own cabinet without the help of all those citizens. So you have to take that risk, take some criticism and blame, but I would argue strongly that it's worth it. And I would argue that in the long term that style of leadership is going to be seen more and more across cities in America, because the issues are too complex, because everybody in the community is a stakeholder and wants a part in the decision making, and because they have the ability to make contributions in these processes in city government. So, as one elected official, I have opened doors, shared the risks, and made some mistakes, but I think it has been healthy.

PEIRCE: I think it is interesting that the question is raised between two Denverites in New York, a city that has traditionally had hero mayors—strong, dominant figures who tell everybody else how to do things and then tell them to get lost when they don't. We outsiders have noticed a change of tone in the last month or two in reporting on New York City, but you know more about that than we do. I think that what you are hearing from outside is that the new form of corporate leadership is also appropriate for political leadership. There seems to be much less swashbuckling, less emphasis on the top, and much more concern with getting all the stakeholders in the corporation to the table. The same tendency is seen in what many people now feel is the appropriate form of leadership in cities—not a charismatic, command-type leadership—the man on the white horse (it was always a man, I think, maybe a woman; usually it was a man) but a new form that also involves the understanding that you are dealing with multisectoral leadership. Equally important is leadership in the business community and unions, if they are to cooperate and work well within the city. Leadership is also important in the downtown development corporations that will be part of the business community—community development corporations—that are part of our effort to bring back our neighborhoods economically. Scott Fosler, with the Committee for Economic Development, has used the term "ad hocing" it, and we're ad hocing all sorts of relationships in the society now. Rich Bradley, with the International Downtown Association, and others are looking at the new model of leadership in the cities now, cooperatively with the Citizens Forum/National Municipal League and some others. It is interesting that we can now begin to see how well these traditional forms of leadership are working and what new ones will be more appropriate. But we still have not resolved the question of how a lower-key, conciliatory leader will gain recognition and acceptance.

HUGHES: I tried to say briefly—and this is not to negate my feeling and support for our oldest citizens—that the newer leadership on both the labor side and the management side are willing to talk to each other. If that continues, we will be able to work in partnership to determine where we want to go.

Mr. Peirce, I'm intimidated by the media, because if you go after me and I happen to be found not guilty, you don't then give that story the same coverage. That frightens a lot of people. And then when good things do happen, there's not enough reporting on it. The media have become a very important part of our lives. People won't even drink a cup of coffee unless the paper is there. You can see the joggers running through the street in the morning to get the paper to get back to the house for a cup of coffee. A positive image of all these things would help influence those who may be reluctant to follow the less charismatic leader, whether he be a mayor or she be a governor, who tries to make things happen. (The use of such terms as "he and she" can have a decisive effect on the direction in which we go.) I believe strongly that we can understand the fears of each other and can recognize that you're not weak when you involve everyone who is affected by a particular issue. It shows that you have a concern about the total community because that same total community is going to make your programs successful or unsuccessful.

STRAUS: Time is running out, so I'm going to ask Mr. Byrom to sum up.

BYROM: Our first renaissance in Pittsburgh was considered exceedingly successful. There was only one thing that I know of that we missed very badly, and we might not have missed it if Jane Jacobs had written her book *Death of Cities* before we went ahead with our renewal. In order to take care of a bad slum situation, we created new housing for a lot of people and did not involve them in the decision making in any way whatsoever. We assumed that since we were giving them better housing that they would be delighted. The problem was that the better housing wasn't a home. We caused great, great problems in Pittsburgh that lasted for a long time. The moral of that is to be sure that all the constituencies are involved in the partnership.

Governor Lamm was nice enough to invite me to speak to his cabinet at a retreat soon after I moved to Colorado. I listened to them discussing things for a while, and they talked about how they were going to solve this problem and that problem and how they would go about it. When I came on I said, "You people are doing what everybody else in the United States always seems to do. You're trying to solve problems that you haven't yet defined. Will somebody explain to me why Colorado exists?" That was the cabinet of the governor, and they looked at me as though I'd gone out of my mind. The problem was that they had not yet decided what the mission of that political entity was. I think that partnerships must not try to solve a problem before taking the time to figure out what the mission of that segment of society happens to be. Then they could identify some realizable objectives that, if implemented, would help them fulfill their mission.

I'd like to say I am delighted to be involved with public-private partnerships in cities other than New York. I don't know how you do it here. It seems to me that public-private partnerships best operate when they are dealing with the problems of a community. I am not satisfied that I understand what "community" means in the city of New York. Is it a series of boroughs? Is it the city? I don't know what it is, and it seems to me that it would help the New York City Partnership if it would address this question. I recognize the need for critical mass and economic scale that are afforded by an organization like the New York City Partnership, but maybe there would be a place for component partnerships that would deal with problems that are unique to a community and not necessarily to all of New York City.

STRAUS: One of the ways I must say that we are able to do it in New York is because of the remarkable leadership we're given by Frank Macchiarola, our president. I'll give you each one minute to sum up.

PEIRCE: I want to talk about this question of what you learn from others, because I think it's important in New York, which tends to view itself as the center of the universe, to realize that some very interesting activities in partnerships are under way in other cities around the country. I think New York could look at the Boston Compact and learn a lot more about how to have a challenge relationship that makes the schools work more productively with the businesses of the city. It could look at Denver and see how to devise a city plan that tries to reach out from the inner city across the no-man's-land and into the neighborhoods that are struggling. It could look at Seattle, which has a "Kids' Place" program on how to make the city a warm and welcoming and enthusiastic place for young people. It could see how the Boston Housing Partnership gets a lot more people around the table than others normally do. It should, I believe, send people out to look at other cities. A lot of learning is negative. Why did other cities fail in what they tried? I think that effort by New York could help a lot, because if you want to take New York today as the equivalent of Olde England, the center of the universe as it sees itself, recall that Rudyard Kipling once said, "Who shall England know, who only England knows."

PEÑA: I hope that at least you got the impression from my remarks that it's my strong belief that in communities across America, at least in the climate and circumstances that exist in this country in this decade and probably in the next few decades, that partnerships are here to stay. They are absolutely critical to the development of our communities. We can no longer, at least at the local level, rely on the traditional resources we have had in the past. The issues today are too complex. They need involvement, ideas, and suggestions from everybody. We are all going to have to work together, compromising, giving up certain positions we have taken in the past, all contributing in one way or another in order to move our cities forward. All of the challenges discussed today—from hunger and air pollution to job training and housing—are much too difficult for one mayor, or one governor, or one government to meet alone. We all have to do it together, and I hope that you see that these efforts are exciting, they are workable, and you can make a contribution.

STRAUS: After this discussion, it is clear that public-private partnerships are here to stay. They're growing. And we all have to work in various ways to make them stronger.

# The Role of the University in Public-Private Partnerships

RONALD C. KYSIAK

Although public-private partnerships have usually been limited to business and government ventures, there is a variation that can be a powerful tool in meeting new economic-development goals — the university-public-private partnership. This partnership has been effective in some parts of the country in promoting a technologically oriented economic-development program.

Joint university, public-sector, and private-sector initiatives in New Haven, Connecticut, and Evanston, Illinois, have forged unusual yet highly effective alliances between city governments and universities, two institutions with a history of conflict. The enmity that characterizes these relationships was pronounced in New Haven and Evanston because of a basic political conflict over the universities' tax-exempt status and the seemingly uncaring attitude of those institutions toward the budgetary and developmental plight of the cities. Yet these fragile coalitions, once built, can be powerful in dealing with the rejuvenation of obsolete economies and depressed business climates.

The benefit of these partnerships is that they strengthen the existing public-private partnership, because the university contributes something that neither the business community nor the public sector has — the prestige and environment of a major institution, including its faculty and physical resources. These attributes were of little import when economic-development programs were built around the seminal strategy of attracting and retaining an industrial base. This was the major urban strategy of the 1950s through the 1970s of most of the cities in the Midwest and the South, while eastern cities were slowly realizing that such a strategy was doomed to fail. The eastern cities, such as Boston, Philadelphia, and New Haven, first suffered the major shift away from manufacturing in the national economy. They came to understand the necessity of a more effective strategy tied to new technology to generate new business. The implementation of this strategy demanded university involvement and opened the doors for mutual discussion among public, private, and university sectors in order to create a nurturing environment for entrepreneurial development tied to new technologies.

Because of the structural changes in the national economy, with the expansion of services and decline of manufacturing and the growing realization that job growth came through the generation of small businesses, the cities required access into the small-business formation and technology arena. As Boston experienced a new economic resurgence along Route 128, other cities began to see how the new service and technology economy was created, and they also clearly understood that the concentration of universities within the Boston area sparked the development.

Economic development in cities was therefore redirected to technology transfer and new-business development; for this the cities needed the expertise and credibility of the university. Thus from an economic-development standpoint, city-university partnerships were natural.

The business-university partnership also began to grow while the dominance of United States industry in world manufacturing was replaced by the creative manufacturing methods of the new industrial giants, Japan, Taiwan, and Korea. American industry had to admit that it needed to go overseas to learn how to produce better and cheaper goods. And it was not long before American companies, stung by this realization, began to seek ways of joining with the educational centers of technological expertise to reestablish American dominance, or at least competitiveness, in manufacturing.

For years, large corporations had provided money to universities to do basic research, with the understanding that they might gain some practical benefit from such research at some point but not counting on it. Businesses found new products and new processes in their own laboratories, but they were slow to implement changes because of complacency born of market dominance throughout the 1950s and 1960s. A prime example of this hesitancy to modernize is the United States steel industry, which is now trying to catch up to its overseas competition with major new investments in equipment and technology. That reinvestment and rejuvenation of the basic manufacturing foundation is slowly under way, but in many sectors it may be too late.

Thus the private sector has come to understand that it needs university relationships on a much more direct level, and new research agreements between businesses and universities, with an applied orientation, are being formed with greater frequency. At the same time, the business community has begun to look to the universities as a major stabilizing force, as a real estate anchor, and as a growing source of applied research and technical professionals. It was only natural that these emerging partnerships between business and industry would connect with the needs of the public sector to revitalize its local communities, and thus the tripartite partnerships have begun to be formed, beginning along the East and West Coasts and spreading to other parts of the country.

These partnerships imply not only a joint sharing of benefits but also a sharing of risks. Both universities and cities are historically conservative institutions that avoid taking risks. Yet without risk there is little chance of gain. Both cities and universities have therefore had to reevaluate their long-standing aversion to risk-taking, and these unlikely partners have agreed to share the risks with each other.

Yet the city of New Haven and Yale University, along with the Olin Corporation, assumed the risk of a major project to convert eighty acres of abandoned industrial land and buildings into a vibrant center for new-business development. The Philadelphia City Science Center is another example of how universities and the private and public sectors can mesh their resources to regenerate a city's economy. In Philadelphia, thousands of new jobs and millions of dollars in new real estate development have been generated by a consortium of twenty-eight universities and teaching hospitals in support of a major science center in the City University area.

In Evanston, Illinois, Northwestern University and the city government are embarking on a downtown-urban research park as joint-venture partners, each sharing equally in the risk and possible rewards. The risk is compounded by the opposition of some in Evanston who have a deep and historic distrust of the university and its motives.

To effect these partnerships, substantial impediments had to be removed between the city government and the universities. These impediments consisted of each side's misunderstanding of the other's respective roles and responsibilities in the life of the city. And this difference of perception has kept these two potential allies separated for many decades in most urban centers.

## *New Haven and Evanston*

The case histories of the partnerships in New Haven, Connecticut, and Evanston, Illinois, have a disturbing similarity in the pattern of city-university relationships over time. Both Yale in New Haven and Northwestern in Evanston are private, independent universities of substantial reputation that draw their students from throughout the country and the world. Both are located in smaller urban communities. Yale is situated in a city of 125,000 people, wedged between the downtown and a poor, deteriorated neighborhood. Northwestern is located just north of Chicago along the beautiful lakefront of Lake Michigan, surrounded by upper-middle-class residential areas and downtown Evanston. Although Evanston has only 70,000 people, it has long been a sophisticated community, the first suburb north of Chicago and the home of a diverse and highly educated population.

Both universities were established around the same time as their respective cities and thus consider themselves at least the equal of the local governments. John Evans was the first president of Northwestern and was instrumental in forming the city that took his name. Yale University existed before the city of New Haven was established. Both universities expanded and achieved national and ultimately world significance and found themselves increasingly removed from the mundane administrative and political issues of city life that developed over time. This separation is physically demonstrated at Yale, where many of the university's buildings were constructed with their walls facing out to the city and their internal, protected courtyards reserved for the students. At one time there were pitched battles between "town" rowdies and "gown" students.

Northwestern University, on the other hand, owned the most desirable real estate in Evanston along the Lake Michigan shore. When additional land was needed for expansion in the 1970s, the city objected and the university had to engineer a major landfill project on its shoreline to create more acreage.

Both Yale and Northwestern have well-defined boundaries that the city governments in New Haven and Evanston jealously guard from expansion. Both universities, because of their size and reputation, have participated little or not at all in local politics, unless it was to gain some necessary legal approval for building or zoning needs. When they needed to expand or acquire additional properties, they did so with little or no warning or explanation to the local political system, leading to harsh statements from both sides and often public outrage. This division widened over the years and has been bridged only since 1980 in New Haven and only since 1983 in Evanston.

Although universities bring great prestige to a community, many citizens perceive them solely as large, powerful, nontaxpaying entities that soak up city services and provide little in return. This perception, combined with the universities' penchant for making unilateral decisions without city consultation, made the relationship between the two entities more and more acerbic as time went on. In both New Haven and Evanston, the university's tax exemption became a prime issue in local elections, with automatic defeat the reward for any candidate who defended the university's exempt position. It has been only recently that mayors in both New Haven and Evanston have been elected while proposing to find ways to cooperate with the university.

## The City Problem

As the fiscal squeeze began to tighten around the nation's cities during the late 1970s and early 1980s, municipal governments began to seek revenues from untapped sources. With cutbacks to cities in Federal development grants, welfare and health-care funds, and revenue sharing, cities began to run into the very real political problem of having to raise property taxes to the point of confiscation. During this time, cities turned once more to their large, nontaxpaying educational institutions and began to either demand or negotiate a contribution to shore up their sagging budgets. Most universities fought this action bitterly, though some reached a negotiated agreement to pay some fee in lieu of taxes. However, both Yale and Northwestern flatly rejected the concept of any financial contribution, calling it a surrogate form of illegal taxation.

Ironically, it was this fundamental disagreement that ultimately spawned the city-university partnership in both locations. In each case, the arguments on both sides supported the need for more tax revenue and a stabilized tax base. It was then a short leap of logic to a new, practical understanding that universities could help cities expand their tax bases by exploiting their scientific and technological resources.

Yale agreed to support a joint venture with the city government and the Olin Corporation to develop an eighty-acre, Olin-owned industrial complex into Science Park. The project was born out of a particularly bitter strike in one of Olin's subsidiaries and fanned by the heat of a mayoral campaign. When the mayor cordoned off all of Olin's property to "prevent violence," the company went to his opponent for relief. The university was soon brought into the fold through the efforts of both the Olin chairman (an alumnus) and some Yale visionaries who had been advocating a partnership with the city for some time. Those meetings resulted in the three parties' publicly announced agreement, in principle, to develop Science Park. The announcement was made within days after the new mayor took office.

In Evanston, a well-reported public dispute over city revenue needs and a proposal by some city councilmen to levy a "tuition tax" on Northwestern students prompted private-sector intervention by an alumnus who knew both city and university officials. He engineered a series of meetings between the two, out of which came a proposal for a nonprofit development corporation, supported by the city, the university and the business community, to increase employment and expand the tax base. This corporation, called Evanston Inventure, was formed in 1983. Shortly after forming Inventure, the university approached the city for a joint venture to develop a research park in downtown Evanston.

The goal of city government has historically been to generate a broader tax base with which it could leaven the tax burden and reduce the cost to the individual taxpayer, the person who votes. To do this, cities have historically attempted to tax businesses at a higher rate, if possible, or have created any number of user fees, which are intended to be a painless way of extracting more funds from the individual taxpayer without political fallout. By the late 1970s and early 1980s, American cities, particularly those in the Midwest and East, had run out of revenue-raising ideas and begun to reevaluate their fiscal future in light of the quickened shift in the American economy from manufacturing to service. As the cities watched their industries leave, taking with them their property and income-tax revenues, many participated in hectic development strategies to lure new industries into urban centers. These programs, supported substantially by the Federal government in the 1970s, had minimum results, since manufacturing was fleeing not only to the suburbs but also to the South and ultimately overseas because of severe cost pressures. Along with that shift often came a corresponding growth of the cities' service economies, but increasing numbers of office workers did not provide the property tax base once supported by major industry. It was then that economic-development strategies began to be adjusted to find ways of converting the new service economy into a taxpaying activity like city-income or head taxes.

Many cities chose to rebuild their downtowns, promoting—with Federal help—large office and hotel developments for new service workers and major in-city retail developments, such as Faneuil Hall in Boston and Harborplace in Baltimore. These developments were geared to capture the urban impulse spender as well as to generate additional sales taxes and, in some cases, local income taxes. At the same time, cities began to look at their longer-term future and many of them concluded that the retention of their remaining industrial base was problematic, as was their ability to attract existing businesses from outside. However, they did see a potential to generate new-business development, capitalizing on the city's historical role as an incubator of ideas and a provider of inexpensive space for entrepreneurial activities. It was at this point that cities began to see the university not as a negative property-tax drawback but as a positive influence in creating an environment for new-business development.

## The University Problem

At the same time, universities were also losing Federal funds, particularly in the area of basic research. The late 1970s were the peak of Federal investment in university research, but a sharp drop-off in nondefense research occurred in the early 1980s as the government began to back out of many expensive programs, including those that supported cities. Universities then scrambled to find private-sector research relationships to replace the Federal money they had lost. At the same time, other Federal actions were attacking many of the support systems that universities had used to grow over the years, including student-aid provisions, such as low-cost loans with deferred interest and outright grants. Faced with both a squeeze on their students' financing abilities, as well as their growing inability to support their own research infrastructure, universities began to seek new sources of income to support their science-department budgets and their capital-building needs. Once again, as cities had turned to the private sector to form economic-development partnerships to build new tax bases, the universities also began to see the private sector as a major partner in supporting and expanding their research capacity.

It became clear to many major universities that their ability to retain scientific faculty was going to depend more and more on not only the quality of the overall research environment provided for these highly skilled people but also opportunities for faculty members to expand their involvement in private business as either consultants or entrepreneurs. Universities in Boston and California, as well as in the Research Triangle in the Southeast, could compete effectively for top scientific faculty talent, because they could offer much more than the standard teaching or research position. They also offered the fertile intellectual environment of many private research companies and a concentration of entrepreneurs.

Both Northwestern and Yale, in order to be competitive in attracting students and faculty, understood that they needed to become part of a larger environment that allowed private-sector involvement for their faculty. Moreover, the two universities depended a great deal on their endowments to provide financial aid for students. Both universities had need-blind admissions policies, which allowed anyone accepted by the universities to attend; any student's financial shortfall was made up through the university's scholarship program, supported by income from endowments and solicited scholarship funds.

With the cutback of Federal-support programs, private universities like Yale and

Northwestern found themselves depending more and more on their endowment base and realized that soon there would not be enough income generated to continue their present policies. And since most, if not all, of their endowment and scholarship funds came from private industries or individuals, universities had another reason to seek new relationships with the private sector.

Finally, both universities had substantial real estate investments. Both cities had aged and faced the possibility of a static, if not shrinking, tax base. New Haven had real problems with urban decay and had undertaken extensive urban-renewal efforts to rebuild the city. But it still had a large, poor black and Hispanic population residing in thousands of public-housing units, many of which surrounded Yale's campus and the downtown. Both universities wanted to secure their real estate investments by stabilizing the neighborhoods around them and creating an atmosphere of development that would enable them to expand their research and development partnerships with the private sector. (It is a standard joke among urban universities that they cannot afford to move out of deteriorating neighborhoods because there is a very limited real estate market for used, gothic buildings.) Both universities, therefore, fastened on a research-park strategy to provide more faculty opportunity, stronger ties with the private sector, and a more stable real estate environment.

## The Natural Partnership

With the city looking for a new tax base, new entrepreneurial development, and more jobs and the university seeking more prestige and more ties with the private sector, it was only natural that the two would soon find each other even in the dark. Northwestern and Yale, embroiled in major controversies over their tax exemption and uses of land around the universities, began to discuss with city officials how the city and university might jointly help each other and create a partnership that would benefit both, rather than continue to expand useless energy fighting each other.

Yale agreed to be a partner with the city and the Olin Corporation to redevelop Olin's existing eighty acres of industrial land, directly behind Yale, which Olin was abandoning as it moved its manufacturing operations away from the city or closed them down completely. It was in Olin's interest to join the partnership, since its potential for obtaining a reasonable price for the land was minimal, surrounded as it was by an older, deteriorated neighborhood that had income, unemployment, and crime problems. In addition, Olin had two operating research laboratories in the complex and wanted to improve their environment. Thus Olin agreed to donate land and some operating funds to such an endeavor if the city and university agreed to join it as partners.

Yale's administration was enthusiastic about the possibility of turning an old, industrial slum at its back door into a new science park; but that enthusiasm was not mirrored by some of its faculty who felt that Yale's historical position as one of the premier seats of learning in the country was somehow being tainted by this pecuniary relationship with private industry. With these kinds of internal problems, Yale had a difficult time in providing any substantive resources for the project, other than some of its land and its "best efforts" agreement to support the development of the park in any way it could. It did, however, create an Office of Sponsored Research to provide business with access to its resources. Yale's internal policy ultimately allowed business access to its faculty on an individual basis through this new office, and it agreed to use its contacts in the corporate business world — particularly New York investment houses and venture-capital firms — in order to provide Science Park companies with increased access to private resources. In addition, the secretary of Yale resigned from that position to become head of the nonprofit Science Park Development Corporation, which brought his close relationship with many faculty members, corporate officers, and directors into play in support of the park.

Northwestern had already moved to gain direct congressional financing for a new applied-research laboratory. Through the efforts of its local congressman, Sidney Yates, Northwestern had obtained a commitment of $26 million from Congress to develop the Basic Industry Research Lab. Sponsored by the Department of Energy and dedicated to the application of technology and the conservation of energy in the manufacturing process, this "anti–Rust Belt" initiative gave the university a strong incentive to develop a research park around the laboratory as an anchor.

Shortly after the formation of Inventure, the nonprofit, economic-development corporation, the university began discussions with the city on the development of a research park on an underdeveloped triangle of land directly west of the university campus and downtown Evanston. Northwestern proposed an aggressive joint-venture concept that would make the city and the university for-profit real estate partners in the development and would allow them to share in any increase in the value of the land as it was developed over time. Evanston and Northwestern already owned 75 percent of the land required, and the city agreed to acquire the remaining 25 percent through its condemnation process.

All parties in both cities agreed that the development and operation of the parks could not be in the sole hands of either partner because of long-standing jealousies and practical politics. All partners agreed that the parks should be owned and operated by third-party entities, governed by boards of directors elected by both parties, and staffed by development professionals. All parties also agreed that the question of tenant selection had to be removed from the day-to-day deliberations by the city council and university board of trustees. Thus both partnerships took on a similar third-party character. In New Haven the Science Park Development Corporation is a nonprofit entity; all income is turned back into the park for future development. But the Evanston partnership is a for-profit entity so that any real estate development profits to be made from the activity can flow back to both parties over time. It is unlikely, however, that any of the partners in either city will gain any direct financial profit within the next decade or two.

In both New Haven and Evanston, the university and the city knew they needed a third partner to make the development work. Both cities and universities went to the business community for board members to operate their parks. In Evanston, only one director out of fourteen is an elected official. In New Haven, none are elected, though one is a direct employee of the city government. The lesson in both cases was to insulate the developments from the political vagaries of both city governments and universities. To do this the business community was called on to act as managers and policy setters. This function fit them well, since the business community was comfortable in a management role. By including the business community in the decision-making process the two partners also created a real base of business support for the parks beyond university and city interests.

Though the real estate sides of such partnerships are the most visible and the partnership results the most likely to be trumpeted, it is much more the university interaction with the business community that plays a large role in city revitalization and economic development. As universities enter into these partnerships with the business community and city government, they also give new entrepreneurs—hungry for knowledge and assistance—access to an untapped mine of university resources, producing even more entrepreneurial activity through synergism within the university faculty. As these small companies work more closely with the university scientists, those scientists form their own businesses and attract even more entrepreneurs.

An entrepreneurial environment is being created for technology transfer that only incidentally has real estate attached to it. The important factor is that people with ideas, whether they are faculty or, say, a vice president of research in a private corporation or an inventor, all begin to understand that the university-city-business partnership allows them access to financing, inexpensive space through incubator development, and technological and business assistance through university resources. It also allows them access to highly complex equipment at very low cost, major computer systems, and the entire social and academic atmosphere of the university.

Northwestern intends to treat all business people within its research-park development as quasi faculty in the sense that their businesses will have access to most university facilities at reasonable costs, such as main-frame computers, libraries, and rare technical equipment, as well as amenities like swimming pools, racket sports, and football tickets. This powerful marketing tool will entice many inventors, entrepreneurs, and fledgling high-tech businesses to central sites like university research parks in urban areas. This attraction, in turn, generates a need for space and, ultimately, new facilities to house the continually growing numbers of businesses. This development generates a new tax base and for both Northwestern and Yale the taking of existing, non-tax-producing structures and rehabbing them into tax-producing laboratory and office space. The result is a win-win situation for both the university and the city government, because new businesses bring new jobs and a new tax base and require expanded local business services. At the same time the university is providing a fertile environment for its faculty to interact with the private sector and is building strong bridges for private research as well as future endowment assistance.

The university-city-business partnership is a natural one and, though difficult to forge because of historical enmities, it is probably the most powerful partnership in economic development today. Added to this is the fiscal support of many state governments, which are rapidly producing new programs in economic development, and new, creative ways for the private sector to become more active, such as the development of local venture-capital funds and real estate development corporations. The result is a lattice work of many partners, all doing what they do best and not being pushed into areas where they have little or no expertise.

## Who Pays? Who Controls?

An example of how these partnerships work and the give and take required to forge them is the Evanston-Northwestern research park. As explained earlier, the city and the university already owned approximately 75 percent of the twenty-six-acre site needed for development. The site had been used for years by the city for its public-works operations and by the university for its car pool, printing, and other secondary-support activities. Obtaining an agreement between the city and the university to sell their land to a third entity was not difficult, once they understood the practical and political reasons for doing so. Matters of equity, however, had to be worked out, because the city was going to provide proportionately more land than the university to the joint venture. It was finally decided that if any profits were ever made on the land after mortgages had been paid off and operating expenses taken care of, such profits would be distributed on a pro rata basis tied to the respective value of land that each party had provided.

Land contribution, however, was but one issue that had to be resolved between the two parties. The first issue is always "who pays?" but the next one is always "who controls?" Thus the governance issue became a major sticking point between the two parties. After a year of continuous negotiations, an agreement was ultimately forged that moved control of the park from both the city and the university to a third corporation with a board of directors, one-half of whose members are appointed by the university and one-half by the city. Interestingly enough, as mentioned earlier, the university and the city appointed primarily development and technology experts and top businesspeople rather than policy or political representatives.

Other terms of the agreement included a city pledge to spend up to $24 million in tax incremental financing bonds to acquire the remaining properties still in private hands, relocate affected residents and businesses, demolish any remaining buildings, and provide the site with a new infrastructure. At one time the city had proposed that the university contribute half of the required money to acquire the remaining portion of the site as a gesture of good faith in the partnership. The university felt that its contributions were already substantial in that it had to acquire additional property in Evanston in order to relocate its present activities in the research park in addition to absorbing the costs of obtaining the Federal grant for the laboratory and its corollary agreement to support its yearly operating costs. The university finally offered to lend the city $4 million at 53 percent of prime for five years, in order to reduce the city's cash crunch. In effect, the university used its borrowing power to assist the city, without tying up its funds in a long-term real estate transaction. In return, the university agreed to abide by city requirements for minority contracting set-asides and targeted job-training programs. One additional requirement, a ban on all weapons research, was finally accepted by the university as an additional compromise to the city's sensitive political position.

Just as important, however, were the other activities that the university and the city supported in order to establish a creative environment for the success of the park. First, through a grant from the state of Illinois, Northwestern set up a Technology Commercialization Center — an office charged specifically with providing businesses with direct access to the university's Technological Institute and its graduate business school. This center also had the capacity to pay university experts to act as consultants to small companies needing specific help in developing their technology-oriented businesses.

Second, with this technical-assistance mechanism in place, Evanston Inventure, the nonprofit corporation set up by the university, the city, and the private sector, established a $1 million seed-capital and lending fund for Evanston businesses — with a particular emphasis on high technology start-ups in the research park. The money was raised by selling debentures to four local businesses and the university. To obtain financing, businesses must either be located in or move to Evanston, and they had to give first priority to Evanston residents in hiring.

Third, the university agreed to convert one of its existing buildings within the research park into a small-business incubator center, obtaining some state money and putting in its own cash to offer 36,000 square feet of multiuse space to small high-tech, start-up companies associated with the university and the park.

The incubator provides inexpensive space to high-tech start-up companies, which are also provided common business services. They receive technical assistance through the Technology Commercialization Center and can receive financing through the seed-capital corporation. These three activities — low-cost space, technical assistance, and financing — are the major necessities that start-up businesses require to begin operating. The seed-capital fund and the technical-assistance operations also draw business to the incubator, and all reinforce one another.

## Doing What is Familiar

The research park and the federally funded laboratory that the university is now constructing for basic industry research offer a rich environment for entrepreneurial development. The university provided its building at no cost for the incubator, and its access to state government in order to fund the Technology Commercialization Center, as well as contributing to the seed-capital fund. It is also committed to pay half the costs of operating and managing the park. Therefore, Northwestern University is actively involved, using its existing resources in land, buildings, cash, and expertise, to support the total research-park concept. It is doing what it knows how to do.

On the other hand, the city has been most active in obtaining grants from the state to support some of the infrastructure improvements necessary to the park, as well as acquiring the rest of the site through its eminent domain powers. The city has taken on the particular burden of strong political opposition by environmentalists and others to the park plan. It has also agreed to pay half the operating costs of the park's operating corporation. In addition, the city provided a grant to the seed-capital fund for operating purposes and has begun basic engineering on public improvements for the park.

The city's contributions, then, are primarily in the area of public improvements, some funding for the operating corporation, and support for some of the peripheral activities. In addition, its power of eminent domain allows the complete site to be pulled together, an absolute necessity for marketing purposes. Again, this partner is providing its share of support by doing those things with which it is familiar.

With the creation of a third corporation to manage and operate the park, the city and the university will begin to withdraw from direct participation in planning and development. Rather, through their board members, they will financially support activities recommended by the operating corporation. But their partnership must remain strong if the park is to be a success, since much of the university's and city's support is integral to many of the park's support activities, such as the incubator, the seed-capital fund, and the Technology Commercialization Center, as well as the Basic Industry Research Laboratory.

Both parties understand that there will continue to be disputes over matters affecting city and university policy. However, the city and university have agreed that such continued bickering will take place outside the context of the research park; it will not be used by either party as hostage to resolve unconnected disputes.

In New Haven, Yale's contribution included its new Office of Sponsored Research as a universal access point to its resources, a prime piece of vacant land adjacent to the park, temporary office space for the nonprofit corporation, and access to its well-connected alumni, especially those in Fortune 500 corporations. Since the formation of the Science Park concept, Yale's relationship with the city has improved substantially. Yale has assisted the city in a number of ways since that initial agreement and has been generous with its time and faculty whenever the city sought its help. The university, for the first time, invested in a major downtown development, because it understood its self-interest in stabilizing New Haven's retail base.

City government in New Haven, like that in Evanston, concentrated most of its efforts on providing direct city support for infrastructure development as well as obtaining state and Federal grants to assist in that activity. New Haven had already established a seed-capital corporation and was thus able to connect this activity directly into the Science Park, once it was established. That corporation is used as a marketing device to bring additional companies to the park.

The Yale-New Haven Science Park is now known as one of the great success stories in partnerships. It boasts a roster of over eighty companies, most of them small but growing. It has also been successful in luring the high-tech subsidiary of the New England Telephone Company as well as a major engineering firm to its park. Much of this success is due to the board of directors and its staff, headed by the former secretary of Yale, Sam Chauncey. Everyone agrees, however, that it has taken the patience and commitment of both the city government and the Yale administration to make everything work. To achieve that goal, much patience, determination, and sensitivity have been required from both sides.

The Northwestern-Evanston partnership has just begun. Mistrust is being replaced by wariness, and real understanding will develop in time. As universities and cities get to know each other better as partners, they will find new ways in which to cooperate, as they did in New Haven. The enmity that has existed between urban universities and city governments took decades to develop. It will not be dissolved in short order.

# Partnerships and Schools

SUSAN D. OTTERBOURG
MICHAEL TIMPANE

If numbers mean anything, partnerships with schools make good business sense. During the past several years, elementary and secondary schools have established more than 40,000 partnerships with business, government agencies, and community organizations. And the number continues to grow in urban, suburban, and rural areas. In New York City alone, there are more than 1,000 partnerships between individual schools and businesses, with a need for twice that number.

These partnerships are collaborative alliances in support of education. They stem from a growing national awareness that business has an important self-interest in the success of schools and that a combined effort of the two partners will be more successful than if either one alone attempted to improve education.

From the educators' point of view, partnerships are not expected to pay for staff salaries or the maintenance of school buildings. They are considered to be a tool to mobilize community, business, and school-district resources for use by schools, teachers, administrators, and students. These resources are used to support and supplement activities that address school needs in such areas as staff development, student enrichment, basic skills, and career education.

Partnerships are also political resources, attracting allies during budget times and encouraging commitment to public funding for public schools. Through local partnership activities, businesses see more clearly how sound public education contributes to their own interests as producers and employers as well as community stability—no small consideration, particularly in urban centers. In the past few years, business interest has turned from the local level to the state and national levels, with business leaders playing important roles in the membership and sponsorship of education-reform proposals and reports. The range of policy issues of interest to business has been broad, from employability to school management to enhancing the vitality of the teaching profession.

Ironically, this activity is growing at a time when the Federal government has maintained a schizophrenic attitude in its policy toward and support of education. On the one hand, Federal commissions and their subsequent reports have spearheaded nationwide efforts to improve instruction and educational opportunities for students. President Reagan proclaimed 1984 the National Year of Partnerships in Education, establishing a White House office that continues actively to support private-sector initiatives. On the other side are the many attempts to cut Federal support to education, coupled with increasing pressures to shift more and more of the funding burden for education to state and local levels.

Many businesses have committed human, material, financial, and political resources in support of education. More businesses will follow in these leaders' footsteps. Before undertaking a partnership venture, however, businesses should address the following critical issues: Why will an alliance be helpful to schools and business? What factors make programs work? What does it take to get these programs in place? What are the ongoing problems? What are the specific short- and long-term implications of partnerships?

This essay responds to these questions, with a status report on current developments and some consideration of future directions for partnerships in education. The essay begins with a discussion of why business and schools need each other. Then it outlines the components necessary to establish successful partnerships: assessment of all partners' needs and resources, program leadership, planning, and implementation. Finally, it reviews what partnerships can and cannot do, how partnerships can and should be evaluated, and what might be the best long-term role for business in partnerships with education.

## Business and Schools Need Each Other

Why, now, are businesses becoming increasingly involved in partnerships in education? From the mid-1960s to the late 1970s, business and schools were often isolated from each other. Earlier corporate influence on local, state, and national public-education policy had been reduced by the entry of new advocacy groups from local communities, Federal and state programs, unions, and public-interest agencies.

Business and the public schools have gradually reestablished connections since the mid-1970s. Since 1983, these ties have grown swiftly. Current and future demands of the economy and the labor market, together with wide-ranging public attention to excellence in education, have spurred this renewed interest in and subsequent involvement of business with public education. The corporate community as well as small, local businesses are responding concretely to their own needs as well as to national concerns by expending resources on school alliances — on partnerships.

*Economic considerations.* The relationship between the stability and vitality of the immediate community and its schools and the economic well-being of local business has become a central concern of business, one that is voiced across the country. Southwestern Bell Telephone, for example, noted that "one in every four blacks in St. Louis, 25 years and older, has less than a high school education. Of the black labor force, 22 percent is unemployed and about half of the city's black households are living on less than $10,000 a year. As corporate citizens, with large resources and large responsibilities, located in St. Louis, we feel it our duty to address this problem."

For firms tied to a specific community, partnerships are seen as one tool to address a central business concern, that is, maintaining an adequate pool of skilled labor in the community. At the International Business Machines' Southwestern Area Marketing Division in Dallas, management noted the long-term benefits of the schools as suppliers of "quality products." IBM efforts aimed at supporting area schools in the development of productive graduates include such programs as Communities in Schools, which focuses on keeping high-risk students in school; Adopt-A-School, featuring volunteer activities by IBM employees, ranging from clerical assistance to tutoring and demonstrations; and Junior Achievement programs in which fourteen IBM managers teach two courses (Applied Economics and Project Business) in fourteen schools.

Business hopes that, in some cases at least, these alliances will enable the school to furnish job-ready workers at a lower cost to the firm than post–high-school retraining by business. Southwestern Bell, for example, has for many years supported a work-study program with a local high school, providing more than 400 youths with part-time employment and job experiences. HealthWest in Los Angeles reflects the same view; through shadowing, mentoring, and demonstration activities, HealthWest seeks to interest young people in the health-care field, a profession with persistent manpower shortages.

Miss Elaine, a lingerie-manufacturing firm in St. Louis, faces all the problems of the shrinking American apparel industry. It pins its hopes for long-term survival either on automation of its manufacturing operations or on capturing the interest of a skilled younger generation in the apparel industry. Thus, tours to manufacturing sites, demonstrations by personnel from all departments of the company, and donations of approximately $80,000 worth of fabric and machines to all home-economics departments in St. Louis high schools have become part of the company's program to encourage interest in careers in manufacturing.

This labor-market interest will predictably grow throughout the national economy. The technological and managerial demands of new jobs, the need for increased productivity in the face of international competition, and the decreasing numbers and increasing heterogeneity of young people entering the labor market—all of these factors will keep the attention of business riveted on the schools for many years to come.

*Maintaining community stability.* States and local communities, seeking to attract new businesses, are often asked about the quality of local schools. Companies relocating want a good education system, as do the companies already in the community that will benefit from the new corporate activities. As Southwestern Bell said, people want to locate where the best schools are, and relocation "means business to us."

*Improving community relations.* The rationale for entering into partnerships with schools is further strengthened when these alliances improve community relations and public images of businesses. Television station KTVI in St. Louis looks to its partnerships as a way "to give back to the community" that the station serves, a way to get involved and, at the same time, uncover new subject matter for programs.

The Los Angeles Dodgers Corporation's corporate headquarters, located at Dodger Stadium, had long been aware of its immediate neighborhood's feelings toward the corporation. The community was greatly concerned when the stadium was built, displacing people and their homes. The partnership developed by the Dodgers with the neighborhood elementary school has helped reestablish the corporation as a good neighbor in the community. The partnership sponsors activities to encourage school attendance and improve basic skills, particularly English. Tours of the stadium, presentations related to all aspects of running the corporate side of the Dodgers' enterprise, tickets to games, and graduation ceremonies on the Dodger field involve students at all grade levels, as well as their parents. Interestingly, the team has now developed a second partnership program at its winter training camp in Florida.

*Extending business staff-development efforts.* Managements of many businesses think that the participation of their employees in school partnerships improves staff morale and contributes to the development of skills in leadership and management. More than 160 employees from IBM's Houston and Dallas offices volunteer on company time in public schools each week. At Foley's (a division of Federated Department Stores) Distribution Center in Houston, executive, administrative, and operations employees are released weekly to tutor students in mathematics, reading, and English for non–English-speaking students. In some departments, the opportunity to volunteer is considered to be a reward. Also in Houston, several architectural firms partially satisfy the professional and community-service requirements for state licensing for new architects by assigning their interns to a range of activities in public-school partnership programs.

*Financial support to schools.* Business has also taken on new roles in contributing directly to the schools. These limited funds can only supplement public funding of local educational programs and services, but they often have a strong multiplier effect, providing enough aid to help the local school community put new energy and excitement into its programs. Thus, business contributions have supported staff training, curriculum-development projects, work experiences for teachers and students, school redesign and improvement projects, and educational research.

In many cases, the business community has become the catalyst in the development of communitywide business organizations focused on the financial support of school-improvement efforts; the Boston Compact, the New York City Partnership, and the Allegheny Conference for Community Development in Pittsburgh are prominent examples of this function. Moreover, business has participated in the development of more than 200 state and local education foundations to raise monies for the public schools through nongovernmental sources. The largest of these ventures, created by the Bank of Boston, sponsors projects supporting students and educators, including scholarships, assistance in gaining financial aid for post–high-school training and education, a teacher fellowship program, and school-based project grants. With business support, local education foundations throughout the nation have been especially successful in launching minigrant programs for teachers — small (sometimes tiny) amounts of money to add vitality to their classrooms. These minigrant programs are based, in turn, on careful developmental work in twenty-two communities across the country supported by the Exxon Education Foundation.

The business community has also become more active in seeking adequate public funding for schools. Around the country, businesses are working with their communities to support the passage of larger school budgets. At the state level, business has greatly moderated its earlier enthusiasm for tax-limitation measures like California's Proposition 13 and Massachusetts's 2½. In fact, the states increased expenditures for schools by $10 billion or more in legislative years 1984 and 1985, often with business support. For example, new taxes or school-finance formulas for education have been enacted with business encouragement and assistance by Texas, Oklahoma, Utah, Arkansas, Iowa, Tennessee, South Carolina, Florida, and Mississippi. A few years ago, California dedicated most of its budget surplus to enacting the education program of the California Business Roundtable.

*Involvement in school-improvement efforts.* At the local level, members of the business community have become actively involved with schools and other partners (government agencies, universities, and nonprofit groups) to form alliances that support a range of education projects. One notable example is PATHS (Philadelphia Alliance for Teaching Humanities in the Schools), a program focused on staff development in the humanities. Another is the New York Alliance for the Public Schools, whose programs include professional development for New York City high school principals, a GO PUBLIC! public-relations campaign in support of the city's public schools, and MENTOR programs in law, engineering, education, and advertising.

At the state level, business representatives have joined the more than 200 commissions or task forces in education established in the past few years. The recommendations of many of these bodies, covering such areas as curriculum requirements and standards and teacher qualifications and preparation, have been or are being converted into new legislation or new regulations in every state. National commissions and task forces, such as the President's Commission on Excellence in Education and the Task Force on Education and Economic Growth of the Education Commission of the States, have also included substantial representation from the business community. Most recently, the Committee on Economic Development's Task Force on Business and the Schools has examined the nature and extent of the emerging business interest in the schools in a major report, *Investing in Our Children*. This report, distributed to tens of thousands of business executives, presents the new gospel of business's enlightened self-interest in the improvement of schools.

Finally, specific national corporations have seen it in their interest to finance, through their corporate foundations, education projects of national significance: ARCO supported Ernest Boyer's study of the American high school; Metropolitan Life has supported annual surveys of the American teacher; American Can Company has stimulated new studies of dropouts and supported the expanded activities of the National School Volunteer Program.

## What Does It Take to Set Partnership Programs in Place?

In the development of long-term alliances between education and business, successful programs have usually followed particular planning and development steps and have involved particular "key players."

1. *Knowing the territory.* When Security Pacific National Bank, Los Angeles, decided to establish a partnership in education, bank leaders investigated the programs of other businesses that were already involved in these alliances. Their research included discussions with the director of the Adopt-A-School program for the Los Angeles Unified School District and syntheses of materials from the Private Sector Office of the U.S. Department of Education and from *ProEducation*, a magazine that focuses on partnerships with education.

As a result, Security Pacific initiated a series of programs: Project STEP, a training program for entry-level banking jobs; COOP, a cooperative education program; a Summer Career and Economic Education Program for Educators (SCEEP); Blue-Backs, simulated currency to be used as a teaching aid; and Adopt-A-School, wherein the bank's Community Affairs Division provides a Conversational English Project, a speakers' bureau, and curricula for students who are recent immigrants at the Evans Community Adult School in Los Angeles. Careful "homework" and program development are indispensable in this, as any other, enterprise.

2. *Someone must take the leadership.* In the past, schools often reached out to businesses for support in forming partnerships, but recently businesses have also taken the initiative. Whatever the sources, the initiatives are usually high-level executive actions: letters from the school superintendent inviting participation or memorandums from a company's division head or chief executive officer directing subordinates to explore such a venture. Security Pacific National Bank contends that the active support of senior management from business and the school district is needed to ensure the success of the programs that it launched.

In Texas, when the board of the statewide Communities in Schools program wanted to expand its activities from Houston to Dallas, San Antonio, and El Paso, it sought help from IBM. IBM thought the initiative important enough to ask the corporation's vice president and area manager of southwestern marketing to provide leadership and coordination as well as to recruit volunteers from area offices to work directly with students.

In large corporations, the decision to participate is made at both the regional and the national levels. At IBM, commitment to Adopt-A-School programs comes from a combination of corporate and field management. Involvement is a team effort within the company, in which "top management is requested to be part of community involvement," thereby setting an example and encouraging employee participation.

In smaller businesses as well as in some larger companies, partnership decisions are made by the president-owner. What is important is ensuring that whoever makes the commitment can enforce it. Only then can the depth and breadth of commitment necessary to pursue the given project successfully be communicated to the staff, who will actually make partnership activities work.

For some partnerships, a relevant professional association or school district's education department can also provide leadership. For example, in Houston, the school district directs the community's Business/School Partnership Program. When architectural firms want to participate in school partnerships, the program's director refers their requests to the director of the Houston chapter of the American Institute of Architects (AIA). The two directors then bring teachers and representatives of the firms together, pair them off, and help them establish program activities at the individual schools.

A major concern in many communities is the depth and breadth of the business community's involvement in the local partnership program. In St. Louis, Southwestern Bell Telephone — knowing that no single corporation, regardless of its size, can operate alone — uses a variety of strategies to attract other businesses within its region to participate in local partnerships. Recent mailings, sent to customers along with their bills, discussed the Southwestern Bell program; the mailing attracted more than 200 inquiries from potential partners.

3. *Planning for the partnership.* Once the partnership program is broadly defined and unequivocally endorsed by the corporate leadership, there is still essential work for both business and education to develop specific and effective activities. First, representatives from participating partners must form a working group, committee, or task force to identify the schools' needs, place them in order of priority, and determine the business's ability and willingness to respond to them. Within a reasonable time, the partnership task force should develop a plan of action and determine workable policies and guidelines. It should also select a partnership format compatible with its needs and resources and complementary to its proposed activities. The activities chosen might include "adoption" of a school, a volunteer tutoring program, a career counseling project, a staff-development program, a speakers' bureau, or minigrant programs.

In Los Angeles, for example, the Thrifty Corporation determined, with school personnel, that it should adopt a school and help it to improve attendance. The corporation therefore concentrated on an incentive program focused precisely on that area.

The McKesson Corporation in San Francisco pursued its research efforts with guidance from the Corporate Action Committee of that city's public schools. After reviewing its resources, McKesson found a small alternative high school in which students' involvement in a work-experience program with the corporate headquarters was manageable and the principal and teachers wanted the support of McKesson.

Television station KTVI in St. Louis worked with middle, junior high, and elementary schools, primarily at school sites, to develop activities exploring how television stations operate. The KTVI staff provided tours, demonstrations, and teaching units covering such station components as engineering, technical and administrative areas, and program content. Each activity was designed to enrich instruction in science, mathematics, social studies, reading, and oral and written language.

4. *Implementing the partnership program.* An executive from the Monsanto Corporation in St. Louis noted that "it's very important for someone at the company to be identified as the program manager." Most school districts also have a central-management person or team to run the partnership program. In St. Louis, for example, staff from the school district's partnership program seeks the interest and commitment of school site staff. When leadership from business and school develop a workable plan, volunteers from both partners facilitate and coordinate program activities.

Program coordination may be informal, as is the case at the Memphis headquarters of Catherine's Stout Shoppe, a division of Allied Stores. More than half of the company's 300 employees have been involved in the partnership program with the neighborhood elementary school since 1982. The company's construction coordinator informally coordinates the program from the business side, eliciting support and help from all management and staff levels as needed.

In contrast, IBM has extended its community-service activities throughout the country, creating "external program managers," who will head departments responsible for identifying, exchanging, and communicating information regarding good community practices and programs to all divisions, areas, and branches of the IBM corporate network.

Large corporations can usually draw leadership from a variety of departments and levels, but small businesses need to develop different strategies. At the St. Louis office of Dorf & Stanton Communications, the nine members of the public-relations staff participate directly with its middle-school partner. Activities with school's eighth graders include instruction in language through projects that help students identify, plan, and execute public-relations programs they could undertake for their own school or community. The principals of the firm noted that as a small business, Dorf & Stanton has developed ways to share responsibilities with educators, streamline activities, and enlist assistance from other business and community resources (in the media, for example). Encouraging this extended participation helps to offset scheduling and time-management problems.

Financial accounting, management, and staff development related to partnership activities are best achieved with a system paralleling the standard operating procedures already established within the school district. The use of businesses' communications networks and strategies to support the partnership generates enthusiasm and disseminates information on partnership activities to a large audience. Partnership activities should receive ongoing evaluation for purposes of revision, refinement, and elimination or extension of project activities.

## Ongoing Problem Areas

No partnership is free of problems. Those that commonly occur include communications, expectations, expanding commitment, and maintaining a project's momentum.

*Communications.* A consistently high level of communications among all program participants must be sustained. The breakdown of communication networks discourages productive initiatives of volunteers and reduces the enthusiasm of the education staff that is necessary for effective partnerships. Poor communication also blights the image of the program, encouraging perceptions that partnerships are at best frill activities and at worst useless ones.

*Expectations.* Expectations concerning the amount of human resources and time to be devoted to the project must be realistic. Businesses often do not know what resources they have to offer schools, and schools often do not know what to ask for beyond a financial handout. Expectations regarding needs and available resources may therefore be too low or too high. Unrealistic expectations related to program goals, objectives, and activities can lead to difficulties in retaining a high level of commitment to the program.

*Expanding commitment.* Few corporate or education participants have a partnership program as their only responsibility. Individuals' responsibilities are often divided among tasks, diluting productivity and program effectiveness. In addition, there can be disagreement about what activities can or should be accomplished with available resources. Business partners accustomed to working with colleges and college students may be dubious at first about the possibility of improving public education and apprehensive about working with urban schools. School districts, for their part, have had new special programs thrust on them before, particularly by state and Federal departments; they may be reluctant to have another intrusion on their turf. These concerns can be overcome only as partners experience some success in their initial efforts.

Ingenuity is often required to extend the circle of people who continuously participate in the partnership. Middle managers, who must approve employee participation on company time, are often difficult to convince, since they are also faced with regular business assignments. The same is true of the public managers in hard-pressed school districts.

*Maintaining the momentum.* Schools are accustomed to public enthusiasm, which produces a temporary windfall of support but soon disappears. They may not expect a continued supply of human, financial, and in-kind resources. Both businesses and schools must be educated to think of their alliances on a long-term basis.

In Memphis, the Adopt-A-School staff works to extend its program beyond the initial "adoption" of all 155 Memphis city schools. It is seeking multiple "adopters" for programs and schools as well as the use of bartering strategies through which the schools' business and community partners exchange resources to supplement individual activities. An executive of the Holiday Inns Hotel Group noted that the program can become "stale." As a long-time partner with two high schools in Memphis, Holiday Inns and its school partners consult regularly to keep activities fresh and to sustain both partners' enthusiasm.

## Future Implications of Partnerships

*1. What partnerships can and cannot do.* Critics say that alliances between schools and business function as public-relations gestures, and some partnership activities do indeed focus on "buttons and T-shirts." A more savvy view is that business involvement with schools attracts intelligent consumers of both services and products and supports the development of a more capable work force. Of course, the additional opportunities to show a range of community audiences that business has a keen sense of social responsibility cannot be dismissed lightly.

Businesses like those discussed in this essay have committed human, financial, and in-kind resources in support of education. They have done so — and have shown a willingness to continue this commitment — because they want to participate in their communities and enhance their organizational image as good neighbors. For the long run, and of broader potential significance, they believe that these programs can encourage future generations of intelligent consumers and an educated work force from which they will recruit.

These expectations may be unrealistic. Partnerships are expected to help both business and the schools by:

- Training school staff in new instructional strategies, in new technologies, and in management areas.
- Extending areas of basic instruction through tours, tutoring, speakers, presentations, workshops, events, and demonstrations.
- Introducing students and teachers to the world of work through mentoring, lectures, simulated and actual work experiences, job skills orientation, career fairs, and shadowing.
- Providing assistance with or guarantees of employment for high school graduates.
- Supporting post–high-school training and education through direct financial aid, scholarships, prizes, and counseling activities.
- Building community and political support for program improvement and adequate financing of schools.

That is a tall order. Partnerships can only supplement, not supplant, the schools' basic instructional and staff-development efforts as well as their funding. With the level and depth of resources needed, particularly in urban areas, it is clear that no one company can "do it all." Many companies try to act as catalysts and recruiting agents to rally other businesses and community agencies to join in supporting school-improvement efforts through partnerships, but few local business communities would claim that they have yet devoted the resources necessary to do the job.

In the current business climate, moreover, many companies—including some of the largest—are reducing staffs at all levels. Since successful partnership programs are built on the commitment of human resources, these reductions in staff mean cutbacks in partnership efforts. A Monsanto executive noted that the company's partnership with a high school in St. Louis has been flourishing for more than six years and that the volunteers who teach lessons or make presentations take their corporate citizenship responsibility seriously. But, he added, "in the entire chemical industry, the short-term implication is the financial cost of employee released time for these programs. It's got to be charged somewhere, and all programs are cutting back. It may be that employees will have to partly take personal time or their vacation time to participate in these programs." If this is a realistic view of the future, and if there is a widespread belief that partnerships have an educational value to students, then educators and their business community partners must be prepared to find new ways to support partnership activities or craft new means for delivering resources to students and school staffs to support school-improvement efforts.

*2. How partnerships can and should be evaluated.* So far, business appears to be neither hasty nor mechanical in evaluating school-business partnerships. In the short run, corporate management, asking whether partnerships with schools are effective, may be frustrated. Earlier studies of public-school and private-sector interaction in twenty-three United States cities in 1983–84, conducted by Professor Dale Mann at Teachers College, Columbia University, concluded that unless partnerships between business and education engaged core issues like the quality of classroom teaching, they would "wither on the vine" during the next few years. Today, Mann and other observers directly or indirectly involved in these programs have noted that both in size and in nature partnerships are growing more substantive and, in some cases, showing a staying power in their communities. But these observers also agree that it is too early to make sweeping judgments regarding the quality and impact of these programs on schools, educators, and students.

State departments of education, which have the resources to evaluate all kinds and levels of education programs, are finding it difficult to "get a handle" on partnerships by using their usual evaluation strategies and instruments. Indiana is organizing a statewide evaluation of partnerships and, at the same time, developing a data bank on the state's partnership resources. In the meantime local school districts have begun to evaluate programs at school sites and at the district level. Some older and more established local programs have been partially evaluated. Published results—usually through annual reports—are available, including some data on the number and kind of partnership activities, as well as some determination of the extent to which they are a contributing factor in such areas as improved school-staff skills and student achievement. The reports indicate that partnership programs are increasingly addressing substantive community problems, such as dropouts, literacy, and substance abuse. The reports also indicate that partnerships have helped inform consumers, enabled high school graduates to find employment or continue their education, created new political allies for the public schools, and developed stronger local community coalitions.

Withal, most of these locals partnerships are less than five years old, and it is surely too early to draw conclusions regarding their "success." Indeed, some partnership leaders question whether the evaluation techniques used in more traditional education programs will ever be useful, because of the variety of purposes and designs that these programs manifest from school to school and district to district.

What may be more useful is to develop new evaluation strategies for partnership programs that reflect the variety of interests and objectives held by both business and education in each locality. Another possibility is formative evaluation of specific programs at the school or district level solely for purposes of program refinement, extension, or elimination. McKesson, after reviewing its five-year-old partnership to determine what parts of the program could be replicated across the country in connection with its regional offices, recently extended its programs from its headquarters in San Francisco to Phoenix. Program activities being planned and developed in Phoenix are based on the San Francisco experience but adapted to meet the needs and resources of McKesson's Phoenix division and its local school partners.

3. *The broad impact of partnerships on school programs and education policies.* Both businesses and schools have been concerned about partnerships in education. Educators worried that these partnerships would seek too much of a vocational focus for school programs at the expense of academic subjects. But a review of partnerships across the country indicates little basis for this concern. Historically, business's interest in trained labor led it to support vocational education, but this interest has now been extended greatly. Business leaders seek a broad general education for all students, indicating that they will train them for specific jobs in their firms. As a result, their current support for education has been broadly expressed and has furnished assistance to students and staff as well as advice to policymakers covering the entire range of educational offerings, from mathematics and science to the humanities.

School leaders have also worried that business would intrude on managerial prerogatives that are normally the province of school boards and administrators. Once again, reports from school partnership leaders around the country indicate that business has not intruded into the school's domain. Business leaders do not want to run the schools, and nothing reinforces that conviction more than regular visits to the schools and a growing appreciation of the complexity and difficulty of school management.

A final area of concern has been that of educational equity, and the actions of business have sent mixed signals. On the one hand, worried about the need for an increasingly skilled labor supply, business has put great rhetorical emphasis on better education for poor and minority children. It knows that 20 percent fewer young people will enter the labor market within the next ten years, and more of those who do will be minority youth. All of these students must be better educated, with the necessary range of complex skills for a technological work environment. On the other hand, it is not clear that the policies being promoted by business leaders — namely, higher standards and greater accountability of student and staff performance — are fully consistent with this imperative. Such policies could simply bring about a higher rate of student failure and dropouts unless they are embedded in a larger policy context that improves the performance, status, and rewards of teachers and the effectiveness of all schools. Each of these issues — distortion of goals, control of programs, and inequity — bear watching in the future of partnerships. The rise of any one of them could and should discredit partnerships in education.

## Conclusion

Will business continue to have a long-term, substantive interest in partnerships with education, and if so, why? Historically, business interest in public education has been sustained by three concerns: an adequate supply of skilled labor, strong educational institutions that produce an informed and productive citizenry committed to free-enterprise democracy, and positive community relations and attractive community settings for the business enterprises. There have been periods, particularly in the 1970s, when educators got little or no interest or support from the business community. In the 1980s, however, business attention to education has heightened. This interest was first expressed in local partnership projects and has now extended to deliberations about education policy at state and national levels.

Of course, many businesses have demonstrated a long-term commitment to their partnerships with schools. Southwestern Bell in St. Louis have been involved in partnerships in education for more than twenty years. Students, teachers, and employees remain motivated and enthusiastic. The company believes its partnership helps to improve its community-relations image, to enlarge the body of informed customers, and to train employees who can perform capably at all staff and managerial levels. Its Missouri division president said, "Southwestern gets something back — it's just that simple."

For those firms that have recently been introduced or reintroduced to partnerships with education, such programs have exposed businesses anew to the realities of public education. This participation has been helpful for the schools and their students and most instructive to the business people involved, helping to bridge the chasm of misunderstanding created during the 1970s.

Partnerships directly related to instructional goals and objectives have only begun to flourish. Localities are just beginning to recognize their potential to address such concerns as substance abuse, dropouts, literacy, technological change, and access to post–high-school education and training.

Leadership appears to be one key factor in the continuing development and extension of business-education partnerships. Leadership must continue at the top levels for both parties and not be relegated to lower levels of management.

In addition to leadership, it takes communication to maintain and extend business's claim that partnerships make sound business sense — that is, that such alliances can help to develop informed consumers of both services and products, a necessary and more capable work force, and improved community relations. Communication that dispels ignorance on both sides regarding each other's true interests, expectations, and appropriate modes of conduct and collaboration.

The issues that partnerships are addressing will not be solved overnight. To realize the country's hopes for improvement in the curriculum and revitalization of the teaching profession, education will need business as a partner all year, every year. Business, because of its own concerns and self-interests, will need education just as much.

# Partnerships and Public Policy Advocacy

JAMES P. GIFFORD

In discussing public-private partnerships it is difficult to resist the question of the relationship between doing good and doing well. Julius Rosenwald of Sears-Roebuck said, "You have to be able to do good to do well."[1] But at least in the American political and economic systems it is possible to do well without doing good, and it is possible to do good without doing well. It is also possible to do both. Experience with many public-private partnerships suggests that they generally involve measures of altruism and self-interest. To deny that both factors are at work seems, on the one hand, unduly cynical and, on the other, unusually naive.

Although a growing body of literature confirms the mixed motives of partnerships in general, comparatively little has been written about the public-policy-advocacy roles of partnerships. This essay explores why some partnerships become involved with advocacy and why others choose to avoid it. Although it discusses some basic questions about partnerships in general, it is not a comprehensive, comparative study of a broad cross section of advocacy by partnerships in the United States. Such a study deserves to be made, but this modest effort speaks mainly from the experience of the New York City Partnership, an association of business and civic leaders founded in 1979 under the leadership of David Rockefeller.

### Reasons for Partnership Advocacy

Most partnerships of any consequence mount one or more programs designed to bring together the resources of the public and private sectors. Among the more common endeavors are programs devoted to economic development, housing, job creation, and job training. Whatever programs it chooses, a partnership can confine itself to their actual operation. Delivering one or more services is, after all, one of the principal reasons for the creation of partnerships.

Whatever the original intentions of an organization, experience indicates that it will reach a point where decisions made by various levels of government have an impact on it and its programs. If politics is the process by which scarce public resources are allocated, a partnership soon finds itself deciding how to respond to that process. Few organizations, if any, can avoid feeling the impact of the political process, but an organization can remain essentially passive and accept the political outcomes determined by others. The alternative is to become involved in some way, perhaps at first defensively and later more aggressively.

The phenomenon of organized interest groups is part of the fabric of the American political process, and it is impossible to describe accurately that process without considering interest-group activity. The scenes in the corridors outside the congressional committee rooms where the Federal tax-reform bill was debated and written serve as vivid reminders of how pervasive is the impact of government decisions and how extensive — even frenetic — is the organized effort to affect those decisions. Whose interests are served in the process may be debatable but the centrality of interest-group activity is not.

A group devoted to cooperative relationships between the public and private sectors has to confront the question of whether it will lobby. Although the question is inevitable, the answer is not simple. There are rewards for becoming involved in the policy process, but there are also costs. At the least, political involvement increases the complexity of the environment in which a partnership operates. A partnership must consider a number of questions: Does it lobby against as well as for the public component of the partnership? What happens when the public sector itself is divided, either horizontally between the executive and the legislative branches or vertically among local, state, and Federal levels? What happens when a partnership aligns itself with the losing side?

Whether a partnership decides to become active in lobbying depends on several factors. The nature of the partnership's membership or board will affect the decision. If the formal structure of the organization includes public officials as well as private executives, the public-sector representatives may resist the organization's intruding onto what they consider their turf. They may find it inappropriate, awkward, or even unethical to be part of an organization that makes representations in formal public policy-making processes in which they have a role. What, for example, would a mayor do if a partnership on whose board he sat came before him on a matter involving the distribution of city funds for a partnership-run day-care program? What would he do if the partnership advocated tax incentives to encourage economic development? Under these circumstances, the partnership could desist from lobbying, avoid questions on which the public board member has direct responsibility, or pursue whatever advocacy it believed necessary without the public board members' involvement in the decisions. People in different jurisdictions may not agree on these matters, but the point remains that the questions facing a partnership board that includes elected officials differ from those before a board composed solely of private-sector representatives.

One can easily imagine a partnership board with mixed public-private membership concluding that it should not lobby at the level of government from which its members come but that it should lobby at other levels. Local officials might argue that lobbying locally is inappropriate, or they may suggest it is unnecessary because the officials already know what the partnership advocates. On the other hand, they may contend that the partnership should lobby at the state or Federal levels to ensure that the locality gets its fair share in the distribution of funds or programs.

Although the public members of the board are a key element as to whether a partnership lobbies, the private members' opinions are important as well. Some individuals may personally oppose any lobbying because they think it is unnecessary, unseemly, or risky. Others may oppose it because they represent private organizations or firms that seek to avoid possible political contentiousness that might redound to their disadvantage.

Because of the nature of the organizations that they represent and because of their personal predilections, board members are crucial in the public-advocacy question. Those who organize a partnership should therefore consider the lobbying issue even before the final board is chosen. If one goal of a newly organizing partnership is to influence the government structure, it makes no sense to select a board that will preclude that activity.

The nature of a partnership's board constitutes one element in whether it will lobby; another element is the nature of its program. The narrower the program, the less likely is the need to lobby. If its program is broad and dependent on governmental decision making, it has a greater need for advocacy. Running a job-placement program can be done productively without lobbying, although one can envision advocacy issues that could tempt those people involved with job placement. However, if a partnership's central concern is the local business climate, refraining from public-policy advocacy would reflect either exemplary faith or extraordinary restraint.

Another element affecting a partnership's decision on lobbying is the law. Probably the most important consideration is the Internal Revenue Code and, more specifically, its provisions for charitable organizations. If a partnership is organized under section 501(c)(3), donations to the organization by individuals or corporations are deductible as charitable contributions. Although a 501(c)(3) organization may make some representations on issues of concern to it before legislative bodies, the law imposes significant restrictions on lobbying. There are limitations on the extent of its activities and the percentage of its funds that can be devoted to lobbying. Considerable care is therefore essential and may make a board reluctant to be involved at all.

An alternative is to incorporate the partnership under section 501(c)(6) of the Internal Revenue Code; this section is designed for business leagues, professional associations, and chambers of commerce. Such organizations can devote as much attention to advocacy as they choose. A third possibility is to divide the partnership between the two sections and be scrupulous about the allocation of contributions and the distribution of funds.

In addition to the Internal Revenue Code, any partnership interested in lobbying must be familiar with Federal, state, and local laws regarding the registration of lobbyists. The issue is not whether a partnership constituted under section 501(c)(6) can lobby but the imposition of reporting requirements, the limitations on expenditures, and the regulation of conduct. Usually separate from these yet equally important are Federal, state, and local regulation of campaign contributions.

## Organizational Philosophy

Like other organizations, a partnership may approach the political process with a systematic political philosophy or with ad hoc responses to individual political situations. Or the partnership may find itself, as is frequently the case, on a point somewhere between these two ends of the spectrum, combining a loose ideology with considerable pragmatism.

Obviously, one organizing theme is a belief in the validity of public-private partnerships. This belief translates into a commitment to some kind of cooperative arrangement between the public and private sectors. The exact nature of that arrangement must be worked out in each instance, but the starting point is always a faith that both sectors have unique resources and that there are benefits to their working together. Furthermore, there is an assumption that it is possible and legitimate to work together.

The founders of the New York City Partnership were impressed by the cooperative arrangements developed during New York City's fiscal crisis in the mid-1970s. Some leading business executives concluded that the distance and occasional disdain that had marked the relationship between the two sectors was counterproductive. While some of the joint responsibility was institutionalized in newly created boards like the Municipal Assistance Corporation and the Emergency Financial Control Board, the founders of the New York City Partnership thought a vehicle that would go beyond the city's fiscal affairs was necessary. This philosophical commitment persisted and found frequent articulation in the public and private comments of board members.

Partnerships are also likely to develop an interest in a particular geographic area, usually a city or a metropolitan region. This regional commitment can also become an organizing theme in the pursuit of public policy. Reacting to others' proposals or initiating its own, a partnership gauges its position on what the impact is likely to be for its area. How narrowly that geographic base is defined will vary, but many partnerships have proved relatively sophisticated in thinking fairly broadly.

At its inception, the New York City Partnership made the deliberate decision to go beyond the usual Manhattan focus not only for its board but also for its programs. Leaders like Board Chairman David Rockefeller, Vice Chairman J. Paul Lyet, and Policy Committee Chairman Richard Shinn took as an organizing premise that the long-term strength of New York City depended on the economic and social health of all five boroughs, not just the borough of Manhattan south of 96th

Street. In addition to geographic diversity, there was also a commitment to ethnic and racial diversity. Those concepts found expression in both the rhetoric and the actions of the board. Board members continue to be drawn from all boroughs and from a wide range of backgrounds.

The New York City Partnership's choice of programs reflects its commitment to all sections of the city. A city map shows Partnership housing projects in every borough and in some of the poorest neighborhoods. It also shows Join-A-School and public-safety programs citywide. The organization's economic-development projects started in Brooklyn and continue to emphasize boroughs other than Manhattan.

Similarly, the choice of public-policy positions carried out this five-borough philosophy. A Partnership priority has been to lower energy costs in New York City. When the mayor advanced an initiative that benefited companies expanding in boroughs other than Manhattan or in Manhattan north of 96th Street, the Partnership supported it even though the many board members from companies in the core of the Manhattan business district stood to gain nothing. The same support came for a mayoral proposal to lower the city's occupancy tax in these areas, again excluding Manhattan below 96th Street. In its support for state efforts that produced economic-development zones comparable to enterprise zones in other states, the Partnership lobbied successfully for changes that benefited these areas.

Advocating the interests of one area can too easily lead to hostility toward other areas. But at least some partnerships have opted for a philosophical orientation that tries to pursue a variable-sum game rather than a zero-sum game in regional economic development. For example, the New York City Partnership was an early supporter of the joint New York-New Jersey effort to win designation of a site in one of the two states for one of the navy's homeports. A broad public-private coalition, organized in part by the Port Authority of New York and New Jersey, sought the home port in the belief that wherever it was located in the port area the whole region would benefit. Obviously, jurisdictions on both sides of the Hudson River preferred that they win the designation, but there was a sustained commitment to the regional effort.

The relations between New York and New Jersey have not always been cooperative, and the last few years have seen some bitter comments and divisive actions. The incidents have resulted in large part from competition for corporate locations and development projects. Some New York City officials accused some New Jersey localities of pirating jobs or of violating Federal regulations on the use of Urban Development Action Grants (UDAGs). In turn, New Jersey officials complained about the effects of New York City's sewage and the proposed construction of Westway, a major highway along the west side of Manhattan. One of the complaints about Westway was that landfill from the project might raise the level of the Hudson River and flood the New Jersey lowlands.

In these interstate skirmishes, the Partnership privately advocated that the rhetoric be moderated and confrontation avoided. Although strongly committed to the economic development of New York City, Partnership leaders thought that hostile talk and actions would be counterproductive. They also assumed that the metropolitan area needed to think in regional terms as much as possible. As a result, the Partnership added to its board the chairman of the Regional Plan Association (RPA) and worked with the RPA on a variety of projects. In addition, the Partnership sponsored a conference on possible joint biotechnology projects between New York City and New Jersey. The featured speaker was the governor of New Jersey, Thomas H. Kean.

One spin-off of the philosophical interest that partnerships develop toward their own geographic area is an orientation toward cities in general. Because most partnerships are city-based or include a major city, they are likely to conclude that some of the problems in their own city are generally found elsewhere. This conclusion can lead to involvement with organizations in other cities on urban issues. In 1985, the New York City Partnership joined a broad coalition, focused mainly in northeastern cities, in response to the Federal budget. Proposed sweeping cuts in programs benefiting urban areas galvanized mayors, council members, civic groups, unions, and others to sponsor a rally and lobbying campaign in Washington.

Another philosophical orientation for partnerships is a belief in growth. "Less is more" is an unlikely motto for a partnership. Since many cities in the 1960s and 1970s suffered from slow growth or decline, those interested in such cities learned the penalties of economic contraction. In fact, concern about the future viability of their cities is what prompted the formation of many partnerships.

The value of competition elicits varying responses from partnerships. Because of a commitment to a particular city or region, a partnership may endorse public policies that give preferences to the area. Some municipalities and states have enacted legislation that gives advantages to local firms in procurement. On a national level, some regions and organizations have fought hard for protectionist trade policies. In a period when many industries, employees, and jurisdictions are enduring major economic dislocations, some conclude that a form of protectionism is warranted. To these partisans, it is as natural and as justified as the concept of self-defense articulated by political and religious commentators. This philosophical view is not universal, however. The New York City Partnership believes that in most instances competition is preferable to the alternative and has opposed protectionist legislation at all levels of government. New York State legislation limiting municipalities to buying American steel, for example, did not win Partnership support. The Partnership agrees that both Federal and local governments should ensure that competition is fair, but it is also mindful that support for policies of fair competition is sometimes a guise for sanctioning exactly the opposite.

For the leaders of the New York City Partnership, a belief in the value of competition also means a belief in the freest market possible. While accepting the nineteenth- and twentieth-century reforms that ensured various employee protections and curbed predatory economic practices, the Partnership resists what it regards as excessive public regulation of the private sector. This orientation applies to all levels of government, but it takes on particular importance when the Partnership considers the impact of the local business climate on the area's competitive position. Since doing business in New York is more expensive than in other areas and since New York firms are subjected to requirements not imposed elsewhere, there is a danger that companies will expand elsewhere.

A sense of balance is important in determining how much regulation is appropriate, and Partnership board members are sensitive to that. Whether native New Yorkers or not, most Partnership board members are imbued with elements of the civic culture of the city and state, which traditionally is accepting of governmental activity.

## Partnership Goals and Issues

If the philosophical framework of a partnership denotes the general boundaries of its political actions, a set of programmatic goals provides the destination points it will seek. As is the case in the underlying philosophy, these goals may be organized systematically or may develop haphazardly. Some attempt at a coherent set of goals surely is preferable, but organizations have an astonishing capacity to be diffused and even disorganized. After about three years in which it gradually found it was overextending itself, the New York City Partnership charged a committee with reviewing resources, assessing options, and recommending priorities. The result, *The Partnership Blueprint: Strengthening New York as a World City*, became the strategic plan for the Partnership.

The *Blueprint* served to determine both program and policy choices. As a result the Partnership focused on economic development, broadly conceived. Included under this rubric were not only the usual interests in expanding economic activity and improving the business climate but also interests in education, youth employment, housing, and public safety. All these were seen as part of a sound, long-term effort to make New York City more viable. Although the Partnership's stated goal was to make New York City "a better place in which to live, work, and do business," the *Blueprint* helped set some limits. The organization's board, committees, and staff used the *Blueprint* to make choices. Saying "no" became somewhat easier and certainly more rationalized.

With these basic goals, the New York City Partnership over the next three years developed positions on a range of city, state, and Federal issues. Although many issues were exclusively limited to one jurisdiction, others involved two or all three levels of government.

One of the first issues on which the Partnership took a position involved Federal, state, and city jurisdictions; the issue's complexity and controversy were hallmarks of the New York City political process for a decade. The issue, known simply as Westway, was a proposal to build a major highway and related projects on the West Side of Manhattan between 42d Street and the Battery. Projected to cost more than $2 billion, Westway included a four-mile arterial, a ninety-three-acre riverside park, and reconstructed municipal facilities, such as a Transit Authority bus depot. In addition, the plan called for landfill in the Hudson River that would serve as part of the base for the road as well as land for new housing and for commercial development.

The undeniably grand scale of the plan and its perceived benefits to the city's development attracted organizations like the Partnership and the Regional Plan Association. The same plan and its possible impact on the environment, as well as the use of public funds that some preferred to direct to mass transit, produced long and bitter opposition from an array of individuals, groups, and politicians. The struggle over Westway demonstrated to the Partnership that its conception of what benefited New York City was not shared by everyone involved. Westway made it clear that once one moved beyond the generalities of economic development to specific projects one should expect not only opposition but also hostility. Although there are still places where a strong consensus exists for almost any kind of economic development, whatever the side costs, that is certainly not true everywhere. In New York and a growing number of other areas, projects much smaller than Westway are guaranteed to trigger opposition in the planning and zoning processes, in legislative bodies, in the media, in the courts, and even in the streets.

Ultimately, a Federal deadline required the state and city to decide whether they would gamble on approval of Westway in the courts or trade in the money for Federal aid on other transportation and transit projects. Although they had been supportive of Westway, the governor and mayor decided that the certainty of some trade-in dollars outweighed the uncertainty of final court approval of the project.

Westway occupied the Partnership's agenda for the first five years of the organization's existence. Some issues are more discrete in their time frames and in the levels of government involved. Such was the case with the decision by the mayor of New York City to tax the real property of certain nonprofit organizations. The issue reached a climax in the spring of 1983, and the Partnership decided to oppose such a tax. Many board members sat on one or more nonprofit boards in the city and thought that these organizations would be jeopardized. They argued that taxing nonprofits ran counter to long-standing local policy. They also pointed out the many economic, social, and cultural contributions that nonprofits made to the city. The ad hoc coalition that developed on this issue and in which the Partnership actively participated convinced the mayor to return to the past policy of not taxing nonprofits. From this effort came a new organization, the Nonprofit Coordinating Committee of New York (NPCC-NY), which developed a membership of 200 nonprofits and continues to represent their interests.

The New York City Partnership's tax agenda extends beyond nonprofit organizations to the profit-making sector, because the Partnership is committed to economic development and it represents the business community. In fact, no other public issue has been as important as taxes on any level of government. One of the Partnership's major objectives has been the lowering of the overall tax burden in New York State and in New York City. It was one of the leading voices in a campaign that culminated in the state's 1985 decision to lower taxes on personal income derived from salaries and wages as well as from savings and investments.

A second priority for the Partnership is fiscal reform. For many years the state committed some expenditures in one fiscal year and made them in the next. The fiscal gimmick required the state to engage in massive short-term borrowing, finally reaching over $4 billion annually. The Partnership joined with State Comptroller Edward Regan and Governor Mario Cuomo in urging the legislature to end such practices that it considered fiscally unsound. Starting in 1985 and continuing in 1986, the state committed the necessary funds to end the so-called spring rollover. While the financial community and others agreed that this was a good decision, it was not an easy one, since it used up budget dollars that might have been spent for politically more appealing programs. That made it all the more important for prestigious organizations and individuals to make it a priority.

Another major issue mainly played out at the state level is the cost of energy. New York City has had the unfortunate distinction of having one of the highest, if not the highest, energy costs of any city in the country. State and city taxes, reliance on imported oil, and the additional cost of low-sulphur fuel to meet environmental requirements all contribute to these high costs. For several years the Partnership has pointed out to state and city government leaders that companies considering moves from the metropolitan area often cite energy costs as a significant factor. In response the Partnership has advocated increasing the downstate share of low-cost hydropower generated by the New York State Power Authority. The organization has also proposed various alternatives for reducing state and city utility taxes, which are passed on directly to customers.

The Partnership's programs generate many of its public-policy positions. The Housing Partnership, the entity devoted to facilitating and financing the construction of middle- and moderate-income housing, for example, has generated a number of important recommendations, including support for the state legislation making it easier to construct factory-built housing and for measures providing various tax incentives for housing construction. The Housing Partnership also served as the principal model for a new $25 million program funded by the state to replace some of the withdrawn Federal housing subsidies. Since 1984 the Partnership leadership has made the inclusion of these funds in the state budget a priority, and the Partnership staff has assisted in drafting the language of the bill and implementing the program.

The Partnership's concern for the public schools has resulted in advocacy for increased state funding for education and for an increased share of that funding going to New York City. Joining with the mayor, the New York City Board of Education, and other groups concerned with city education, the Partnership urged the legislature to consider the city's current disadvantage in the state aid formula and the unique demands on city schools.

Early in its history, the Partnership turned to Washington for help in determining what would happen in economic development, housing, youth employment, and education and in improving the competitive position of the city and state. The Partnership has lobbied at the Federal level on such issues as enterprise zones, Urban Development Action Grants, and Targeted Jobs Tax Credits. On a wider scale, it has also joined those advocating significant Federal deficit reduction on the grounds that continuing deficits imperil the entire national economy.

When the campaign for Federal tax reform began to move appreciably in late 1984, the Partnership was among those convinced that the elimination of the deductibility of state and local taxes would be an enormous disadvantage for New York. In 1985 Partnership leaders helped establish a coalition cochaired by a Partnership board member, Lewis Rudin, the chairman of the Association for a Better New York. This group mounted a major campaign to bring together representatives of the public and private sectors. Against enormous odds, including the president's position in favor of eliminating the deductibility, this coalition helped produce a tax-reform bill that maintained the deductibility of state and local income taxes and property taxes but not sales taxes.

## Partnership Advocacy Process

Once a partnership has decided to be involved in the public-policy process and has determined its goals, the next question is how it will advance those goals. There is, of course, a broad spectrum of options, ranging from occasional letters to elected officials to sustained lobbying. The New York City Partnership opted for a more comprehensive agenda and a more systematic involvement with the legislative and executive branches. The organization now has a small full-time professional staff devoted exclusively to setting the policy agenda, working with the board and its committees and with staff who have substantive expertise in program areas like housing, education, and economic development. The public-issues staff, registered as lobbyists in New York City and New York State, is also responsible for working with elected officials and their staffs. Although the full-time staff oversees Federal advocacy and occasionally works in Washington, the day-to-day activities are assigned to a Washington law firm on retainer to the Partnership.

From the beginning, the Partnership's board members have played significant roles in the lobbying process, even since the addition of full-time lobbyists. At the beginning of each state legislative year, a group of about a dozen board members spend a day and a half in Albany hosting a reception for the legislature and meeting privately with legislative leaders and with the governor. This annual visit to the state capital allows board members to present the Partnership's priorities to those with whom they meet. The Partnership delegation consists of its chairman, David Rockefeller, and key board members and committee chairs (usually chief executive officers of major corporations or institutions). In addition, some senior staff members of the Partnership also attend. Because of the nature of the board and the organization, state officials are ordinarily accessible, and in these sessions the board members rather than staff speak for the Partnership.

If there were no follow-up to these meetings, they might prove to be merely ceremonial exchanges. With the addition of full-time staff the entrée gained by the board can be built upon by the staff as well as by the board members. As the legislative session evolves, the staff works with the members of the legislative and executive branches, and staff members selectively call on board members to send telegrams, place telephone calls, or make personal visits.

Because of their prominence and their activities outside the Partnership, the board members have proved to be a special resource. Whether in the White House, the New York Executive Mansion, or Gracie Mansion, board members frequent the meeting rooms and dining rooms at the highest levels. Besides their corporate responsibilities and their activities on the Partnership board, these executives are often on a host of governmental commissions and advisory panels. These board-member activities are sources of information and influence. The informal network resulting from overlapping responsibilities and multiple involvements is one of the more effective ways in which the political process builds consensus. For organizations like the Partnership, this has proved advantageous in advancing its policy agenda.

Board member and staff involvement in other organizations and in the political world has another implication for the way partnerships engage the political process. In some instances a partnership is the sole advocate for a particular position. Generally, however, effective public advocacy means coalition building. On most issues, the New York City Partnership has been involved in existing coalitions or has helped to organize coalitions. Sometimes these are quite formal in nature and transcend legislative years, but frequently they are loose arrangements that focus on one issue and then disperse. On tax reform, education aid, new housing programs, Westway, Homeport, Targeted Jobs Tax Credits, and many other issues, the New York City Partnership has been part of coalitions. Although some coalitions consist only of groups or individuals from the private sector, others involve public and private representatives. By their nature, partnerships are more likely than many other groups to engage in joint advocacy with public officials. On Westway, Partnership members and staff joined city and state officials, labor leaders, and representatives of other civic associations in lobbying members of Congress. The coalition that fought to retain the Federal deductibility of state and local taxes was even broader, consisting of almost every major public official in New York, local school boards, individual companies, unions, nonprofits, and professional and civic groups.

### Advantages and Disadvantages in Partnership Advocacy

A number of advantages accrue to partnerships that choose to become involved in the public-policy process. First and most important, by deciding to be active they have a much better chance to affect those decisions that affect them. Like other advocacy groups, they will sometimes get less than they want. However, they enter the political arena with more resources than some; they must organize those resources effectively. John F. Kennedy often cited the truism that victory has many fathers, and defeat is an orphan. Partnerships sometimes wonder how much a difference they made; their voice may be only one of many, but it can make the difference. There will also be occasions when their voice will absolutely make the difference, but they choose to keep that knowledge to themselves.

Reference was made earlier to doing good and doing well. A partnership may gain a special advantage by being associated with an agenda that does good; it may find it easier to win support for goals that have direct benefits for the sectors of the economy they represent. One does not have to dwell on the merits of exchange theories of politics to recognize that reciprocity is a powerful dynamic.

In addition to the political credits earned for finding work for young people or building housing, a partnership may enjoy some publicity that wins the organization wider visibility. If visibility becomes public approval, the organization will be stronger in all its endeavors, including advocacy.

There can be a side payoff for those involved in partnership advocacy of programs that benefit those beyond their own membership. Whether one regards this as civic pride or psychic income, those who see their efforts produce worthwhile programs may gain satisfactions that go beyond those won from greater income or more political influence. Undoubtedly, this feeling of doing good is one of the motivations for those who have done well.

Anyone contemplating advocacy should be aware that, while a partnership involved in lobbying enters the process with some advantages and gains others, there are also costs, risks, and disadvantages. First, there are the monetary costs. Hiring full-time staff, maintaining offices, covering travel and entertainment expenses, and sometimes making campaign contributions require resources that obviously mount if a group chooses to be active at more than one level of government.

Some of the advantages that partnerships enjoy can easily turn into disadvantages. Visibility, for example, is a mixed blessing. While some may respect and appreciate board members involved in public projects, others may see the rich and powerful interfering where they are not wanted, and still others will assume their involvement has base motives. Increased exposure may generate resentment against a perceived elite.

That exposure may also produce demands that neither the partnership nor its board members can meet. The public may expect more houses and jobs and turn against those who supposedly could provide these needs if they wished. In addition, once politicians are aware of the organization, they may expect it and its members to provide special favors in a plethora of forms to constituents. Even closer to the hearts of elected officials may be campaign contributions for themselves.

Another advantage that could become a disadvantage is psychic income. Winning a legislative battle or seeing a project succeed may be gratifying to the ego, but losing a vote or seeing a project fail may take its toll, particularly for board members unaccustomed to politics. Some of the rough-and-tumble taken for granted by those who have served time in political clubhouses is foreign to corporate chief executive officers. One may go away from a political battle not only having lost but also having been publicly embarrassed or privately ridiculed.

If one weathers these political storms, one is still left with the question of balancing interests. The balancing takes many forms. How many issues does it get involved with? Which ones should be chosen as priorities? Just as a partnership may spread itself among programs that are too diffuse, it may find its legislative program growing out of control. An inchoate policy agenda will drain limited resources. It also invites disrespect among policy-making professionals.

The most serious issue here is how a partnership balances its inclinations to recommend public spending and its proclivity to favor tax cuts. As was observed earlier, taxes—especially tax cuts—are high priorities for partnerships. Then is it inconsistent for a partnership to advocate program enhancements? More than once, a high official has put this question to the New York City Partnership.

One can support some additions in programs along with tax cuts if one does it with a sense of responsibility and with a recognition that there are limits to budgets. Public revenue growth may make the necessary funds available. One may ascertain areas where costs can be controlled or lowered, and one may establish priorities, just as elected officials do. To accomplish this while developing an advocacy agenda, it is useful for a partnership to have some unit that can integrate and rationalize the program. At the New York City Partnership this is largely the responsibility of the Committee on Public Issues, currently chaired by James D. Robinson III, chairman and chief executive officer of American Express. Receiving recommendations from various program committees and staff, the Committee on Public Issues functions much like the House Ways and Means Committee. Although there is no attempt to construct an entire budget, there is an honest effort to achieve a reasonably balanced agenda. In other organizations, the full board or an executive committee might assume the responsibility.

This search for balance raises a related question. When does a partnership pursue goals beneficial to a wider community, and when does it seek policies that will redound to the benefit of its own members? Failure to resolve this issue can result in confusion over the organization's purposes and goals. A successful partnership should recognize that there is a time to do good, a time to do well, and a time to do both. Successful partnerships help provide the capacity to do good and well, both in programs and in policies.

## Note

1. Peter F. Drucker, "Doing Good to Do Well: The New Opportunities for Business Enterprise," in *Public Private Partnerships: New Opportunities for Meeting Social Needs*, ed. Harvey Brooks, Lance Liebman, and Corinne S. Schelling (Cambridge, Mass.: Ballinger, 1984), 285–86.

# Partners for Downtown Development: Creating a New Central Business District in Brooklyn

PERRY DAVIS

Breaking ground for "Atlantic Center" in downtown Brooklyn signals the physical start of one of New York City's most ambitious construction projects. Costing approximately $500 million, the mixed-use development will eventually comprise up to 3 million square feet of commercial space clustered in four office towers, over 100,000 square feet of ground-level retail establishments, 643 moderate-income, owner-occupied residential townhouse units, and a new public park. The project will be located on more than twenty-four acres of land.

The groundbreaking signals an even more historic event—the renaissance of downtown Brooklyn and the physical extension of the country's largest business district, Manhattan, across the East River and into the city's boroughs. As recently as 1980, large-scale office construction outside Manhattan in New York City was inconceivable. But by late 1986, over 10 million square feet of office space had been planned for construction in Brooklyn alone, and Citibank had already begun work on a 1.2 million square foot tower in Long Island City, Queens. The public-private partnership mechanism stood at the heart of this dramatic development. Shared risks and opportunities brought government and business together for the benefit of all.

### The Borough of Brooklyn

The borough of Brooklyn, with its 2,230,936 residents, emerged from New York City's mid-1970s fiscal crisis and the national recession of the early 1980s in a state of economic disarray. It had suffered a substantial loss of manufacturing jobs. At the same time, the vigorous growth of New York's service industry had become an economic dynamo, fueling the expansion of the financial services, insurance, and real estate sectors. The job growth and real estate boom associated with this dynamo were having a positive effect on the Manhattan Central Business District. And yet the impact of this expansion was not spreading east to the outer boroughs but west to New Jersey and north to Westchester and Connecticut.

Between 1977 and 1983, 7 million square feet of office space was leased in the suburbs surrounding New York City, according to the Regional Plan Association. Some 2.6 million square feet of that space had formerly been leased in Manhattan. Brooklyn's political leaders and Edward Koch, mayor of New York, saw Brooklyn as a viable alternative to the suburban space, but private-sector tenants did not agree.

In 1983, for example, Bankers Trust Company moved 1,200 employees to a new computer center in a renovated building in Jersey City, New Jersey. The site was ten minutes away from downtown Manhattan via mass transit and benefited from line-of-sight telecommunications capability with its headquarters. A Bankers Trust vice president said, "We did look at several sites in other boroughs. But location and availability—to coincide with our need for expansion—were at a disadvantage compared to the site we chose. Energy costs were a consideration and the cost of space."[1]

The political, civic, and business leaders of Brooklyn were intimately aware of a different side of the story. Brooklyn, particularly the downtown area, had a great deal to offer. It had affordable, publicly owned land, short and direct transportation links to Manhattan and the other boroughs, a large labor pool, the sixth largest retail center in the country, a broad array of residential properties ranging from luxury brownstones in Brooklyn Heights to public housing in Fort Greene, seven universities, and renowned cultural institutions like the Brooklyn Academy of Music and the Brooklyn Museum.

But the bankers were also correct—construction costs were high, taxes were uncompetitive, and energy costs were double those of New Jersey. And most important of all were the perceptual obstacles. Brooklyn was seen as crime ridden and squalid; its labor force, ill-trained and undependable. An undercurrent of racial prejudice permeated some locational decisions. Somewhat less malevolently, Brooklyn—in the eyes of Manhattan business leaders—was a step down. At least New Jersey was uncharted. Donald Moore, president of the world-renowned Brooklyn Botanic Garden, put it well: "Sometimes I think we get more visitors from the island of Honshu than we get from the island of Manhattan."[2]

Brooklyn needed validation. Building office space for government workers would not help much. Something more than boosterism by the borough president and the Brooklyn Chamber of Commerce was needed to make an impact on private developers and tenants. Symbolic of the changes in perception was an article by society writer Lindsy Van Gelder in the September 1985 issue of *Town and Country* magazine. The article's placement told half the story and the rest was clear from the title of the piece—"Beautiful, Bountiful Brooklyn." Social validation was crucial, but a real private-sector commitment required a more substantial investment: new office buildings, retail revitalization, and new service-sector jobs.

## Brooklyn and the Private Sector

Early in 1983, the New York City Partnership formulated a blueprint for its future. Extensive research by a committee of its most prominent board members, led by John Whitehead (then head of Goldman, Sachs & Co.) and including Partnership Chairman David Rockefeller, preceded the selection of five priorities for Partnership projects. One of these priorities was the retention of back-office space in New York City. Back offices handle the largely clerical and support functions for key service industries. These facilities were quickly deserting Manhattan for New Jersey, Westchester, and farther destinations. The Regional Plan Association estimated that by the start of the twenty-first century up to 45 million square feet of back-office space could leave Manhattan.

The Partnership decided on a three-part strategy designed to keep back offices in New York City. First, it sought to avoid any publicly imposed market restrictions, such as restrictive zoning and new regulatory limitations, on the Manhattan Central Business District. Additional back-office space was available on the outskirts of the Manhattan Central Business District, and the Partnership along with the Real Estate Board of New York encouraged the development of these sites. Second, through its lobbying activities, the Partnership moved to lower taxes and energy costs and to improve the overall business climate of the city. Both of these approaches were traditional chamber of commerce-type business-retention strategies.

A unique third strategy, however, was added to the traditional package. Borough sites were to be surveyed, and special pump-priming government incentives and subsidies would be recommended to encourage pioneering deals that would begin the commercial-development process outside of the Manhattan Central Business District. This third approach presented significant problems to Partnership board members. Some were themselves eyeing New Jersey for potential sites. Most were quite ambivalent about Brooklyn's lackluster image. Others were philosophically troubled that steep public-sector subsidies were inappropriate market-tampering devices that might be more than pump primers and could become massive public-spending programs. Nevertheless, in late 1983 the president of the borough of Brooklyn, Howard Golden, challenged the Partnership to apply its resources to the potential economic revitalization of the area. That challenge, along with an effective presentation by Partnership board member Eugene Luntey (chairman and chief executive officer of the Brooklyn Union Gas Company), a key report on Brooklyn by the Regional Plan Association, and a short but important bus tour of the area for key Partnership leaders led to an active commitment to the borough. Frank Macchiarola, the Partnership president and a lifelong Brooklyn resident, argued forcefully that if a borough strategy would work anywhere in the five boroughs it would work in downtown Brooklyn. The Partnership, representing the business community, was convinced that Brooklyn was a manageable risk.

## The Atlantic Terminal Urban Renewal Area

When the leaders of the New York City Partnership agreed to focus on Brooklyn as a likely alternative to New Jersey in real estate competition, they went far beyond the borough president's challenge and demand. His notion of public-sector validation would have been satisfied with a public statement of support and encouragement and a set of letters to developers and potential tenants touting the assets of the area. Instead, the Partnership staff was given an explicit charge by the board. First, an in-depth report of the back-office market would be necessary. The competitive strengths of the suburbs would be evaluated. Manhattan fringe-area alternatives would be assessed, as would key business-climate disincentives. Then a borough alternative could be surveyed and, if identified, one or two specific sites in the area would be selected for closer analysis. Most important, a report was not enough; the Whitehead committee overseeing the project wanted to see concrete action leading to a tangible real estate development.

When the Partnership report "Competing for Back Offices" was completed and released in late 1984, all of the Whitehead committee's instructions had been fulfilled. Two sites in downtown Brooklyn were identified and described. The first, Metrotech, was truly the pioneer development in Brooklyn, centered on the campus of the Polytechnic Institute of New York. Polytechnic, the developer of the project, planned over 1.8 million square feet of commercial space on sixteen acres of land. Brooklyn Union Gas Company indicated an interest in relocating its headquarters to the Metrotech site and another prime private tenant was being sought.

But discussions with public officials and business leaders revealed a more intriguing site at the heart of Brooklyn's transportation hub — the Atlantic Terminal Urban Renewal Area (ATURA) and an adjacent site, Brooklyn Center. Rights to the area belonged to the state's transit agency, the city, and — more specifically — the city's Public Development Corporation.

The ATURA site was not only publicly owned, available, and cleared, but it was also the busiest and most accessible transportation nexus in the city. All of the city's three subway systems met at ATURA, fourteen bus lines crossed the intersection, three major vehicular arteries came together, and the Long Island Rail Road had a terminal under the site. Forty percent of the Manhattan work force passed under or through the ATURA site. Yet the site still begged for a developer.

High hopes for ATURA were hardly new or novel. As early as November 1970 the Park Slope Civic Council *Civic News* noted that the project had "its first stage in design with construction of 800 apartments, local shopping space and related community facilities expected to begin next summer." Despite a cleared site of over twenty-two acres and ambitious plans for a college campus or a new baseball stadium to replace Ebbets Field, the ATURA site lay fallow and embroiled in controversy for decades.

By 1984 the demand for back-office space, the renewed interest in Brooklyn by the city's business leaders, and a firm commitment by the mayor and the borough president to match or beat any New Jersey offer to tenants or developers sparked a renewed interest in ATURA. The city hall offer followed several years of balanced budgets, which signaled the official end of the city's fiscal crisis. Surpluses and Urban Development Action Grant (UDAG) funds were dedicated to commercial development projects in the boroughs. Kenneth Lipper, a new deputy mayor for economic development, who was recruited from Salomon Brothers, enjoyed a collegial relationship with the city's key private-sector leaders.

Jonathan Rose, a principal of Rose Associates, a real estate firm, heard of ATURA when he was engaged in new moderate-income housing development in Brooklyn under the New York City Partnership's affordable housing program. Rose, a son of Fred Rose, a Partnership board member and company chairman, saw the attractive aspects of ATURA before he became aware of its political history. By then his commitment to a major project was quite strong and the company was supportive. The road from a personal, instinctive commitment to a deal to a groundbreaking was tortuous. The public-private partnership vehicle, however, was key to negotiating the obstacle course.

### Structuring a Deal: Partnership as Catalyst

Rose Associates was quite aware of the obstacles they faced in structuring a multisector deal for ATURA. They had previously tried to consummate an agreement for a project in Manhattan involving a public-bidding process. The results were unfavorable. The Roses felt that bids by incompetent or unscrupulous companies made the overall bidding process untenable. To reach an agreement on the ATURA site would be even more difficult, and Fred and Jonathan Rose asked for the Partnership's full support and involvement in the deal-making process.

A wholly contained private-sector negotiation has common elements with the multisector format. In essence, one party seeks a site for a cost designed to allow maximum use at a price that will permit market-favorable rents as well as a profitable return on the original equity investment. The owner of the site wants the highest possible sale price. Simply stated, cash and land are the currencies and resources on the table as the negotiations proceed. Lawyers and accounting professionals are the support team for the real estate principals. Traditional risks attend the deal; if the seller gets too little or the buyer pays too much to be in a favorable leasing position, then land or buildings remain unoccupied, generating costs rather than profits.

Rose Associates, the Partnership, and the city were partially aware of the significantly more complex nature of a proposed ATURA acquisition. First, in addition to the common currency on the trading block, land and cash, new stakes were added by the city. While the city wanted a favorable financial settlement, its profit would be measured in noncash terms as well. The prestige and favorable publicity of the largest mixed-use development project outside of Manhattan in decades would translate into popular support and ultimately votes for the mayor and the borough president. Additionally, the public legacy attached to the renaissance of the boroughs loomed as a more intangible but significant plum for elected and senior appointed officials. The size and setting of the project made the project historically significant for the developer. The Roses realized as well that in addition to the land the city had the potential for financial support and the ability to improve the site's appearance and readiness for construction. It could provide crucial city services and infrastructure improvements at little or no cost. Ultimately, the city saw more traditional public-sector success factors resulting from the project—neighborhood revitalization, new homes, new retail businesses, retained or newly created jobs, and the tax revenue they bring to the city coffers. A final currency brought to the deal by the city—an anchor tenant—turned out to be crucial for the Rose decision to proceed with the project.

As much as the currencies of success varied in this multisector deal, the related risks to both sides were even more diverse and complex. The Roses' risk was clearly the greatest. First, the developer risked some design-tampering from a public-bidding process that was defined and controlled by the city. The Roses wanted (and received) as much freedom as possible in the design of the mixed-use development. Second, the Roses faced serious political obstacles and negative publicity, because the project would have to go through a lengthy public-approval process that allowed the local community, the City Planning Commission, and the elected leadership of New York to snipe at the project. The gentrification objection would surely be raised. Third, the developer risked severe fiscal and prestige losses resulting from a lack of tenants. The Roses' willingness to be urban pioneers might easily result in the public embarrassment of the firm if millions of square feet of office space stood vacant, glaringly visible in the heart of Brooklyn. If approval delays increased, if the city's booming real estate climate turned sour, if the borough could not overcome its image problem, and if costs of acquisition and construction forced uncompetitive rental costs, the project would fail. The Fantus Company, a real estate site-analysis consulting group, had already told the Roses that any Brooklyn office site would have little likelihood of tenanting success and suggested that square-foot rents would have to be well below $20 to be competitive.

The city's risks were not as extensive as the Roses' but were quite significant. First, political reputations were on the line. The mayor and the borough president were making lofty promises of a borough commercial revitalization. Similar predictions had been made in previous years; indeed, some earlier commitments had been made to the same ATURA site, with developers pulling out at the last minute, sometimes with parting shots critical of the public officials involved in the deal. The city also had to provide special tax abatements and heavy public subsidies to make the project possible. Land would have to be sold or leased at a very low cost. In the short run the media, some political opponents, and the general public might see the mayor in a less than arm's length deal with "fat cat" developers. At best, some would describe the agreement with Rose as a naive deal for the city. In retrospect the Roses saw the deal as a "poor" one, with city agencies delaying certification unfairly for more than nine months.

The New York City Partnership leaders also faced risks as they put the organization's reputation on the line for a deal that could easily fall apart. If Brooklyn remained a public-sector office domain and New Jersey continued to attract key private back-office tenants, Partnership companies would come under increasing pressure to be pioneers and opt for the Brooklyn alternative. The broad economic and civic goals of the Partnership board would clash with the "bottom line" necessities of individual Partnership chief executive officers. Such a clash of goals would threaten the very foundation of the organization.

Ironically, the complexity of a multisector deal, as in the case of the ATURA project, also held the seeds of an effective resolution. Since both sides faced significant risks, mutual concessions were more likely to be structured. Both sides could claim that original positions were flexible and key demands could be forgone because the other side was willing to accept higher levels of risk.

The Roses, for example, originally refused to acquire the site on the basis of a public-bidding process. They wanted to be awarded the rights to the property on a "sole source" basis. Furthermore, they demanded major public subsidies and supports to permit a low rental cost. The Roses adamantly refused to build anything without committed tenants. They reluctantly accepted the inevitability of a difficult public-approval process but welcomed a chance to work with the local community as the project was being designed. The final design, however, would be the one developed by Rose Associates and Peter Calthorpe with help from the architectural firm of Skidmore, Owings, and Merrill.

For its part the city had a fundamental difficulty in awarding the site without a bidding process leading to the lowest cost for the city. Massive subsidies were politically dangerous and acceptable only if the Roses built in anticipation of tenants. In other words, fiscal support would come only if real construction, not merely land acquisition, occurred. As an early inducement, the city offered to locate the headquarters of the public Health and Hospitals Corporation in one of the site's two towers. The city was reluctant, however, to give Rose acquisition rights on a second major site, the Brooklyn Center, a block away from ATURA.

Parties on both sides and the Partnership staff and directors helped bridge the gap between the city and the Roses. The Partnership's input came at the Roses' invitation. Before the Roses met with the city, their interest and that of the Partnership were put before Deputy Mayor Lipper and Mayor Koch by Frank Macchiarola, president and chief executive officer of the Partnership. The Partnership senior staff also attended the first meeting held between Borough President Howard Golden and the Roses. The city was therefore aware that the Partnership, representing the broad business community of New York City, stood at the shoulder of a member firm and that a successful deal with the Roses would be translated as an economic-development coup of citywide proportions. The reverse was also obvious, and a degree of political pressure was added to the negotiations. At various points during the negotiations, the Roses presented their plans to the leadership of the Partnership. In turn, senior staff and key board members contacted the mayor and other officials to give encouragement and support for the deal. As John Whitehead reported to the Partnership board in early 1985, "As you remember, last October, the Roses presented their formal plans for the project to David Rockefeller and our Committee. All of us reacted enthusiastically and conveyed our enthusiasm to the Mayor and the Borough President at a critical point in the negotiations."[3]

An early and crucial breakthrough came when the city acceded to Rose and the Partnership and agreed to deal with the developer as a sole source for the project. There would be no public bidding. The Partnership officially intervened in support of Rose at the request of Deputy Mayor Lipper, who wanted a first-test case for his new "sole source" procedure for difficult sites like ATURA. In a politically effective alliance, he enlisted the business community to support a new policy that was valuable for the development community in New York and equally crucial for the future of borough revitalization.

In November 1984, the logjam broke. The Roses committed to new speculative construction in addition to the Health and Hospitals Corporation headquarters. The city in turn approved a substantial financial package consisting of Municipal Assistance Corporation surplus funds, a UDAG capital budget support, and lower-rate Industrial Revenue Bond support. The deal was made in late December, just as the Partnership released its back-office report to the public. The report hinted at the project and the Partnership's role in it. The project was formally announced in January 1985.

And so each party had accepted some risk and made concessions to the other party. The Roses got their sole-source designation and a major multimillion dollar financing package of low loan rates and outright grants (including the city's agreement to construct a parking garage for the project and provide infrastructure improvements). They promised to build 250,000 feet of the project without any tenants committed. For its part the city gave an anchor tenant for a second tower and sole-source designation outside of a public-bidding process but got an ironclad commitment of construction of at least one tower plus 250,000 square feet of space. Both sides got favorable rental costs as a result of the low land costs and major subsidies. Favorable publicity followed the announcement, and the Partnership got its share of the credit. The *New York Daily News* commented that "nothing solid happened until the New York Partnership took an interest."[4] The Partnership's new-homes program was also designated to facilitate the construction of 600 new townhouse units on the site.

The project as announced in January 1985 would comprise approximately 3.1 million square feet of office and retail space and 600 housing units. It would be linked to a satellite telecommunications center by fiber-optic cable. Retail space would include restaurants, a major cinema complex, and a supermarket. Rights for additional developments of the Brooklyn Center parcel were given to the Roses. The city estimated that if the project reached full potential it would employ up to 12,000 people.

*The Final Stage: Finding Tenants and Public Approvals*

In the year following the announcement of the deal, the Roses, the Partnership, and the city faced significant additional problems. Foremost was the search for private-sector tenants. John Whitehead had committed the Partnership to helping promote the downtown Brooklyn area as "a new central business district — a 'Wall Street East' right across the river."[5] The Partnership brought several prestigious companies to the Roses as prospective tenants and sponsored a well-publicized bus tour of the area for Manhattan business leaders, yet not one new private tenant was willing to commit to a lease at ATURA or any other borough-development site.

Finally, later in 1985, the city announced that it had reached agreement with the investment-banking firm of Morgan Stanley & Company to build and occupy a major computer center in Brooklyn Heights. By January 1986, construction for the Morgan Stanley building was under way. From the start of negotiations to the groundbreaking the city had never moved faster or more effectively to keep a major tenant in the five boroughs. The city had clearly demonstrated its ability to make deals in the time set by private industry and had added the major missing component to validate the new Brooklyn Central Business District — a prime private-sector tenant.

Crucial to the ascendancy of downtown Brooklyn was the sense that the city and state were responding to the uncompetitive business climate facing prospective developers and tenants. A state income-tax cut and a citywide cut (excluding the Manhattan Central Business District) in utility and rental tax rates was put in effect in 1985. The Partnership had lobbied actively for each of these items, and together they added to the increased credibility of an economically competitive city and state. Borough deals were no longer special deals. Six months after the Rose deal was announced, large, privately owned parcels of land had been acquired in the vicinity of ATURA. More significantly, a nearby city-owned site had been put up for public bidding, and six major developers submitted proposals for the property. In a matter of a few months, the Hilton Hotel chain had agreed to build a new hotel in downtown Brooklyn, a major waterfront warehouse area was being reconverted into office space, and the Metrotech site had attracted the Securities Industry Automation Corporation as an anchor tenant. Potential new and refurbished office space added up to nearly 10 million square feet in downtown Brooklyn. The market was now self-propelled; the critical mass necessary to sustain the growth of a new central business district had been attained.

As the number of prospective tenants interested in the Rose site grew, the project faced one final obstacle — the public-approval process.

Neighborhood groups and citywide advocacy groups attacked the Rose project for being insensitive to the employment needs of the minority community and for neglecting low income housing requirements. Jonathan Rose's promise to open the project up to public scrutiny helped quell much of the dissent. In addition, some local political leaders were supportive of the project and helped split the opposition camp.

Most important, the design of the Rose project blunted a great deal of potential criticism. Jonathan Rose found a mutually reinforcing element in the need to attract tenants to the site and the local community concerns. Tenants, he decided, were essentially choosing between urban and suburban sites as they looked for new space. Downtown Manhattan was one alternative; the other was the bucolic

Connecticut office campus. Rose would provide a third alternative, an "environment that has the ambiance of the suburbs, but the labor force, the transportation links and all of the excitement of New York City."[6] Additionally, Rose thought that a fortress setting was not the way to overcome the crime that prevaded the area. Engaging large numbers of people in dawn-to-dusk activities would be the best way to keep the site safe—not a sterile office-park bastion. Rose therefore saw the supermarket and the multiplex cinema as a way of keeping the area busy and open to the community. The new home owners would have a park in their midst. They would be responsible for its maintenance and security, and it would be open to all from dawn to dusk. As for employment, tenants could draw from the Brooklyn and Queens labor pool. The resulting work force would form a multiracial community similar to Fort Greene, the handsome neighborhood nearest the project. The Rose project would enhance land values, but the neighborhood was increasingly middle class; thus, gentrification would not be initiated by ATURA's development. The alternative, the continued neglect of the site, was politically and socially unacceptable to the local residents.

Therefore, sound design and a welcome attitude to the democratic process kept the public-approval process on track. A series of city scandals, problems with the transportation agency that controlled some of the land, and environmental concerns about air quality associated with the increased traffic in the area did delay the final approval of the project about six months, but by early 1987 groundbreaking and the start of construction were imminent.

*Lessons Learned*

Within the panoply of issues—such as job programs, educational assistance, and safety projects—that can be aided in the context of public-private partnership solutions, real estate development projects are rare. Their dollar costs are usually higher than other so-called softer partnership priorities. They also face fairly rigid timetables. In the real estate industry, time is truly money. Preliminary negotiation and public-approval requirements can add years to the length of projects, and while the clock ticks toward the official groundbreaking, soft costs measured in lawyers' billable hours and consultants' per diem fees mount up. The Roses estimate that their preliminary design and approval fees amounted to $4 million. Simultaneously, the cyclical real estate market waits for no one developer, and lease costs carefully computed at the start of the negotiation process may be woefully uncompetitive as the construction process nears completion. The risk of a poor market may increase the likelihood of a failed project, with empty office buildings standing as monuments to poor timing and lost investments.

On the positive side, successful partnership-assisted commercial development projects—as well as housing programs—have unique attributes that bring all participants a high sense of satisfaction. First, they are visible for all to see. Successful projects provide the community with more than just new buildings. They can also spur the dramatic revival of a neighborhood, reduce crime, improve housing, and provide jobs for hundreds or thousands of people. These projects are graphic examples of public-private partnerships at their best.

Those engaged in a multisector commercial development project must be keenly aware of both the similarities and the differences between such a deal and an intra–private-sector negotiation. Risks as well as rewards are different for the two sectors, and these differences have an impact on the very process of negotiations. Again, for the ATURA project, the Roses needed to have maximum privacy as they approached the final configuration of a deal with the city. As Jonathan Rose said, "We have different needs than the public sector. Our return is in dollars and theirs is in votes. They have the need periodically to stand up and announce things and take credit." There were no press notices of the ATURA project during the period of negotiations. The news blackout, according to Rose, made the city impatient—moving toward an agreement, "so that the Mayor could have a news conference."[7]

Additionally, the resources available in a multisector negotiation differ markedly from private deals. Tax abatements, lower energy costs, public-sector anchor tenants, inexpensive land, and outright grants and subsidies are powerful incentives held out by the government. In the ATURA project, all of these resources carefully balanced the risk being taken by Rose Associates in pioneering the commercial development of a neglected part of the city. Together they made the deal and the project a reality.

Integral to any market transaction is the trust the parties feel for each other. Some permanence of key negotiators is essential for a continuous and trustworthy deal-making process. Common backgrounds and similar cultural definitions of career growth and aspirations are also helpful as negotiations progress. Jonathan Rose's observations relative to these issues are instructive:

> My capital and reputation are tied up in this project. I deal with public officials whose futures are not so closely dependent on the outcome of this project. They have different timetables to work with and different constituencies and individuals to satisfy. Since we started this project, Rose Associates has added one person to our staff. Everyone else remains the same. At the public level almost everyone is new: the Deputy Mayor, the key assistant to the Borough President, the head of the Public Development Corporation. Who did we make the deal with? These are fine people but not real partners in the sense that you really know them, that you went through the trenches with them. Still and all, the deal is still a deal.[8]

Some of the factors that differentiate sole private transactions from multisector deals—like special added resources, a strong sense of timetables, and deadlines—actually promote commercial public-private projects. Others present major obstacles. These obstacles can be overcome in several ways.

First, the vision of decision makers on both sides is essential. It takes "urban entrepreneurs" to bridge the cultural and economic gap between the sides and find the common ground of economic-development potential inherent in a site. This common ground ensures profits and jobs, the crucial ingredients of a successful project. While there is no plethora of visionary leaders, they are increasing in number and fortunately are found in both the public and private sectors.

Second, public officials must unequivocally express their intention to optimize their support for any area targeted for commercial revitalization. Words must be followed by deeds. Competitive early deals along with pump-priming abatements and subsidies must be promised, but improved service delivery and infrastructure investment must begin immediately—not after the private sector announces its investment intentions. If a mayor wants to create a new or enlarged central business district, the city must act as though the area already exists and target police, sanitation, and infrastructural improvements accordingly. Neighborhood chambers of commerce and business groups must be involved in boosting the area at the earliest stage.

Third, if there is a potential value in the site under consideration, the city's business leaders will have to validate the prognostication of the mayor and other public officials. Public support alone, even the relocation of key government offices, will rarely lure private investment to an area. In the ATURA case, both the private Regional Plan Association and the New York City Partnership provided key validation for downtown Brooklyn. In other cities, downtown revitalization has occurred without formal partnership organizations, but the "blessing" and support of one or more of the city's leading chief executive officers was provided.

As a prelude to site identification and support, however, the business community should agree that downtown commercial revitalization is high on its list of priorities. Professional staff and chief executive officer commitments should be directed to this priority. Commitments are best aimed at action by a set deadline. Though riskier, the business community's intentions should be communicated publicly. The ATURA case is illustrative.

In the ATURA case the major challenge was one of overcoming negative images. Despite proximity to Manhattan, excellent transporation, cultural institutions, a large retail area, a good labor pool, cheap land, and potentially cheap power, downtown Brooklyn suffered from an image of decline and tawdriness. The New York City Partnership's approach affected both the perception and the reality. It helped market the potential of the area and thus helped to realize that potential. It added its voice to the area's public and private leaders in further convincing the city to treat the area as a vital central business district and thus helped it to become one.

Essentially, the New York City Partnership served as a promoter and a broker—roles for which it is well suited. It pooled the prestige and acumen of its corporate members to validate project feasibility, elicit public-sector concessions, entice private developers, and help package a deal that no governmental entity or private entrepreneur could have easily consummated alone. It shared risks with the city and the developer by enabling its members to put their reputations collectively on the line without jeopardizing returns to the separate enterprises they lead. Of course, one Partnership board member did put his company in jeopardy—Fred

Rose. Rose Associates may gain significant profits from its ATURA project, but a successful outcome is far from assured. The private equity and reputation of Rose Associates remain at risk. The continued support and active involvement of the Partnership and the public sector are essential for the Roses and for downtown Brooklyn. Clearly, however, the future of public-private partnerships for downtown commercial revitalization depends on city governments attuned to the needs of economic development and visionary risk takers like Fred and Jonathan Rose.

## Notes

1. *New York Times*, 22 April 1984.
2. *Town and Country*, September 1985.
3. Minutes, Meeting of the Board of the New York City Partnership, 12 March 1985.
4. *New York Daily News*, 21 Jan. 1985.
5. Minutes, New York City Partnership.
6. Comments at "Public-Private Partnerships," a conference sponsored by the New York City Partnership, Inc., and the Academy of Political Science, New York, N.Y., 13 June 1986.
7. Ibid.
8. Ibid.

# Partnership New South Style: Central Atlanta Progress

CLARENCE N. STONE

Race-consciousness, metropolitan fragmentation, and economic growth provide the context for Atlanta's public-private partnership. One could even say that the interrelationship among these three factors is the partnership's main concern. As one of the fastest-growing regions in the country, the Atlanta area now ranks thirteenth in population among the country's metropolitan areas; and it is experiencing a high level of office development and expanded employment, indicating continued economic and population growth in the near future. The city of Atlanta fits into the metropolitan area in a noteworthy way. The city is the main force behind area growth, yet the city itself is locked into boundaries largely formed by a major annexation in the early 1950s. That annexation pushed the city's population up to just under a half million. With some fluctuations, the city population has remained in that range since then. In the meantime, the population of the metropolitan area has grown to more than 2 million.

While the city's population has been relatively stable for some time, its racial composition has changed substantially. From a level of 38 percent black in 1960, the city moved to a black majority by the 1970 census and then rose to 67 percent in the 1980 census. Thus, Atlanta—the capital of Georgia, with its Deep South tradition—has become a predominantly black city. In the state and the metropolitan region, each of which is only one-fourth black, the city of Atlanta is conspicuously different from its predominantly white surroundings. This fact has had an enormous impact on both politics and private-development decisions. A major challenge for this predominantly black city is to garner a fair share of the region's economic growth. The harsh fact is that some investors are skittish about investing in a predominantly black community.

For city officials, there is the frustrating possibility that investment money could, as it did for a time in the 1970s, concentrate in the "golden crescent" outside the city along the northern portion of its perimeter highway. For private establishments with fixed investments in the central business district, that possibility is as unappealing as it is for city hall. In this regional and racial context the downtown business community and city government have joined efforts to try to shape Atlanta's place in the economic future of the metropolitan area. In formulating a collective stance on development policy, the business community acts through its partnership organization, Central Atlanta Progress, a member of the International Downtown Association.

## Central Atlanta Progress

Central Atlanta Progress is an action-oriented organization. Its constituent members are around 200 major property owners in downtown Atlanta. Its executive committee and board of directors are composed of chief executive officers of major firms and institutions in the city — people not inclined to tolerate endless discussions of plans that will not be implemented. As an organization, Central Atlanta Progress aims to have a major impact on the community. Its conference room is known as "The War Room"; the organization's standard response to problems is the task force, established to accomplish a specific objective and then to be disbanded, clearing the way for other task forces to pursue their specific projects. Within the board of directors and the membership, there are no standing committees, and the seven-person permanent staff of the organization is too small to be caught up in bureaucratization.

The current organization evolved from the Central Atlanta Improvement Association, formed in 1941 to represent the collective interests of the major property holders in the downtown area. From the beginning it was involved in development planning, and it encouraged particular property holders to think of the interests they shared with other property holders in Atlanta's main business district. To act on shared interests meant taking a long-term view; thinking about the relationship between the central business district and the burgeoning regional economy; and planning, especially in transportation and its effect on the central business district's place in the area economy. It also meant supporting infrastructure improvements and promoting a central role for business in the city's redevelopment program.

As the updated version of the Central Atlanta Improvement Association, Central Atlanta Progress is organized as a private, nonprofit organization. In addition to development planning, it is involved in the execution of specific projects, such as Bedford-Pine urban renewal, a large multiuse project to the east of the business district, and Fairlie-Poplar, a renewal project in the old downtown. Thus, while strictly business-oriented, much of the partnership's effort is directed into the public arena. The upgrading of the area in and around the central business district is a task too large and expensive to be accomplished exclusively by private means. The special role that Central Atlanta Progress plays in Atlanta's civic life is that of putting together projects of cooperation between the downtown business community and local government. It is this particular partnership that it promotes.

Central Atlanta Progress is engaged as a contributing partner with the city of Atlanta and Fulton County in a major planning study of how to improve the quality of life in Atlanta's central business district. This study, Central Area Study II, is the successor to an earlier one in which Central Atlanta Progress was also a partner. Central Area Study I focused on maintaining Atlanta's central business district as the transportation hub of the metropolitan area. In line with the partnership's standard mode of operation, Central Area Study II is proceeding with a set of task forces concerned with such topics as downtown housing, arts and recreation, urban design, and public safety. By involving business people and others from the community on these planning task forces, Central Area Study II aims to obtain support for a body of specific actions to protect Atlanta's position as a major convention city (it ranks third in the country) and make the downtown into something more than a concentration of offices. The goal is to change downtown Atlanta from a ten-hour city that virtually closes down at 6 P.M. to a twenty-four-hour city, with a night life of culture and entertainment.

Paralleling Central Area Study II is the project to redevelop Atlanta's Underground District, the old railroad district that enjoyed a revival as a thriving area of night life in the late 1960s and early 1970s, into a major food and entertainment area. Underground redevelopment illustrates the role that Central Atlanta Progress plays as a catalyst for projects involving public and private cooperation. The development of the project will be coordinated by a nonprofit corporation, Underground Festival Development Company, created at the request of city hall. The board of directors for this nonprofit corporation is composed of prominent downtown business figures. The management of the enterprise will be through a joint venture involving the Rouse Company of Maryland (developers of several similar projects in other cities, including South Street Seaport in New York City, Harborplace in Baltimore, and Faneuil Hall in Boston), and two black-owned firms in Atlanta, Herman J. Russell and Company and Kinley Enterprises. The project involves complementary land-use actions by the state of Georgia and Fulton County, since both the state capitol and the county courthouse are nearby. The city itself, however, bears the responsibility for acquiring land for the festival marketplace, using the power of eminent domain. The city is also to prepare the site for redevelopment.

Central Atlanta Progress has been involved at every stage of this project, from the initial feasibility study through the creation of the nonprofit corporation to the raising of $15 million of private investment money as part of an overall budget now estimated at $140 million. Joe Martin, the director of the Underground Festival Development Corporation, is a former staff member of Central Atlanta Progress and has headed other projects initiated by the partnership. (One of the factors that makes Central Atlanta Progress an influential participant in the civic and economic life of Atlanta and an effective catalyst for numerous projects is the administrative talent of present and past staff members.)

Central Atlanta Progress's main concern is land use and investment activity in the inner core of Atlanta, yet it does not take a narrow view of its role. Public safety is a continuing concern. At one point, to counteract Atlanta's image of being crime-ridden, Central Atlanta Progress initiated the idea of a horseback patrol to police the downtown area. Facing a skeptical police department, the partnership underwrote the training program for Atlanta police officers with the United States Park Service. Today the horse patrol is a permanent part of the police department. In another instance, Central Atlanta Progress, working with an aggressive county prosecutor, led the drive to remove prostitution, pornography, and illegal drugs from the streets of the area now known as Midtown, an area straddling Atlanta's famed Peachtree Street just north of the central business district. A special fund-raising drive for a day-care center and an "urban walls" program of outdoor art are also among the projects that Central Atlanta Progress has promoted. It also joined the city during Maynard Jackson's mayoralty in promoting the creation of the Atlanta Economic Development Corporation, a multifaceted partnership between the public sector and the business community.

The special accomplishment of Central Atlanta Progress, however, is not the particular projects that it has initiated and supported, though it has played the key role in many. The partnership's most impressive achievement is its close and ongoing working relationship with city hall. Central Atlanta Progress has been successful, first of all, in setting an agenda for planning and promoting the revitalization of the city's central business district. This agenda was one around which Atlanta's business community could be mobilized, and that sets Atlanta apart from many other cities. Second, Central Atlanta Progress has had remarkable success in interesting elected officials in its agenda for the revitalization of downtown. To be sure, city hall and Central Atlanta Progress have a shared interest in a thriving business district, but opinions differ on how that can best be achieved. The redevelopment of Underground, for example, has been widely criticized as too risky and too costly. In the judgment of some observers, the city and Central Atlanta Progress should simply write off the southern section of downtown and concentrate their efforts on other areas more strongly supported by the private market. Yet the partnership has been able to work with the Chamber of Commerce and other groups to maintain a public show of business unity behind the project and keep it high on the community's agenda of decision making. Thus, nothing has been automatic about the commitment of public resources to the redevelopment of Underground Atlanta; that commitment owes much to the unyielding support given by Central Atlanta Progress.

It is worth noting that the relations between city hall and Central Atlanta Progress have had stormy periods as well as smooth ones. It is useful, then, to consider how this biracial public-private partnership came into being and was put on a basis of strong cooperation.

### The Evolution of the Partnership

More than thirty years ago, Floyd Hunter wrote *Community Power Structure*, an analysis of the informal public-private alliance that in many ways was the real government of Atlanta. Writing in the period shortly after World War II, Hunter described a situation in which a small number of white business leaders set policy while local government and various civic organizations carried it out.

This was the era before *Brown* v. *Board of Education*, when the Jim Crow system prevailed throughout the South. Hunter found that Atlanta blacks constituted a separate subcommunity, connected to the overall power structure only through informal links to the mayor's office and secondary civic leaders. In that era of racial segregation, blacks were a subordinate group in Atlanta's civic life, making their presence felt mainly as one of the key voting blocs in the city. Their electoral influence, however, was quite limited; for they were not only socially segregated but also a distinct numerical minority. Today, the racial climate has changed, and Atlanta's black community makes use of its majority position to control the city's political apparatus as well as to exercise a wider influence. Andrew Young is Atlanta's second black mayor, and blacks are a two-thirds majority on the city council. A black city council member, Ira Jackson, chairs the Atlanta Regional Commission, the planning agency for the metropolitan area. Another black political leader, Michael Lomax, chairs the Fulton County Commission, the governing body for the county in which most of the city of Atlanta is located. Blacks have served as president of the Atlanta Chamber of Commerce, and no major civic effort is undertaken without significant black participation.

The Atlanta that Hunter studied has changed, yet there are continuities. Mayor Young works in close alliance with the white business community, and, despite the shift in racial control of city hall, white business executives remain among the top leaders of the community. Community decision making is much more complicated than in the past, but public-private cooperation is no less characteristic of the Atlanta of today than it was of the Atlanta described by Hunter in an earlier era. Mayor Young has stated that he cannot govern the city without the cooperation of the business community and that no project can be successful without business support. However, the change from white to black control of city hall was not an entirely smooth transition, and during the administration of Maynard Jackson — Atlanta's first black mayor — there was a great deal of friction between the city government and Atlanta's white business leadership.

Maynard Jackson's election in 1973 was part of a dual "revolution" in the politics of the city. Not only did Jackson's election represent a new level of empowerment for the black community, but it also coincided with the implementation of a new city charter under which Atlanta's recently mobilized neighborhood movement gained substantial representation and citizen participation procedures were mandated. Clearly, the past pattern of cooperation between business and city hall was in for some change, and the change proved to be abrupt. Jackson was young, assertive, and thoroughly committed to the idea of making Atlanta's political *and* economic life more inclusive. Whereas past mayors had been responsive and accommodating to business interests, Jackson pressed business to be responsive and accommodating to his demands. Although Atlanta's public schools and public accommodations had been integrated barely a decade and the women's movement was even newer to the city, Mayor Jackson asked Atlanta bankers to put women and minorities on their boards. And Jackson did not move quietly and cautiously; he insisted that Atlanta's major public-works project, the building of a new airport, provide opportunities for minority contractors and that the operation of the airport include minority business enterprises.

Mayor Jackson regarded his election as a mandate for social reform to which the business leaders as well as other sectors of the community should respond. The clash of personalities was sharp and, given the mix of actors and circumstances, predictable. Friction was inevitable. Although polarization was possible, it was avoided. After tensions began to surface, Mayor Jackson invited representatives of the business community to an ongoing series of "Pound Cake Summit" meetings at which they could exchange views with him and his staff.

The mayor's office and the business community have survived the conflict because of a long history of biracial cooperation and because some strategically important moves were made in the late 1960s and early 1970s. The events of these years demonstrate that biracial cooperation comes about only through an accumulation of efforts and experiences in which a large number of individuals learn how to work together and to trust one another.

Biracial cooperation in Atlanta has evolved through several stages. When the Federal courts invalidated the white primary in the mid-1940s, Atlanta's black community registered to vote in large numbers and became a part of the city's governing coalition. Atlanta's mayor at that time, William Hartsfield, saw that a workable alliance could be created around the themes of economic growth and racial moderation. As this alliance took hold, Atlanta's leadership began to characterize the community as "the city too busy to hate." But more was involved than a slogan and a voting coalition that supported white moderates running for public office. Atlanta's white business leaders put money into and maintained contacts with black businesses, educational institutions, and civic organizations.

In the 1960s, a new age of protest and direct action as well as a process of generational change strained biracial cooperation as Atlanta entered a period of rapid change. In 1961, Ivan Allen, Jr.—white, old-family Atlanta, and immediate past president of the Chamber of Commerce—was elected mayor over segregationist Lester Maddox. The old coalition held together. Allen proceeded with an ambitious and controversial redevelopment agenda, some of which was opposed by substantial segments of the black community, but the mayor avoided polarization. He became a national spokesman for civil-rights legislation and for various urban and antipoverty programs. Moreover, he organized a symbolically important biracial dinner honoring Martin Luther King, Jr., when he won the Nobel Peace Prize. Later, when King was assassinated in Memphis, Mayor Allen went immediately to Mrs. King to express the sorrow of the city. Thus polarization was again avoided.

Although the 1960s were turbulent, communication between the races was never broken. However, in 1968 and 1969—Ivan Allen's last two years in office—two events signaled that contacts between a small number of black and white leaders were no longer enough to maintain an ongoing political coalition. In 1968, the first referendum to launch the newly initiated Metropolitan Atlanta Rapid Transit Authority (MARTA) was defeated in the city as well as in the suburbs. In 1969, the candidate for mayor backed by Ivan Allen and other white business leaders was defeated by a candidate who received overwhelming support among black voters. The 1970 census confirmed what these two electoral contests had suggested—that Atlanta had become a black majority city. The elections thus presaged the black political empowerment that would reach fruition in the 1973 election.

From the perspective of the business community, black political empowerment represented a potential danger. The community could be polarized along racial lines into a white business elite with economic power and a black electoral majority—a majority mobilized around resentment against the white elite. Portents of such polarization were present in both the MARTA referendum of 1968 and the mayoral election of 1969. Working against such a polarization was Atlanta's long tradition of biracial cooperation. Several steps were taken to build on that tradition and make accommodations for black electoral power in Atlanta. The black middle class was one key. Quiet moves were made to provide opportunities for black and white business and professional people to interact around a set of civic concerns. In 1969, the Chamber of Commerce played a role in creating Leadership Atlanta, an organization designed to give younger business and professional people an opportunity to build personal networks around the consideration of civic issues and the examination of community problems. At about the same time, Mills B. Lane, a white banker, launched an organization called Action Forum to provide an opportunity for black and white business leaders to meet on a monthly basis to discuss major community issues. Much of the initial discussion centered on Atlanta's proposed MARTA system, scheduled for a second referendum. Even though MARTA is now an accomplished fact, Action Forum continues; it provides valuable networking for black participants eager to gain full access to business opportunities in the city.

On another front, to help turn around blacks' opposition to MARTA, the mayor appointed Jesse Hill, a black business executive and civil-rights leader, to the next vacancy on the MARTA board of directors. Hill was its first black member. MARTA also began a program of minority hiring. Concurrent with these steps, the boards of the Atlanta Chamber of Commerce and Central Atlanta Progress were also racially integrated. The Atlanta Chamber of Commerce has now had two black presidents, and blacks have served on the executive committee of Central Atlanta Progress in recent years. Thus a number of steps have been taken to draw the black middle class into the business and civic life of downtown Atlanta, making the prospect of racial polarization less likely.

In 1973, with a new city charter providing greater neighborhood access to city government and mandating citizen-participation procedures as well, the political scene promised to become more complicated, and business influence even more tenuous. A strategically important move was made at that time. The board of directors of Central Atlanta Progress decided that a new and more politically sophisticated executive director was needed. If the business community, particularly the major downtown business interests, was to continue working in close partnership with city hall, someone with exceptional skill and experience would be needed for the city's new and still-changing political circumstances. The Central Atlanta Progress membership turned to Dan Sweat, at that time the director of the Atlanta Regional Commission, the planning agency for the metropolitan area.

Sweat's background was in politics, not business. He had attended college in downtown Atlanta at Georgia State University and first worked as a reporter, including a stint covering city hall. Sweat was known for having a good sense of diplomacy in presenting an issue, a skill some link to his early training in journalism. He made the transition from journalism to politics through a position as public information officer for Charles O. Emmerich, commission chairman for DeKalb County—a largely suburban county that includes a portion of the city of Atlanta. Sweat advanced within the organization to become Emmerich's assistant. Subsequently, Emmerich headed the area's antipoverty program, Economic Opportunity Atlanta, and again Sweat became his assistant, carrying out various responsibilities from overseeing community organization to pursuing Federal grants. From the antipoverty post, Sweat shifted over to city hall as Federal grants coordinator for Mayor Ivan Allen. Then Sweat became Ivan Allen's chief administrative officer. He also served in that position under Allen's successor, Sam Massell, before taking the position of executive director of the Atlanta Regional Commission. Journalism, public administration (in several capacities), race relations, and community organization in the 1960s provided an extraordinary background, especially for a man only thirty-eight years old, to assume the directorship of a major downtown business association. But the times were also extraordinary. Sweat's background proved highly appropriate. Central Atlanta Progress is involved as an administrative and financial partner in public projects. Federal grants are an integral part of the process. Race is overridingly important in contemporary Atlanta, and Central Atlanta Progress must deal with a variety of community organizations—some on an adversary basis.

Sweat is personable, but he does not hesitate to disagree with the mayor or other political figures. He is energetic, not only running his high-powered organization but also serving on the boards of ten other organizations, ranging from the Junior League of Atlanta to the International Downtown Association (of which he is a past president). He also serves as president of the Metropolitan Atlanta Community Foundation, which gives funds to various kinds of community work.

Sweat pursues an ambitious agenda and monitors an even broader area of activity, mindful of what can promote the improvement of downtown Atlanta. He is skillful at forming alliances, and he does not hesitate to create allies if they do not already exist. The Midtown Business Association, for example, represents and promotes the interests of businesses, residents, and the arts community in the recently revived area immediately north of Atlanta's central business district. Sweat helped organize the association, and Central Atlanta Progress underwrote its expenses in its first few years of operation.

Sweat's appointment to head Central Atlanta Progress coincided with the election of Maynard Jackson as Atlanta's first black mayor. As indicated earlier, Jackson's ambitious program of social reform and his statements were controversial, including his promotion of the idea that blacks and women should be assured entry into the economic life of Atlanta through a minority-participation requirement for city contracts and grants. Although there was initial resistance in the white business community to such guarantees for minority business enterprises, the requirement is now written into a city ordinance and is widely accepted city policy. While the relationship between Mayor Jackson and Dan Sweat was fraught with considerable friction, they did work together on a number of projects. Moreover, the joint venture arrangements and other minority business opportunities that Jackson pioneered proved to be an important ingredient in smoothing cooperation across racial lines. When Andrew Young became Atlanta's second black mayor, the way was already prepared for a close partnership between city hall and Central Atlanta Progress. Young has courted business cooperation, and business has reciprocated.

## An Uncertain Future

The close partnership between city hall and Central Atlanta Progress rests on multiple supports. Each support is important, and a change in any of them could alter the prevailing climate of cooperation. Cooperation is never certain, and it is all the more tenuous when racial polarization is an ever-present possibility. These supports for the Atlanta partnership are thus worth examining.

One support is the long tradition of black and white cooperation that the Atlanta business community has worked actively to maintain. But this tradition is not self-perpetuating; it has broken down on occasion in the past and could do so again.

Another support underlying the partnership is the economic competition between Atlanta and its suburbs, which gives the partners a strong set of common concerns. These concerns draw the two parties together, as a common threat always does. And through joint efforts, relationships of trust develop and are nurtured. Still another support is the political skill and knowledge that Dan Sweat brings to his position in the partnership. When Central Atlanta Progress has to search for a successor, it will be difficult to find someone with a background and skills comparable to those of Dan Sweat.

Finally, the present pattern of close partnership rests partly on Mayor Young and his cooperation with Central Atlanta Progress. Young is doubly important. First, his background in the civil-rights movement taught him that business leaders are important in setting community policy. No matter how much they avoid political exposure, they are part of the community power structure. Mayor Young understands that and makes his alliances accordingly. After all, the civil-rights experience in Alabama — the shaping experience of Young's early career — taught him that business leaders could be convinced to accept racial change more readily than could the "Bull" Connors, George Wallaces, and Sheriff Jim Clarks of the world. Young's civil-rights background has also helped him unify the black community. His appeal and his symbolism cut across class lines. But again there is the question of his successor.

The poverty rate in Atlanta is nearly 30 percent, and 40 percent of Atlanta's children are in poverty-level households. Economic growth is necessary to alleviate poverty, but the Atlanta figures indicate that growth alone is not sufficient. There is a potential for class resentment, and it may develop in some future city election. That it has been largely dormant during Young's administration is no guarantee that it will not flare up in the future. While Andrew Young can promote his version of "supply side" development without significant opposition from within the black community, future mayors may be unable to do so. Already there are scattered signs of discontent and some questioning of the city's priorities. A more serious signal came from a recent summer festival, the 1986 version of Light Up Atlanta. By police estimate, more than 200,000 people came to the event, but it was marred by roving gangs of youths operating on the fringes of the celebration, particularly as it was breaking up. These incidents were a major embarrassment to the city and a sharp disappointment to everyone who had been working to promote downtown Atlanta as an entertainment center for the area.

The city's initial reaction was the creation of a special police unit on youth gangs to serve notice that officials were not complacent about the problem. But the incident itself invites some thought about the root causes of youth criminal activity. That issue has not been debated publicly and perhaps will not be. Yet the persistence of poverty and the problems that go with it are significant. Whether Central Atlanta Progress will become involved in such matters that are not directly connected to development is uncertain. The organization maintains a high level of concern about public safety, but in the view of some black leaders it has been more concerned with police visibility than with the underlying causes of crime and more interested in the immediate problems of making the downtown attractive for conventioneers than in long-range social and human-development programs. For its part, Central Atlanta Progress thinks that the city's economic future must be secured before other problems are addressed.

The partnership between city hall and Central Atlanta Progress must set some priorities. The easiest to set are those immediately related to development and the protection of downtown property values, but, if a high level of poverty continues and social problems worsen, those priorities may be politically vulnerable.

Cooperative action is most easily pursued if the partnership participants are small in number and rich in resources. But restricted partnership — even when city hall is part of it — is vulnerable to the charge that it is unrepresentative and insensitive to important community needs. That was the message of the defeated MARTA referendum in 1968 as well as Maynard Jackson's concerns about the exclusiveness of Atlanta's power structure in 1974. The issue was divisive in relations between city hall and Central Atlanta Progress, but the experience may have been constructive over the long run. Responses to the divisiveness brought about renewed cooperation between blacks and whites.

There is a natural tendency to rely on relationships in which trust is well established, since those make cooperation easiest. The danger is that other groups may feel left out, and they may express their grievances through the ballot box or, like youth gangs, engage in anomic behavior. The challenge for any "power structure" is to maintain enough unity for effective action while being open to the concerns of the wider community. That unending challenge makes the future uncertain even for partnerships like the one in Atlanta.

The Atlanta partnership concerns itself mainly with the external challenge of economic competition in a setting in which urban growth continues outward. But there is also the internal challenge of combating poverty, mental illness, youth crime, and a potential breakdown of civil order. While these problems are certainly not unique to Atlanta, no well-defined strategies exist for attacking them, and no partnership effort to confront such problems is visible. Inattentiveness to these problems could jeopardize the long-range character of the partnership, because the future of the city's politics is uncertain. The partnership rests on a close alliance between the black middle class and white business interests, but it remains to be seen how well the supports for that alliance hold up when Mayor Young leaves office at the end of 1989. The city charter limits mayors to two consecutive terms, thus ensuring that new leaders will be in city hall. Continuing biracial cooperation is likely, but it is not certain. As conditions and personalities change, new efforts will be required to sustain Atlanta's pattern of public-private partnership.

# Partnerships for Housing

KATHRYN WYLDE

"Housing" appears on a local partnership agenda when the independent efforts of private enterprise and government fail to satisfy community needs for decent and affordable housing. In urban centers, evidence of this failure may include the highly visible presence of the homeless, dilapidated apartment buildings, and the more insidious phenomenon of middle-class families relocating from areas with a chronic shortage of housing and a lack of stable neighborhoods. The failure may also emerge in rural areas where the elderly are unable to keep up their homes, as well as in affluent suburban communities where the younger generation has been priced out of the local housing market. And, virtually everywhere, a disproportionately inadequate supply of affordable housing is apparent among racial and ethnic minorities.

Although the manifestations of housing problems vary among localities, solutions universally depend on the cooperative application of both public and private resources in some form of housing partnership. The concept of a public-private partnership in housing is a commitment to sharing development risk, financial obligations, and program responsibilities among government, private financial institutions, builders, developers, and — to the maximum extent possible — nonprofit organizations and the larger business community. This shared commitment and exposure to financial risk allows the community to form a consensus on a response to its housing needs. Successful program implementation generally requires a formal and institutionalized public-private vehicle, with a mandate to serve as the intermediary agent for all participants in the partnership program.

When interest rates and the national economy are relatively stable, a serious imbalance between housing needs and supply can be attributed to three conditions. First, the cost of building and maintaining housing exceeds what people can afford to pay for it (known as the "affordability gap"). Second, the cost of building and maintaining housing is greater than its market value, as determined by what people are willing to pay for housing in a given location. Third, the profitability of private development, ownership, or investment in housing is insufficient, often because of government-imposed regulation or taxation that is not offset by public subsidy incentives.

To correct these conditions, housing partnerships can reduce the cost of housing construction and finance and help expand the capacity of the private-development community to respond to local housing needs. The partnerships also stimulate appreciation in property values in blighted areas with readily available land and buildings. Further, they generate both private contributions and new public resources to bridge the "affordability gap" for the households that remain unserved by private enterprise alone.

Extra impetus for local mobilization of housing partnerships has come in response to changing Federal housing policy. During the 1970s, the Federal government assumed virtually exclusive responsibility for the production and financing of low- and moderate-income housing, relieving pressure on state and local governments to address housing issues. New and rehabilitated housing was financed with Federal Housing Administration (FHA) mortgage insurance guaranteeing repayment of construction and permanent loans. Section 8 rental contracts provided monthly subsidies sufficient to pay all costs of maintaining and operating low-income housing for up to forty years, and income-tax benefits were structured to ensure advantageous tax shelters for investors in low-income housing. By the end of the decade, the potential cost to the Federal government of constructing and maintaining a single unit of low-income housing in New York City approached $500,000. For those in the private subsidized housing industry, building and financing housing for the poor was a highly profitable business.

This environment of Federal largesse did not encourage housing partnerships. There was little incentive for state or local governments to monitor or help reduce housing costs. Private lenders, with every dollar guaranteed by the FHA and often with a commitment from the Government National Mortgage Corporation to refinance construction loans at a subsidized rate, had little reason to scrutinize the cost, quality, or creditworthiness of projects. By 1979, even Congress was alarmed at the trillion-dollar price tag associated with housing production programs that placed all of the risk and financial obligation on the Federal Treasury. With White House leadership, between 1979 and 1982, Congress eliminated most housing production subsidies and returned the responsibility for subsidized housing to state and local governments.

This action spurred renewed interest in public-private partnerships, primarily as a replacement for Federal financing of affordable housing and community renewal. Over time, however, the fact that chronic housing problems do not disappear has encouraged the evolution of more realistic expectations and greater responsiveness on the part of both private leadership and government at all levels. Housing partnerships have emerged as the only practical approach to financing essential housing construction.

Partnership programs in areas where housing problems exceed local resources must depend on continued support from the Federal government. This support will clearly not take the form of past subsidy programs. But it can include catalytic Federal commitments of direct financing, technical assistance, third-party mediation, or simply enhancing the prestige of a local program. Aside from funding,

Federal participation demonstrates to private partners the possibility of securing the long-term public commitments required to sustain development activities that local government—far more vulnerable to political pressure that can effect abrupt changes in development policy—cannot provide.

Successful examples of public-private housing initiatives all seem to follow a formula that maintains a role for Federal as well as state and local government. One national housing partnership is the Neighborhood Reinvestment Corporation, which has been funded by Congress since the early 1970s to organize and support neighborhood housing-rehabilitation programs. The Reinvestment Corporation illustrates the effectiveness of a nonideological, results-oriented approach that is endorsed by all levels of government, as well as community leadership, and, importantly, the home loan industry's prime regulator, the Federal Home Loan Bank. Community-based efforts outside New York are exemplified by the Boston Housing Partnership, which has built a production program around the highly leveraged use of Federal Community Development Block Grant funds and tax-exempt mortgage revenue bonds. In Minneapolis and St. Paul, a Family Housing Assistance Fund pioneered the use of Federal Urban Development Action Grants together with private grants and loans in a local trust fund to build and rehabilitate low- and moderate-income housing.

Another reason for continued Federal support is that housing is less attractive to philanthropic contributors than other charitable activities. Unless supplemented with public dollars, private contributions do not help much in building or maintaining housing for low income households, which generally require a 100 percent write-down in capital costs (i.e., no debt service) plus perpetual rent supplements. In 1985 former president Jimmy Carter visited New York City to lead a fund-raising drive as a volunteer carpenter in a vacant apartment building on the Lower East Side. He was promoting a national program to produce low-income housing entirely with private donations and volunteer "sweat equity." The fact that it required a former president to raise enough funds to renovate two dozen apartments in a neighborhood with hundreds of abandoned buildings and thousands of homeless people illustrates the futility of housing programs for the poor that do not enjoy direct support from all levels of government.

The private sector generally perceives a substantial downside risk associated with housing development in such areas as cost overruns, faulty construction, political controversy, accidents, delays, foreclosures, and conflicts inherent in the public-private relationship. Problems arise, first, from competition among members of the private sector over sharing information and responding to demands for cooperation that may be contradictory to narrow business interests. Beyond that, there is a lack of trust between the people who work for government as policymakers or regulators and the bankers, builders, and landlords who are essential to any housing program.

Even if ideological differences are put aside and all partners can agree on a single definition of what constitutes the "public interest" for purposes of the partnership initiatives, on-going tension over "political" versus "economic" priorities is likely at every stage of program implementation. Members of the real estate and finance industry point out that they are prepared to evaluate and assume economic risks, but they cannot deal with political risks. Publicly sponsored housing development is a politically charged activity, and public partners are vulnerable to pressures from constituents that can derail commitments. The danger of political disruption is a constant source of tension in the development process, whether it arises from trade-union objections to the introduction of building technology that reduces labor costs, neighborhood protests that new development on a given site will lead to secondary displacement and gentrification, tenants rebelling against rent increases that are necessary to finance rehabilitation, or simply an election that brings a "fresh approach" midway in a project.

New York City offers an extreme but instructive example of a "partnership response" to local housing needs. Its experience may well anticipate what other areas of the country will face as their housing inventory, infrastructure, and economies mature. The severity of the older cities' problem is illustrated by the fact that New York City measures progress in housing production not by its ability to build housing but by the reduction in the numbers of housing units lost annually to abandonment—from 40,000 units a year in the 1970s to only 23,000 in 1985. It has been estimated that New York City requires a capital infusion of more than $20 billion to assure each of its current 2.7 million households a decent, safe, and sanitary home or apartment. Another $30 billion will be needed by the year 2000 to finance the new housing required to support the projected expansion in local employment opportunities.

As New York City has been forced to rely on its local tax base to generate subsidies for housing the poor, evidence of the accelerated exodus of middle-class taxpayers and a qualified labor pool—often in search of affordable home ownership not available in the city—is particularly alarming. In 1985, the Regional Plan Association identified the inadequate supply of housing as the "Achilles' heel" in an otherwise positive economic projection for the metropolitan area over the next decade. This forecast is confirmed by analyses indicating that corporate decisions to relocate or expand outside the city are significantly influenced by the unavailability of reasonably priced housing for employees.

The direct relationship between the health of the New York City economy, an adequate supply of housing, and the preservation of the city's residential neighborhoods was first articulated by David Rockefeller when he was chairman of Chase Manhattan Bank in the mid-1970s. His observations led immediately to the first citywide housing-partnership initiative, the New York City Community Preservation Corporation (CPC). This nonprofit organization was established in 1975 by twenty-four commercial and savings banks. Recognizing the impossibility of financing the replacement of housing units being lost to abandonment, CPC's purpose was to reinvest in the repair of existing buildings to preserve that inventory. Participating banks committed a pool of funds to CPC, which its staff used to underwrite and originate loans for private rehabilitation and refinancing older apartment houses in target neighborhoods.

Since its inception, CPC has financed the renovation of more than 15,000 apartments, concentrating on upgrading tenanted buildings that would otherwise have fallen out of the housing inventory. The average cost of preserving an apartment for an additional half century is less than a third of the cost of rebuilding that unit once it has been abandoned. The pooled investments in CPC by banks and, more recently, pension funds total more than $300 million. Recently, with the New York City Partnership, the CPC has enlisted the participation of the city's insurance industry in the formation of the Housing Partnership Mortgage Corporation, a nonprofit originator and packager of permanent financing for new and rehabilitated housing. Five insurance companies have pledged an initial $50 million to the Mortgage Corporation. Importantly, they will commit to an interest rate on permanent loans at the beginning of construction, permitting developers and lenders accurately to predict expenses and rents after construction.

The Community Preservation Corporation was established as a lender of last resort for buildings that could not support conventional investment because of low rent rolls, low valuations, inexperienced ownership, or the condition of the property. The CPC had to depend on a partnership with government to carry out this work. The city and state provided from fifteen- to thirty-year abatements of real estate taxes proportionate to the extent of rehabilitation carried out on a property. The state also established a Mortgage Insurance Program, capitalized with a surcharge on the State Mortgage Recording Tax. The State assumes up to 75 percent of the default risk (100 percent for pension funds) for rehabilitated apartment buildings. The state and city collectively addressed the need for raising tenant rents to cover the cost of rehabilitation and refinancing by legislating the authority for rent restructuring in apartment buildings renovated with government assistance.

Federal participation with the CPC initiative took two forms: (1) rent subsidies for tenants-in-occupancy who could not afford the restructured rents after rehabilitation and (2) Community Development Block Grant funds that the city channeled into a Participation Loan Program. In participation loans, the city committed long-term mortgages at rates as low as 1 percent for up to 60 percent of project financing needs. This program allows CPC to finance the renovation of the more deteriorated buildings with larger numbers of low-income tenants, since the blended interest rate results in lower debt service and the risk of the private lender is significantly reduced by the public participation in project financing.

The renovation and preservation of occupied apartment buildings is a highly specialized area of construction management and finance in which the CPC has become expert. For banks, it makes sense to invest in a joint initiative that pools the expertise and resources required to carry out this type of difficult rehabilitation lending. Government has an advantage in using the underwriting and construction lending expertise of the private sector, with the assurance that public funds advanced in a participation loan will be administered with the same prudence as the private investment. The CPC is self-sustaining through its income from fees and is expanding into other areas of construction lending that are not being adequately addressed in the private sector. The primary limitation on CPC's activities is that it will not compete with private financial institutions, since its success as an intermediary vehicle for public-private partnerships depends on the goodwill and confidence of the for-profit lending industry.

New York City suffers from housing capital and subsidy needs on a scale unmatched elsewhere in the United States. Wherever a significant level of poverty exists, the local treasury and charitable resources are inadequate to mount a low-income housing development or rehabilitation program without Federal assistance. It was no mere coincidence that when David Rockefeller announced the formation of the New York City Housing Partnership in 1982 he did so at a luncheon with President Reagan. The president's participation in the birth of this ambitious venture has served as a point of reference in garnering the extraordinary level of private and government resources necessary to make some progress in solving the city's housing needs.

The impact of Federal cutbacks on New York City housing programs precipitated a decision by the New York City Partnership to expand on the successful model of the CPC and establish a citywide Housing Partnership New Homes Program. The prime objectives of the program were to increase home-ownership opportunities for working families priced out of the conventional market and to produce new homes on vacant, city-owned land in neighborhoods that could not attract private residential development. The Partnership was asked to secure participation by banks and builders willing to construct, finance, and sell homes at the lowest reasonable cost in locations and for income groups designated by the city.

In New York City, the median resale price of a home is more than $130,000, well beyond the means of the $16,500 a year median-income household. The cost of residential construction ranges from $75 a square foot for small homes to $175 a square foot for high-rise apartments, resulting in luxury sales prices and rentals for new housing. In fact, 95 percent of the city's households have annual incomes of less than $50,000 and are absolutely priced out of the market for privately developed housing. The consequence is an annual production rate of less than 10,000 units in a city of over 7 million people, and a migration of the home-building industry and middle-income households to areas outside the city where development is less expensive and less difficult.

The nonprofit Housing Partnership Development Corporation (HPDC) was established in 1983 by the city and the New York City Partnership as the intermediary agent to carry out a New Homes Program that would provide access to new home ownership for about one-third of the city households, earning between $25,000 and $48,000 a year. The HPDC board of directors includes key city officials as well as private-sector members, embodying the public-private approach. The role of this corporation is to preprocess sites for development, secure public approvals and financing commitments, and contract with the private builder-developers to carry out construction. The HPDC has a core professional staff, supplemented by "on-loan executives" contributed by private corporations for one-year tours, retired Executive Volunteers, and in-kind assistance from banks, law firms, utility and insurance companies, the real estate industry, and the larger business community.

In addition to its role as intermediary, advocate, and packager, the HPDC must be prepared to fill the vacuums in the marketplace that are encountered in the course of establishing a new program. For example, one of the first issues raised by bankers and builders was whether homes built in blighted areas could be sold. Before a single house was under construction, a citywide marketing program, put together on a pro bono basis by the Madison Avenue firm of Young and Rubicam, had identified thousands of home buyers prepared to purchase homes in the target neighborhoods. The partnership's marketing approach highlighted the fact that the private sector as well as the government was taking the financial lead in rebuilding long-blighted neighborhoods, assuring home buyers that their own investments would be secure. One community leader in the South Bronx summed it up: "If the Rockefellers are investing in this neighborhood, I sure am gonna get myself one of those houses."

The typical profile of prospective buyers is a two-earner family of three with a total income of about $32,000 a year and accumulated savings of $10,000. The average age of the head of the household is thirty-seven, or about ten years older than first-time home buyers in the rest of the country. Documentation of demand and definition of the market provided the basis for private commitments to the program. It also defined the objectives for the design and cost of the housing to be built under the New Homes Program and the minimum levels of public subsidy necessary to achieve feasibility and affordability for this market.

The huge oversubscription for homes in previously "unmarketable" locations illustrated the pent-up demand for home ownership that New York City, which once focused exclusively on rental-housing development, had largely ignored. This evidence of market potential — particularly among the city's minority and ethnic middle class — encouraged banks and private home builders to expand their moderate-cost, private-development activity beyond the Partnership program. Since 1983, when the Partnership announced the first new private homes to be built on the North Shore of Staten Island and in the Southeast Bronx, Harlem, Northcentral Brooklyn, and Southeastern Queens, each of these areas has begun to attract unprecedented private investment in residential rehabilitation and new construction of housing directed to a previously ignored moderate- and middle-income market.

More than 75 percent of the construction and permanent financing for the New Homes Program has come from private financial institutions. The primary sources of public subsidy are Federal Urban Development Action Grants and city capital budget funds, which help pay for site preparation, infrastructure, and public improvements on city-owned sites. The average Federal subsidy is about $13,500 a home, to reach purchasers in the $25,000 to $40,000 income group. The subsidized portion of a construction loan bears no interest. As homes are completed and sold, purchasers qualify for a rollover of all or part of the construction subsidy as an effective write-down of the cost of the home, depending on their income. The city makes land available at a nominal cost and provides abatement of real property taxes for up to twenty years. In 1985, New York State adopted the New York City Partnership model in creating the State Affordable Homeownership Development Program. The state has committed an annual budget allocation of $25 million to provide capital grants of up to $15,000 a home to help finance new and rehabilitated housing that cannot be provided by the private sector alone.

Unlike the Federal housing programs, in which neither the builder nor the bank was significantly at risk, the Partnership model permits only partial subsidies, which, in turn, create an incentive to keep the cost and attendant risk of development low. Builders guarantee their costs, and their profit is limited, so there is no incentive or opportunity to increase house prices. The program is equally appropriate for vacant lots in developed communities and large tracts of land in devastated areas. The program has demonstrated that by offering home ownership opportunities, the city can reclaim neighborhoods that previously could support only deeply subsidized rental housing.

The private sector, dependent on local market values to justify investment, has brought to production programs a clear understanding that the concept of housing is inseparable from that of the neighborhood. Government housing programs of the past built thousands of units with little regard for the community that existed before or after construction. The Housing Partnership encourages and relies on the participation of community-based organizations in planning and marketing homes to ensure that each project reinforces and enhances overall neighborhood-improvement efforts.

The Housing Partnership Development Corporation is in various stages of planning and developing housing in forty neighborhoods. More than 2,000 homes are under construction or have been completed. Through the Partnership, more than fifty private builders have committed and been prequalified to participate in the New Homes Program. Private lenders have committed over $300 million in conventional financing for "high risk" locations. Federal, state, and local grants totaling about $45 million have been invested in onetime capital grants, with no future obligations for public subsidies. The permanent lenders have assumed the full postconstruction risk and the home owners are responsible for housing maintenance, thus freeing public resources for further development activities. In turn, the city has returned property to the tax rolls, retained a resident population that would have been most likely to look for affordable home ownership in other localities, and made a substantial contribution toward the redevelopment and economic strength of many neighborhoods.

A key aspect of New York City's Housing Partnership agenda has been to help revive and refocus the city's residential development and finance industries to carry out the expanded production and rehabilitation of moderate-cost housing in transitional areas. In contrast to either luxury or heavily subsidized housing, the builders and owners of "affordable housing" in the 1980s cannot depend on increased sales prices, rents, or the government to protect them against cost increases and unforeseen problems in construction. The extent of their risk depends not only on their skill in cost estimation and construction management but also on the predictability and efficiency of the government permit and approval processes and the extent to which the full scope of public impositions on a project are both modest and established in advance of construction.

Since 1983, the Housing Partnership has provided a laboratory for the construction industry and government to cooperate in new methods to reduce the cost of housing development, making some breakthroughs that had been resisted in the past. Factory-built modular housing has been introduced in the Bronx and Brooklyn, with the cooperation of the Building Trades' Carpenters Union. Modular components delivered from a Pennsylvania AFL-CIO plant (which retrofitted its product to meet stringent city fire- and building-code standards) reduced development costs of single-family homes by as much as 19 percent over comparable, site-built housing. Despite the cost advantages — primarily due to reduced construction time — it is politically difficult for New York City to expand an initiative that exports construction jobs to an out-of-state plant. Based on the market success and the proven economies of modular housing, the city has recently offered to provide sites and financing for a qualified modular-housing company to establish a local factory. If one or more producers can be attracted to New York, factory technology and prefabrication will likely become a significant component of the affordable-housing industry in the city.

The lengthy predevelopment and construction-permit and approval process in New York City has been another impediment to reducing the costs of housing. More than a dozen different city and state agencies are directly involved in issuing permits and approvals for even routine residential development. Subsidized development that requires special city actions would, if all steps proceeded chronologically, take about eight years from inception to completion. The current average time for completing subsidized projects is six years. The Housing Partnership Development Corporation has worked to collapse the length of this development process, securing in advance the zoning, environmental, and community-planning approvals necessary to prepare a buildable site.

As a knowledgeable advocate for reforms that promote cost-effective development, a nonprofit intermediary may also be more effective in changing government policies and procedures than members of the construction industry, who are perceived as self-serving and motivated only by profit. Recently, New York City announced its commitment to major reform of city regulations in the interest of eliminating government-imposed obstacles to affordable housing. This unprecedented, comprehensive reform is a direct result of actions in the public interest that have been identified in the course of carrying out Housing Partnership projects.

From the New York City experience, several key principles have emerged that are central to the formation and successful implementation of any housing partnership. These principles include the importance of strong leadership, the creation of a structure for policy making and administration, and a careful delineation of the powers and responsibilities of all participants that realistically reflects their interests and capabilities.

A partnership effort requires the leadership of participating private institutions and government to make personal commitments to its success. Because of the extraordinary political and financial risks of development activity, the staff must have a clear mandate to carry out the actions necessary to achieve program goals. Above all, the message must come down that the partnership is not "business as usual" for public agencies or for-profit participants. The power to deliver and enforce this message is at the chief executive level.

The partnership must also have a policy board or corporate structure responsible for program implementation that institutionalizes the partnership, defines its public purpose, and ensures a continuity of commitment and support that survives the tenure of individuals. Housing development and finance depend on sustained, consistent efforts over many years and cannot be carried out on an ad hoc basis. A nonprofit intermediary organization may be necessary as a vehicle for staffing partnership efforts, representing something of a buffer and conciliator among parties with inherently conflicting interests. A new structure may also help neutralize stereotypes and prejudices that could interfere with the development of creative programs and solid public-private relationships.

Finally, from its inception, the partnership must establish clear lines of decision-making authority between the public and private participants. Government needs to maintain accountability and control over public resources committed to joint initiatives, while private financial institutions must uphold their fiduciary responsibility to stockholders, depositors, and regulatory authorities. Lines of authority are essential because of the divergent and conflicting demands imposed on the private sector and government that can surface at every stage of a development project.

In the selection of a builder-developer for a project, for example, government is under pressure to accept the low bid, while bankers look for financial strength and track records. In the targeting of tenants or home buyers, government aims to serve the lowest-income groups, while lenders and developers look for the most creditworthy or stable households. In designating project sites, government selects areas of most urgent need, whereas the private sector prefers those with the least risk. There is public-private tension in the definition of *reasonable profit*; the goal of keeping costs down conflicts with the need for allowing sufficient return to attract and keep a quality developer. As for the level of public subsidies, the government's commitment to the minimum amount required to start a project may not meet a lender's idea of a level sufficient to protect against contingencies and cost overruns.

A format for addressing and resolving these and countless other program and policy issues must be put in place, with the assurance that the needs of public and private partners will be acknowledged and balanced through a dynamic but predictable process. This format must respect government's need to withstand public scrutiny over such issues as the disposal of public property to a private entrepreneur and favoritism in the selection of the beneficiaries of assisted housing. On the other hand, the process must recognize that banks cannot lend depositors' funds to builders with poor credit or for locations with no market value.

Housing partnership initiatives began to proliferate in the 1970s as a somewhat grudging response to the threat of increased government regulation of the banking industry. Laws such as the Community Reinvestment Act of 1978, enacted to counter alleged disinvestment and redlining in low-income areas, provided a "stick" that Federal and state regulators used to secure private investment in a public agenda. Federal housing subsidies and mortgage insurance, on the other hand, provided a "carrot" that permitted financial institutions to respond to public pressures without compromising business interests or fiduciary obligations.

In the 1980s the "carrot and stick" strategy has not been effective in generating housing partnerships. The Federal government is unlikely to mandate investment in high-risk, public-benefit activities while there are serious concerns about the financial underpinnings of the country's banking system. States and localities use the regulatory "stick" at their peril, in an age when financial institutions can easily relocate jobs and tax revenues to a more congenial environment. As for positive incentives, without Federal subsidies local government cannot readily offer competitive or even prudent investment opportunities to attract private dollars.

The current political and economic environment demands new strategies for attracting private participation in a public-housing agenda and depends on inspiring commitments to "partnership" in the purest sense. It requires that key local officials and corporate leaders define and promulgate policies that support the convergence of enlightened self-interest and the public interest. The product of a successful housing partnership will be greater than the sum of individual contributions to a particular project or program. Through the process of building a cooperative effort, all parties transcend traditional roles and demonstrate how existing resources can be applied in new ways to achieve greater objectives. A successful housing partnership will enhance public-private relationships generally and reinforce efforts to improve all aspects of community life.

# Ingredients for Successful Partnerships: The New York City Case

DAVID ROCKEFELLER

When we began the New York City Partnership in 1979, we selected *partnership* from a list of a dozen or so names to signify a new and greater unity among the many components of New York's private sector. While we had government and organized labor very much in mind, the word *partnership* had not been conceived as a new model for social problem-solving through joint public-private ventures. Many people then thought of partnerships only in terms of law firms, tax shelters, or perhaps living arrangements between consenting adults.

A great deal has happened in the intervening years. From a somewhat tentative initial concept, the New York City Partnership has matured into a vigorous organization with solid programs in such areas as youth employment, education, public safety, affordable housing, and economic development. Work with the public sector and advocacy on public issues are central to all of the Partnership's activities. Its position with respect to the public sector is greatly strengthened by the fact that its 120-person board represents a cross section of New York's private sector.

The timing of the creation of the Partnership was in many ways fortunate; it corresponded with a shift in Federal policy that placed new emphasis on private-sector initiatives. Thus it was not accidental when President Reagan agreed to speak at the first annual luncheon of the Partnership in January 1982. He made it clear that many traditional Federal urban programs were going to be cut back or eliminated and that he expected the private sector to play a far greater role.

New York City had a head start in this regard because of its experience with the 1975 fiscal crisis. This crisis forced the financial community, business, labor, and public officials to work together as never before. This was a painful way to create mutual understanding and joint efforts, but it was certainly effective. Indeed, in retrospect at least, the best thing that happened to New York may have

---

These remarks were presented at "Public-Private Partnerships," a conference sponsored by New York City Partnership, Inc., and the Academy of Political Science, New York, New York, 13 June 1986.

been the famous 1975 *Daily News* headline, "Ford to New York: Drop Dead!" That really got our adrenaline going!

I would like to touch on some of the ingredients of a successful partnership — with a small *p* — that I believe helped to save New York from the undertaker.

*First* is a *strong and comprehensive private-sector organization.* In the case of New York, for instance, the private sector was highly fragmented before the creation of the Partnership. Many different business groups, pursuing similar civic goals, tended to represent narrow interests and often competed with one another. The Chamber of Commerce had a distinguished history and became a key component of the Partnership, but its relatively small board represented only the largest Manhattan businesses south of 96th Street. Another group, the Economic Development Council, had the same board as the Chamber, though with a different chairman. The two organizations did not work together effectively, but the Economic Development Council was also incorporated into the Partnership when it was created. The problem was how to get broader citywide representation.

Given this general disarray, the private sector had little political clout, and there was no way in which it could be an equal partner with government. As a result, both the social and the economic climate of the city suffered as political expediency became the order of the day.

We were convinced that the grass was greener elsewhere, and we asked McKinsey & Company to survey how things were done in other cities. Their review disclosed a number of good ideas that were incorporated into the Partnership. Ironically, some of the cities that we considered to be exemplary are now coming back to us and asking us how we operate.

The result was an organization of the private sector that was much more representative and cohesive than anything that had existed previously. Many in the public sector were skeptical at first, but now they realize that the Partnership has credibility. It represents not just a few big-business men but rather a large number and a broad range of voters.

This credibility is due in large part to a *second* ingredient that is critical to a successful partnership — the *personal participation of the chief executives involved.* We have been exceptionally fortunate in the direct personal involvement of our board members, and I think that is the key to what success we have had. A first-rate staff, of course, is essential, but it is the board that makes the difference in terms of key decisions, commitments, and influence. Certain jobs are simply too important to be delegated, and we are blessed by the fact that so many leading New Yorkers believe that preserving the health of their city is one of these. In my experience, at least, delegation is infectious — quickly leading to yet more delegation and the loss of institutional potency.

One way we keep busy people involved is to give them interesting and challenging assignments. Our summer jobs effort, for instance, owes at least some of its continuing success to the fact that it is taken on each year by a different company and a different chief executive. This produces both pride of ownership and some creative competition. I doubt that Ellen Straus, president of Straus Communications, thought several years ago that she would become an expert on public safety. Yet now she can take pride in a program that has helped to solve over 500 major crimes. Much the same could be said of the scores of other chief executives now working on education, housing, economic development, long-term employment, and advocacy.

There is a tendency to think that chief executives have too many weighty business matters on their minds to be concerned about such social issues. But our experience has been exactly the opposite. We have found that it is precisely busy people who most welcome new challenges and the opportunity to work with and become friends with a rich variety of other concerned leaders on matters of true importance to the city.

Good organization and personal involvement are critical, but a *third* component is also essential for success — a *clear mission* and not trying to be all things to all people. Albert Einstein once stated that "perfection of means and confusion of ends seem to characterize our age." I am not sure how perfect our means are, but I am convinced we have made progress in developing well-defined, limited, and measurable objectives. It was clear to us from the outset that we could not possibly take on all of the tasks people would like us to assume without diluting our resources and effectiveness. Thus we identified a limited number of objectives that the private sector could do something about and that were not already being pursued effectively by others. This process was further formalized in 1982 when we created a mission review group, chaired by John Whitehead, then senior partner of Goldman, Sachs & Co.

A year later, this committee produced a detailed "blueprint" for the Partnership, which put priority on job training, the retention in the city of back-office jobs, and the improvement of the business climate. Since then, the Partnership has spearheaded a far-reaching "Adopt-A-School" program by corporations, and it has both produced a report on back-office jobs and stimulated a major development in downtown Brooklyn. It has also created a High Technology Committee, headed by Dr. Joshua Lederberg, the president of Rockefeller University. Booz, Allen & Hamilton recently completed an excellent, sophisticated, and comprehensive study on high tech for this last group — a task that they undertook on a *pro bono* basis.

The job of continually defining and refining objectives may be the most important that any organization faces — be it public or private. Hard choices are frequently necessary, but, without them, it is easy for an institution to stagnate, become flabby, and lose relevance.

So far I have discussed partnerships largely from the private side, but obviously a *receptive and supportive public sector* is also essential — and this is the *fourth* and final component I would like to touch on. There are at least three aspects to this ingredient — good communication, the removal of disincentives, and the creation of sound incentives where appropriate.

I mention communication first because the public and private sectors frequently do not take the time to understand each other as well as they might. Businesses do not often think in political terms, and politicians do not often think in economic terms. Even phrases such as "private-sector initiatives" and "public-private partnerships" can be misleading if they are interpreted as meaning only that government steps back and the private sector steps in. Many tasks in our society rightly belong to government and should stay with government.

Some of the major pitfalls of public-private partnerships involve language. If we are not careful, the rhetoric surrounding the subject can far exceed the substance. If unrealistic expectations are encouraged, the result can easily be buckpassing—with the public and private sectors pointing fingers at each other. This would be in the best interest of no one.

As communication between the two sectors improves, public officials should better understand the disincentives that already exist to private economic activity and job creation. If jobs are a shared bottom line, then it should be possible to focus more sharply on impediments like high taxes, counterproductive regulations, and bureaucracy. At the same time, private-sector awareness will be increased about the importance of the social climate as well as the economic one. Then businesses will also be far more apt to become involved with issues like education, training, and housing.

Removing disincentives by itself, however, will not ensure full private participation in public-private partnerships. Incentives are sometimes required as well. Our Housing Partnership New Homes Program could not have worked, for instance, without a $28 million Urban Development Action Grant. This in turn has stimulated some $300 million of private investment in affordable housing, yet this valuable Federal program is being eliminated. Fortunately, we have helped to develop a similar subsidy program at the state level, but it still seems counterproductive for Washington to eliminate such an effective incentive at the same time that it is urging more private initiatives. The fact is that it is impossible to build affordable housing in New York without some subsidy.

Similarly, the Federal government recently announced that it was giving highest priority in housing to rehabilitation instead of new construction. Now I believe that this is a healthy shift in policy, but rehabilitation in cities like New York will also demand some public-sector support if it is to provide affordable housing for lower-income families. I hope the Federal government will recognize this fact.

The New York City Community Preservation Corporation has rehabilitated over 12,000 units at an average cost of about $12,000 per unit—a fraction of the cost of new construction. Rents must still be modestly restructured to amortize these costs, however, and some families simply cannot afford the new rents. Some form of rent subsidy is essential to help the poorest families, yet, so far, the Federal government is eliminating its program in this area as well. This does not seem to make a great deal of sense. In fact, the Community Preservation Corporation may have to go out of the rehabilitation business unless there is some public-sector assistance for poor families. This could mean the further deterioration and abandonment of billions of dollars of housing that the Federal government says it wishes to rehabilitate. I mention these two housing examples only to indicate that effective public-private partnerships must be a two-way street.

I have focused on New York because I know it best. Others from across the country could cite similar examples of ways in which public policy either impedes or helps private initiatives. An ongoing dialogue would enable us to identify common concerns and to suggest changes in public policy that would stimulate private activity.

# Managing Partnerships: A CEO's Perspective

FRANK J. MACCHIAROLA

   The New York City Partnership was formed in 1979 and began operations in 1980 because the city's business leaders were determined to change their interface with the public sector. The financial crisis of 1975 had brought the city to the brink of bankruptcy, and the business leaders understood that they were unprepared for the tasks that were needed to work more effectively with government. Caught unaware of the extent of the city's difficulties and without an organization in place adequately to represent the private sector, they searched for a way to conduct their public affairs. Consultants from McKinsey & Company told the leaders that existing organizations like the Economic Development Council and the New York Chamber of Commerce and Industry had to be enhanced by an organization that would be more broadly representative of the private sector. The composition of the proposed organization had to be made more inclusive, and the agenda had to include projects and activities that would operate with the support and cooperation of the public sector. The Partnership was to be more proactive and operational — and had to embody the corporate spirit of citizenship.
   The Economic Development Council (which was ultimately absorbed into the Partnership) and the New York Chamber of Commerce and Industry (which is affiliated with the Partnership) had been composed of Manhattan's big-business leaders. The support came from the big-business community of male corporate leaders. David Rockefeller, who assumed the chairmanship of the two boards as well as the chairmanship of the New York City Partnership, had determined to expand the private-sector representation in the Partnership. A sustained effort to include representatives of small business, of minority-owned business, and of women-owned business has resulted in a board of considerable breadth. The decision was also made to expand beyond strictly business organizations. University and college presidents were added, as were the chief executives of major not-for-profit groups in the city, so that the organization could more adequately represent the spirit of American entrepreneurship and capitalism that the Partnership

wished to foster. In addition, it was agreed that representation from the outer boroughs was essential if the New York City Partnership was truly to represent the business spirit in the entire city. As a result, an elaborate and complex governance system was developed, the most broadly inclusive private-sector organization in New York City history, and an elaborate and detailed system for deciding which programmatic activities would be engaged in was also developed.

In January 1983, I was chosen to head the organization as its first full-time president and chief executive officer (CEO), succeeding Paul Lyet, who had recently retired as chairman of the Sperry Corporation. I had been chancellor of the New York City Public School system for five years immediately preceding my selection; therefore, in choosing me to head the private sector's effort to serve as corporate good citizen, the board selected a leader from the public sector and demonstrated to the entire city that it was serious about working with the leaders of government, both in the city and in the state.

Private-sector support for the Partnership has been significant; the Partnership and Chamber of Commerce have more than one hundred employees and on-loan executives committed to the organization's programs. Financial support has also been considerable; almost 90 percent of the funding for the Partnership comes exclusively from private-sector support. Ten major contributors support the Partnership with annual payments of at least $125,000, and substantial and growing corporate support has underscored the extent to which business considers Partnership activities worthwhile.

The growth of Partnership programs has been enormous as well. More than 140,000 disadvantaged youngsters have been employed in a Summer Jobs program over the past six years, including more than 36,200 employed in 1986. Some 2,000 housing units are under construction or have been completed in a program of moderate-income home ownership that has pledged to complete 5,000 new units in sixty neighborhoods of the city by 1988. More than fifty businesses have adopted New York City high schools in a corporate Join-A-School program that has as its goal corporate sponsorship for each of the 112 public high schools by the end of the 1987-88 school year. A Crime Stoppers program has committed more than $100,000 in reward money for anonymous tips that help the police solve major felonies and has solved murders or attempted murders at the rate of one every other week since the program's inception in 1983. A full-time youth-employment commitment has resulted in pledges and programs for entry-level jobs for youngsters who complete their education and who are certified as work ready. An advocacy activity has resulted in access to government officials and represents private-sector interests at city hall, at the state house, and in various commissions and organizations that assist in the development of public policy. An economic-development focus in the outer boroughs has resulted in millions of square feet of office space in commercial projects in Brooklyn and Queens. This ensures the development of new private-sector jobs in these parts of the city for the first time in fifty years. The organization has provided on-loan and technical-assistance consulting to many different city agencies. A high-tech agenda has been prepared for the business community to encourage businesses, universities, and government to cooperate in taking advantage of the opportunities that high-tech offers in leading New York City industries like financial services.

These activities, which are varied in scope and have resulted from the decision to take on new initiatives on a regular basis, require the development of a sizable staff with skills in diverse fields. Since the work of the Partnership has grown enormously, its management has been particularly important to the organization. Operating on business principles, committed to "doing more with less," and expanding into new areas of need have required skill and expertise and, most important, financial assistance.

One of the most important issues that the CEO confronts is the partnership's environment. While the New York City Partnership was built largely because of the city's financial crisis, the growing national trend toward a greater reliance on the private sector to meet people's basic needs helped the corporate leadership to build a "new" New York City. A national reaction against the growth of government was apparent in the presidential victory of Ronald Reagan. While this reaction to big government was apparent throughout most of the country, it was not the critical factor in New York as it was elsewhere. In New York State politics, Governor Hugh Carey was a traditional Democrat in the liberal tradition of Roosevelt, Kennedy, and Johnson. Throughout New York City's financial crisis, business leaders applauded Governor Carey, who did not embrace the political philosophy that less government is good government. Instead, he emphasized increased efficiency and productivity and somewhat successfully challenged service providers, particularly labor unions, to make do with less. In seven of his eight years in office from 1975 through 1983, Governor Carey held the state's budget growth below the rate of inflation; he was also responsible for the greatest tax cut in the state's history. But the issue was pragmatic, and the public in New York State has not accepted the philosophy of "less government."

Governor Mario Cuomo was elected in 1982 on the same program, and his 1986 reelection has reinforced that perspective. At the city level, Mayor Edward I. Koch, while committed to running New York City's government on a businesslike basis and insisting on living within the budget, has in fact increased the cost of government dramatically and has continued to promote the growth of government programs. Such political perspectives necessarily shape the activities and agenda of the Partnership. It is also important to remember that when the Partnership was formed in 1979, political leadership needed the support of the business community in order to save the city. The economic future of the city and state was in jeopardy, businesses were deserting the city, unemployment was on the rise — and the city and state leaders were totally lacking in the credibility that is necessary for civic viability. Today the situation has returned to normalcy. New York continues to be the country's highest tax state, the budgets of the state and city are growing at substantial rates, and public-sector jobs have become a leading component of the expanding economy, but from the standpoint of the political leadership, the private sector can deal with these difficulties. The CEO of the Partnership has to realize that the limits of private-sector power are largely determined by the relationship between business and the public sector.

The environment within New York City and New York State remains a difficult and sometimes uncongenial one for an organization that is based on the notion that private-sector contributions are essential. The public-sector attitude toward the private sector has an important role in shaping and defining areas where the organization can be effective. If government leaders are supportive, business will be called upon to deal with issues like the cost of government, taxation, government services, and government regulation. If government leaders distrust the private sector's input and believe that government is the sole instrument to solve the basic problems of citizens, then true public-private partnerships will never materialize. If public officials believe in big government, they will not see a role for the private sector, and they will use partnerships only to placate the public. I am not fully convinced that in New York City the public sector has enough faith in the role of the private sector to sustain partnerships over the long run. A critical task for the CEO is to convince the political leadership through effective programs that the private sector's role is an essential one and that it must be strengthened.

Because of the significance of the environment, the external factors that help establish the conditions under which a partnership can operate, the role or mission of the organization cannot always be readily, or easily, agreed upon. The New York City Partnership spent several years carefully identifying its mission and seeking projects that would effectively fulfill that mission. The uncertainties that were addressed by key board members of the Partnership included the composition of the board; its relationship to the Chamber of Commerce, unions, and government; its committee structure; and the organization of its executive offices and system of governance. Once that was accomplished, a Project Planning and Review Committee was created to help evaluate and determine the programs that were developed as its basic agenda.

The Partnership had to face certain critical issues. Government officials would be allowed to serve on Partnership committees but not on the board. Labor unions, which had played a critical and positive role in dealing with the city's financial crises would help form a Business Labor Working Group but were not included in the governance. Universities and not-for-profit organizations were accorded a full role in the Partnership. As indicated previously, it was important to go beyond the big-business Manhattan leadership to include outer borough representation as well as women- and minority-owned businesses that clearly warranted a place within the Partnership.

The issue of inclusion is always an important one, and managers must always resist the tendency to exclude and close ranks. It is always easier to manage an organization in which key executives share a common philosophy and perspective. By any definition, however, a partnership has to be broadly inclusive. Management must make certain that the system is open to diverse points of view and that it is willing to debate both sides of virtually every relevant issue. An effective partnership needs to hear representatives of the private sector who share the goal of making the community a better place in which to live, work, and do business. That openness is one of the most important aspects of managing a partnership. In addition, the partnership must be responsible for ensuring that outsiders are comfortable in the system. Newcomers often hesitate to express themselves in organizations that they have just joined. Management must therefore make a special effort to bring them into the community and to make certain that they play significant roles in the organization and its committees.

In addition to an appropriate membership, a partnership needs a proper mission. Two New York City Partnership committees were established to play a special role in defining the organization's mission. One special committee was set up to determine how the Partnership would be formed — what its relationship would be to constituent groups like the Economic Development Council and the New York Chamber of Commerce and Industry. The Partnership's governance and committee system was derived from a set of recommendations made by that special committee. A second committee was later established to help define the mission of the Partnership. It set the organization's agenda around the theme of economic development: creating jobs, enhancing the business climate, making the city's services more focused on attracting business, and reducing the cost of government. The committee also directed the staff to focus on the question of New York City's competitiveness within the state and within the region. In practical terms the committee cautioned the staff to undertake only those projects for which it was uniquely suited, and it warned the Partnership against taking on too many projects. This committee was also given the tasks of planning and reviewing projects. Such a structure permitted the board and the staff to deny the many worthwhile requests that were not well suited to the capacity of the Partnership.

This mission-defining responsibility must clearly be part of the work of the board, for the staff should not be given broad freedom to choose the activities of the organization. The CEO must balance the roles of the board and staff and see that each support the activities of the other. An active board will be a supportive one, and a board and staff that interact will develop innovative programs for the organization. The board and staff are working to refine a new Partnership activity — mass transit. The need is great, and an appropriate private-sector role will be helpful to New York City's citizens.

The administration of a partnership has to be certain that corporate support for the program occurs through the personal involvement of CEOs from major business institutions. The leadership of the partnership must discourage the CEOs' tendency to delegate critical responsibilities of board membership to corporate subordinates. The partnership needs top-level support; corporate executives are very conscious of the status of the colleagues with whom they share a place at a board meeting or other partnership function. There must be a constant, direct, and personal involvement of the private-sector leaders themselves if the partnership is to be successful.

David Rockefeller, chairman of the New York City Partnership, has been enormously helpful in conveying to corporate leaders the idea that business leadership in city affairs is an absolute necessity for the well-being of both the private sector and the city itself. On several occasions, when the New York City Partnership has permitted seconds-in-command to assume the position of board member, the result has been less effective. While second- or third-ranking corporate officials can often be personally supportive, they have less influence within their own organizations, and other CEOs notice the absence of their peers from other leading businesses within their industry. The issue of status must be viewed critically by the organization and its administration. Corporate CEOs pay special attention to their colleagues and the signals that they send to one another, and the personal involvement of their corporate colleagues is a necessity.

Another difficulty in sustaining a partnership's success is maintaining corporate interest in the organization's affairs when few dramatic issues face the city. During the city's financial crisis the business leaders had to be involved with municipal affairs on a regular, if not daily, basis. The mayor and the governor called on the Partnership's founders to help the city in its time of greatest distress. Private-sector leaders took key roles in creating and then serving on the Municipal Assistance Corporation and the Emergency Financial Control Board. The city was challenged to convince the public that services could still be delivered to its citizens in an effective way. During these uncertain times the private sector took a leadership role in most areas of the city's life. They shuttled between city hall, Gracie Mansion, and the executive mansion in Albany. Business and labor made concessions; on-loan executives even served as deputy mayors and chief of operations of the city government. Crisis led to involvement, and the private sector was eager to do its part. Today, however, matters have settled down to the level of normalcy or even boredom, which may convince private-sector leaders that there is little or nothing for them to do. Government, can, in short, be left to the professionals. Such a conclusion is unfortunate, for it is not only the extraordinary that needs the assistance of the private sector; the mundane, the ordinary, and the usual also call for private-sector analysis and involvement. In such situations an incipient problem may go unnoticed, and it is hard to get expertise to deal with systemic problems.

In such situations it is hard to get the financial support that is necessary to sustain the operations of a partnership organization. The CEO has to work hard to maintain corporate support, expand into new areas where partnership giving has been weakest, and obtain foundation support for worthwhile projects. The New York City Partnership has reached into the real estate community, the legal community, the professional-services field, and the investment banks for increased support. In some cases we have even introduced them to the concept of corporate support for organizations like the Partnership. We have also shared agendas with foundations and have sought their help in expanding the reach of programs such as youth employment, education, and housing. Projects of importance to different sectors within the city must be undertaken if the organization is to grow in power and effectiveness. In the New York City Partnership, I have tried to strengthen board-member participation by asking our board members to work directly on solutions to some of the city's most pressing problems (such as education, youth employment, crime, and housing) with an agenda that interests the city fathers and the private-sector leaders. In housing, for example, we have focused on home ownership and have worked exhaustively—against great odds—to produce affordable housing for New York City's working middle class. We have worked with three industries (finance, home construction, and development) and with all three levels of government. We have put housing experts and business leaders together in our governance structure. Thus we have a solid program—not without problems—but with a sense of commitment and accomplishment.

Business leaders are inclined to withdraw from partnerships during "good times," and in New York City many corporate leaders prefer international and national issues to local concerns. Often, matters like the international balance of trade, the growth of the national debt, and national tax reform are more significant to them than Join-A-School, the Youth Employment Program, or the Moderate Income Housing Program in New York City. Many corporations headquartered in the city also maintain substantial operations in other places, and it is harder to gain their attention and corporate support.

Fortunately, our role in national affairs, through a Committee on Public Issues chaired by James Robinson of American Express, and the importance of New York City in matters such as Federal tax reform and the Gramm-Rudman-Hollings Act of 1985 has highlighted the need for a strong organization to represent private-sector interests. And, as Governor Cuomo moves to reduce taxes in New York State and uses Partnership board members like James Robinson, John Brademas, president of New York University, and Felix Rohatyn, head of the Municipal Assistance Corporation, the Partnership can have a significant impact. This is understood and appreciated by the Partnership leaders.

Another danger to the Partnership's ability to be objective and representative of the private sector is that the operation of joint programs with the government can often mean that the partnership organization becomes co-opted. In such situations, when the partnership is trying to represent the private sector and still work cooperatively with government, how can it respond to the press's queries about the effectiveness of a related, or perhaps the same, program? At what point does honesty mean the abandonment of discretion? When does honesty destroy a good working relationship?

A frank and forthright answer to these questions may be necessary to maintain credibility with third parties. As a partnership's involvement with government increases, these questions also increase in frequency. Occasionally I have dealt with angry officials who claimed to have been attacked and improperly criticized. More often than not, I have disagreed with them. Telling them what one honestly believes often requires great diplomatic skill. Aggrieved officials have sometimes threatened to withhold cooperation with the Partnership. And cooperation is difficult enough, even when government officials are trying to provide it. The success of more than one project has been held for ransom, and the price for setting it free has been the loss of objectivity and the freedom to criticize.

A problem may occur because a partnership is boosting the community while exhorting government to be more responsive to the needs of the private sector. At the same time that the Partnership is working to convince out-of-state business to relocate to New York City and stressing the advantages of operating here, it is decrying the cost of doing business and warning that excess costs and high taxes are driving business from the city. The fact that the New York City Partnership is both a booster of the city and a critic of its policies poses an operational problem for the CEO.

The best way to deal with that problem is to be discreet but honest. The government should be criticized for failing to compete economically but any progress must be publicly acknowledged. Any criticism must be impersonal and carefully framed. Failure to provide necessary criticism would compromise the integrity of the partnership. I have also found that successful projects, such as housing, summer jobs, and Join-A-School, earn the respect of critics and are sufficient proof that the interests of the organization are tied to the well-being of the body politic. The absence of a partisan political agenda is the best guarantee of the integrity of the organization.

In addition, the relationship of the partnership to other organizations — newspapers, business periodicals, labor unions, and civic organizations — and the development of a public-policy point of view that is associated with the partnership will also be helpful in dealing with the political forces. The New York City Partnership's concern about the competitive aspects of doing business in the city rather than elsewhere has become a well-known position of the organization. The commitment to economic development — as evidenced by our crucial role in the commercial revitalization of Brooklyn and Queens — is well known in the city. Our efforts toward reducing the tax burden on New Yorkers in order to keep business operations in the city is also a well-understood position of the Partnership. Our actions on the legislative front, at the state house and at city hall, are consistent with that position. Our advocacy, even when it is strong and hard, makes us effective. At the same time, we have also tried to encourage public expenditures when the need is clear. Our support of increased aid to education and our concern about an equal distribution of state aid are well-known Partnership priorities. We have not been afraid to advocate government spending when the return has been clear and effective. Such forthrightness has benefited the organization.

Another major concern for the partnership CEO is finding competent executives who understand both the private sector and the public sector. The matter is made more difficult because few executives have had successful and productive careers in both sectors. There is a great deal of difficulty in moving between these two sectors, and very often representatives of one are quite suspicious of those of the other. The corporate cultures in these sectors are quite different. In addition, good private-sector managers often hesitate to leave their positions and risk not being able to return. Compensation levels are also generally more favorable in the private sector, and hence the problems of recruiting good private-sector managers and adequately compensating them in organizations like partnerships are difficult. Their motivation for working with partnerships must go well beyond the monetary reward.

The ideal organization involves a mix of strengths within the staff. Some of the staff who have been successful in the public sector appreciate the demands that occur in the public sector and understand the need to be politically sensitive. At the same time there must be private-sector persons who understand profits and cost-benefits. The staff interaction, through frequent discussion of programs and plans, will result in good partnership programs. In addition, an organization like a partnership should be representative of all the ethnic groups in the city. No partnership can be successful without that inclusion.

An example of the need for different perspectives to come together is found in the housing field. A partnership cannot build subsidized housing alone, but it can help close the gap in understanding what exists between private-sector developers and government bureaucrats. The government should appreciate that for private-sector developers the process of government approvals must be accelerated if affordable housing is to be built for moderate-income home owners. Such an appreciation has been difficult to achieve. When all costs were paid by the government, time was a wasted commodity. Many government procedures and personnel are holdovers from that period. If a housing program based on partnership is to succeed, government agencies must become more responsible.

The knowledge of both public- and private-sector perspectives will ensure that the partnership's options will not cost more than they are worth. For instance, one of the antecedent organizations of the Partnership, the Economic Development Council, had an extensive on-loan and task force program designed to assist agencies such as the Board of Education, the New York City Transit Authority, the Office of Court Administration, and the district attorney. This program cost the Partnership millions of dollars to maintain. Although some useful work was accomplished and the benefit to some of the agencies was worth while, not many of the agencies took full advantage of the results. Some of them regarded the recommendations as too insensitive to the political realities within which they worked. Other agencies resented the fact that reaching a solution often meant disclosing the problem, and that could embarrass or even unseat the public-sector manager. Today, when the New York City Partnership provides on-loan or consultant assistance—which we do, as needed—the work is more clearly developed with both public- and private-sector input. The findings are more focused on their usefulness to a manager who has been charged with improving the situation. We suffer somewhat since the confidential nature of such an approach keeps many of our members unaware of what we have done, and yet their knowledge is helpful in obtaining financial and other support. But the price of anonymity is well worth paying because it makes a partnership more effective and more helpful in building the city's future.

Another difficult task for the partnership CEO involves pleasing different constituent groups within the membership. Nowhere is this more difficult than in the area of advocacy where public interest often meets special interest. The executive must ensure that all options are considered openly and that all elements within the organization have at least the opportunity to be heard and to present their points of view. Such a process of consultation can be painstaking, but it is necessary for an effective partnership.

With all of this, the most difficult aspect of partnership may be determining and measuring success. Few organizations can be used as reference points, and there are few forums for discussing what can be done. Partnerships have yet to organize themselves nationally, although some movement has been made in that direction. New partnerships are being created. New alliances and developing relationships are novel and anxiety filled. Partnerships are still developing a vision of the good life for our cities and our citizens. The goals — self-sufficient citizens and workers prepared to do their jobs and to help achieve basic human needs — remain elusive, but the effort has been quite rewarding.

# Partnerships Redefined: Chicago's New Opportunities

DONALD HAIDER

In the depths of New York City's 1975 financial crisis, national attention turned to the country's second largest city, Chicago. While urban conditions were deteriorating elsewhere, Chicago represented stability. It was "the city that works": no municipal labor strife, no budget deficits, and no lack of public and private leadership. This dynamism, according to several observers, rested on a base of three interlocking entities that included the ward organization, the governmental apparatus of the city and county, and the powerful private interest groups and constituencies in the community. Over the decades, noted *Chicago Magazine*, "the belief persisted in Chicago that no civic problem was so great that it couldn't be solved by gathering a handful of important people — usually the Mayor and the chief executives of the largest local corporations — together in one room."[1]

Chicago's public-private partnerships emerged as the envy of other large cities. But ten years later, the Chicago partnership model was in disrepute. Richard J. Daley had been Chicago's mayor and leader for twenty-two years. His death in 1976 accelerated evolutionary changes that seem revolutionary in retrospect. The Democratic party and its organizational structure came apart at the seams. The building-trade unions no longer dominated Chicago's labor scene. Business and civic organizations were in disarray. The *Chicago Tribune* concluded: "The two factors that have for so long glossed over Chicago's inadequacies — economic growth and Daley political power — are gone for good."[2]

The power struggle resulting from the succession of three weak mayors following Daley's death produced unfavorable media coverage locally and nationally. What the local media termed the "Vietnamization of Chicago" in 1984 led the national press to refer to Chicago as "Beirut on the Lake."[3] Clearly, Chicago in the 1980s does not function as it did in the 1970s; nor will it do so again.

Cities, like most large organizations, pass through phases of growth and decline. They are vulnerable to powerful trends and changes in the external environment that, in turn, affect their viability and governance. Chicago's cycle of growth and stability ran longer than most. But, with the confluence of external forces and internal effects, changes in the late 1970s and early 1980s occurred rapidly.

The alchemy that generates public-private partnerships also works differently in every city. Because urban characteristics and cultures differ, the particular combinations that evolve across sectors to solve problems or to meet human needs vary. Leadership, a basic ingredient that runs throughout successful public-private partnerships, does not appear to be a readily manufacturable or transferable product. After two decades of Daley's strong urban leadership, Chicago experienced a leadership vacuum, a condition that shook the very pillars of this proud industrial center.

The Committee for Economic Development (CED), the prestigious business organization, expressed qualified enthusiasm about the Chicago model of public-private partnerships in the 1970s. Noting the extraordinary accomplishments of the Chicago 21/Dearborn Park Project, which helped preserve the Loop, Chicago's central business district, CED observed that the positive relationship between business and government in Chicago during the Daley years was based on political conditions that were destructive of other values.[4] These "other values" have been amply manifested in the post-Daley era, altering the foundations on which the old Chicago partnership was based.

A new model is still emerging, and in the process Chicago has experienced disruptions, often seen as chaos by outside observers. Political and economic change has been costly—loss of jobs and investment, opportunities missed to husband scarce resources, and delays in forming civic consensus for action. New leadership has been slow to emerge, and so have constituent groups that are needed to enable leadership to appear. The Chicago case, therefore, is a study of transition: a partnership created, largely dissolved, and a process of rebuilding upon new foundations.

The CED study identified certain basic "civic foundations" conducive to successful public-private partnerships: a positive civic culture (participation), community vision, effective civic organizations, a network among key groups, civic entrepreneurs, and continuity in policy. Few cities, particularly ethnically diverse cities with sizable minority populations and established political structures, possess all of these foundations. How the old Chicago partnerships worked and why they no longer serve Chicago's current needs are important aspects for understanding their evolutionary replacements. Such an analysis may also shed light on the particular ingredients of partnerships—their dynamics, situational context, and sometimes fragile structure.

*Partnership Elements*

The partnership concept suffers from problems of general application insofar as it embraces most ongoing relationships that cut across three dominant but not carefully delineated sectors: government, business, and nonprofit. In the 150 years since Alexis de Tocqueville discovered extragovernmental "associations" to be

America's legacy to democracy, partnerships may be found in all sizes and varieties in cities.

The concept of urban partnerships has come to imply a sustained collaborative effort of two or more institutions — one public, the other private — in which each of the participants shares in the planning of projects and programs designed to meet a collective need and contributes resources. Since partnership definitions are neither conceptually neat nor empirically rigorous, one is left with certain basic characteristics that run throughout most successful ventures. These include equality among participants, shared risks, and perceived mutual benefits.

Finally, an understanding of urban partnerships is often conditioned by an earlier period, when the focus centered on massive, multiyear physical projects that showpieced public-private experiments in central-city revitalization: Pittsburgh's Renaissance II, Charles Center/Inner Harbor in Baltimore, Atlanta's Peachtree Center, and New York City's Battery Park, Lincoln Center, and Javits Civic Center. These ventures manifested civic commitment and purpose, and functioned as models of cooperative efforts across sectors.

In some cities, such bold and visible projects have become the building blocks of countless less-conspicuous partnership projects and programs. In other cities, like Chicago, they have also set in motion another agenda: a grass-roots reaction against "downtown attention" and a growing demand for partnerships that address neighborhood development, community services, housing, and jobs. Chicago perhaps epitomizes this rapid shift of attention that involves a still unresolved transition to new partnerships.

## The Old Order and Its Passing

An understanding of how and why Chicago partnerships have been altered begins with an environmental overview: economics and demography that, in turn, fundamentally affect Chicago's politics, leadership, finances, and public agenda. In a dynamic and interactive sense, external factors produced internal changes in Chicago's governance and leadership structure. Demographic shifts have been accelerated by economic transformation and have contributed to the breakup of the city's political structure. The consequences of demographic and economic change came relatively late to Chicago, compared with other urban centers — or at least the full recognition of their impacts was only belatedly understood.

From 1950 to 1970, Chicago's population, like its economy, was stable in size but changing in composition, a function primarily of the massive out-migration of middle-class Chicagoans, overwhelmingly white, and their replacement by immigrants, largely from the South, Puerto Rico, Mexico, and Asia. Chicago lost 600,000 whites during the 1970s, 100,000 fewer than left the city in the 1960s. Chicago in the 1970s became smaller, more black, and more poor. The city's black population increased from 33 percent to 40 percent, the Hispanic composition rose to 14 percent, and the proportion of residents whose incomes fell below the poverty line expanded by nearly 40 percent.

Chicago's population peaked in 1950 at 3.6 million residents and has declined since — by 2 percent in the 1950s, by 5 percent during the 1960s, and by 10 percent during the 1970s. By 1982, the population had fallen below 3 million for the first time in sixty years, and Los Angeles had replaced Chicago as the country's second-largest city.

Chicago epitomized the nineteenth-century city, built on productive power, massed population, and industrial technology. The late Charles Merriam said of Chicago's dynamic economy in the 1920s: "Perhaps in no other great city of the world has there been presented so interesting a picture of modern industrial development, so conspicuous a transition from agriculture to the manufacturing basis of wealth."[5] That was Chicago's heritage and tradition — steel, heavy industry, big business, and "hog butcher to the world."

Chicago's depopulation and the decomposition of its industrial base began in the 1950s, but the rate of change was greatly accelerated in the late 1970s. Private-sector jobs peaked in 1957 at 1.4 million. By 1983, there were 1.1 million jobs — a loss of nearly 300,000 — much of which occurred in the 1979-83 economic downturn, when Chicago alone lost nearly 120,000 jobs. As a heavily industrialized, goods-producing center, the loss of jobs hit those industries at the heart of Chicago's economic base. The stockyards and appliance manufacturing vanished; steel and fabricated metals shrank; and machine dye, tools, and food processing declined. Service-sector employment increased, but not as an income or skill replacement for those jobs being lost. Between 1969 and 1984, the number of industrial firms operating in Chicago declined by nearly 30 percent, 8,100 to 5,800, while manufacturing employment fell by more than 40 percent. In many cases, these small manufacturing firms operated in the city's neighborhoods and were the anchors of neighborhood activities.

Evidence of this rapid shift from the industrial to the postindustrial stage of Chicago's development is perhaps best illustrated by the rate of change in the city's property base. The industrial proportions of the property tax base (assessed value) declined by 26 percent from 1977 to 1983. In contrast, the service-sector transition, concentrated in the growing central business district, accelerated. The downtown commercial component of the city's tax base increased by more than 50 percent in that period.

Both demographic and economic changes that had begun earlier hit full force in the late 1970s. While the northeastern states and their urban centers had the highest unemployment rates in the 1973-76 national recession, the Midwest had the lowest among the four United States regions through 1978. The 1980-83 recession completely reversed these regional jobless rates; the Midwest, particularly Chicago, was the most severely affected area. The turnabout in regional rates was only slightly more dramatic than the shift in city-suburban employment. In the 1960s, Chicago's percentage of the six-county metropolitan-area employment approached 60 percent. It declined over the next twenty years, to 45 percent by 1983.

Cities are shaped by economic and demographic shifts. Because urban political organizations and structures ultimately take their form from urban demography,

Chicago's politics and leadership could resist but could not stem these changes. The passing of the city's old order is exemplified by the breakup of its political structure. While dominant political organizations in other large cities deteriorated, reformed, or simply vanished, Chicago's much-vaunted machine remained the last of the great, big-city organizations. "The machine has had an unbroken record of rule over the City of Chicago and Cook County for forty years," noted Milt Rakove in 1975, "and while it has occasionally suffered reverses, it has always demonstrated an ability to recoup its losses and retain its power."[6]

Chicago's political structure is based on a ward system — a city council of fifty aldermen, one from each of the city's fifty wards elected on a nonpartisan basis. Dating from 1923, when Chicago's ethnic composition consisted of sizable Polish, Irish, German, Scandinavian, and Eastern European populations, the political system and structure accommodated this cultural and ethnic diversity into its political representation system, creating the largest city council of any major city.

Ethnic rivalries and hostilities may have been checked by this system, but never contained. "Irish Catholic dominance of the political and governmental systems of the City is a fact of life in present day Chicago," noted Rakove, "and has been so for many years."[7] In fact, the Eleventh Ward, also known as the Bridgeport community, produced four consecutive mayors, three of whom were Irish, whose tenure at City Hall spanned forty-six years from 1933 to 1979.

In spite of the machine's strength and domination of the Chicago political scene, its composition changed significantly over the years. In the 1950s and 1960s, political divisions ran along party lines and socioeconomic differences; lower classes in the inner-city wards supported the machine, and the outlying middle-class wards supported Republicans and independent challenges. In later years "race began to replace class and party as the City's basic political division," noted Bill Grimshaw, "with the most racially threatened white wards backing the organization against black disaffection with the party."[8] Traditional labels of Republican, Democrat, and independent became increasingly meaningless as race replaced ethnicity and even party identifications in Chicago's vibrant politics.

In 1979, a coalition of angry blacks, lakefront liberals, and dissident white ethnics united against an administration paralyzed by the worst snowstorm in the city's history. They elected Jane Byrne mayor, ending the machine's domination of City Hall. Four years later Byrne, aligned with segments of the old machine, was defeated in a three-candidate Democratic primary by Harold Washington. Upon Washington's election as Chicago's first black mayor in April 1983, the new mayor promptly declared the machine "to be dead." The blacks elected a mayor, but the white politicians responded by seizing control of the City Council, resulting in a daily political saga, known locally as "Council Wars."

Public-private partnerships during the Daley era began with the mayor, in whom the city's political power resided. Daley built the machine around his needs, strengthened the mayor's role in city government, upgraded municipal services, and "worked out a partnership built on mutual self interest with the powerful business and labor elites who provided the major economic underpinnings of the City."[9]

Daley ruled the machine. He allocated jobs and economic rewards to the feudal barons, the ward committeemen. He also held them responsible for their wards and for getting out the vote to produce electoral victories.

The effective political–government–private-sector interest-group system that Daley nurtured did not immediately collapse after his death. Daley left no heir apparent, nor did major elements of that system want an heir or another mayor as powerful as Daley. Moreover, as a highly personal system that depended as much on interpersonal skills as it did on formal powers of public office, the system could be patched, as it was from 1976 to 1983, but not replicated.

The eventual breakdown of the political machine and its loss of City Hall in 1983 spilled across all sections and sectors of Chicago. The stirrings of a new political order had many antecedents, evident even before Daley's death: Dr. Martin Luther King, Jr.'s historic open-housing marches in 1965-66, the 1968 riots on the city's West Side, the anti-Vietnam disruptions at the 1968 Democratic Party Convention in the city, the restlessness of the Young Turks within the Democratic party, the first black mayoral challenge in 1975, the defection of Daley's newspaper support, the constant rattlings of neighborhood discontent over the downtown focus of City Hall, and a changing urban economy that left areas of the city further behind.

Chicago changed, but the gap between image and reality in the post-Daley period required time to close. In 1982, the *Chicago Tribune*, editorializing on "Chicago's Crisis of Leadership," observed that the "so-called power elite of Chicago are for the most part impotent and lost on the political battlefield where things get done, both good and bad."[10] Noting the loss of Chicago's visionary civic leaders — General Robert E. Wood, George Pullman, Cyrus McCormick, Potter Palmer, Philip Armour, and Montgomery Ward, to name a few — the *Chicago Sun Times* labeled current leaders "the toothless lions."[11] Highlighting the city's economic and social problems in a series entitled "City on the Brink," R.C. Longworth of the *Tribune* clarified the new reality through an in-depth focus on Chicago's declining services and economic base, failing schools, and growing "underclass."[12] Amid this turmoil and growing introspection, the old partnership, without City Hall, attempted to rally its members behind a massive civic undertaking — Chicago's 1992 World's Fair.

## The 1992 Chicago World's Fair: The End of an Era

In June 1985, plans for a 1992 Chicago World's Fair ended when the Illinois General Assembly failed to approve permanent funding to allow the fair to go forward. The fair died not in the state capitol but in Chicago, when a loose-knit coalition of civic and neighborhood organizations, academics, single-issue groups, and community activists had an opportunity to work their will on the older order of downtown business interests, corporate chief executive officers, and labor and political chieftains.

Twice in Chicago's history, great world fairs galvanized its citizenry—two world-class events, the 1893 World's Columbian Exposition and the 1933-34 Century of Progress during the Great Depression. The proposed 1992 Chicago World's Fair was conceived as the culmination of a "decade of rebirth," the dream of a transformed Chicago that would be, among other things, a truly world-class city, a center of international business and commerce. The 1992 "Age of Discovery" would leave the "City and State with an impressive set of residual benefits, and provide an unparalleled opportunity . . . to improve Chicago's and Illinois' impressive cultural institutions, tourist attractions and high technology capabilities."[13] The 1992 fair was to be a singular event that would bring a much-divided city together. Its demise temporarily left the city even further divided.

Momentum for the fair began under Mayor Jane Byrne in 1980. Support was enlisted from Chicago's top chief executives and officials of major newspapers, labor unions, financial institutions, and city, state, and Federal governments. The fair's directors, committees, and task forces read like a who's who of Chicago. Tens of millions of dollars were invested in architectural renderings, intergovernmental accords, planning and feasibility studies, affirmative-action agreements, marketing, and endless public hearings. In the grand tradition of building the biggest and best projects, the fair was to be all things to all people. It would be an answer to the city's infrastructure and unemployment problems and a panacea for its neighborhoods. As an economic-development venture, the fair would also be the culmination of Chicago's transformation from a predominantly industrial economy to an international service center.

Whatever its virtues, the proposed multibillion-dollar fair had its shortcomings. It was conceptually shifting from an exhibition focus like previous fairs to an entertainment-events concept developed for the financially successful 1984 World Olympics, environmentally silent on impacts on the Lake Michigan shoreline and surrounding communities, and ambiguous regarding financial risk-sharing and costs. The fair, like Chicago itself, fell victim to crumbling civic foundations. Without leadership, shared vision, and trust, the fair was not to be.

No one will ever know whether the proposed 1992 Chicago World's Fair would have generated benefits that would have remotely approached those proclaimed by its supporters. Once begun, however, it was clear that the fair would have dominated the city's agenda for the next decade.

The fair's demise represented much more to Chicago's leadership. For nearly four years the energies of major business leaders, their companies, and their organizations had gone into a single endeavor whose defeat represented not only an individual setback but a civic one as well. Some retreated from public life, while others reassessed their personal and business commitment to Chicago. All those involved learned painfully from the lesson. That is, clearly a new order was emerging in Chicago, however negatively its force had been manifested. For urban partnerships to be successful again in Chicago, the old and new orders would have to accommodate each other. The city had seemingly lost its economic and civic purpose and had yet to find a new one.

## A New Order Emerges

Chicago's partnerships worked smoothly so long as the city was on the upward side of the economic growth curve. Business, labor, financial, and political alliances functioned effectively in an expanding economy where mutual accommodations produced benefits for major interests. When the economy and politics of the city changed abruptly, economic and political cleavages widened throughout the city. No institution, individual, or event alone could fill the void.

The Chicago business community had remained remarkably stable, cohesive, compact, and definable during the 1950-70 period. Some critics argued that "the price of cohesiveness was a civic leadership that was largely insulated from most of the City's population."[14] But that leadership, no less than the city, would not be insulated from economic forces. International Harvester, the Continental Illinois Bank, and First Federal Savings collapsed, as did several steel firms. Marshall Field, Montgomery Ward, Sunbeam, Chemetron, Fansteel, Transunion, and Northwest Industries — all Fortune 500 firms — were acquired, changed ownership, or even corporate locations. Old families, wealth, and corporate traditions faded. Major industrialists, retailers, and packers departed. Much new wealth and power stemmed from real estate interests and financial exchanges, whose leaders emerged as the business activists in Chicago's changing economic and political order. It remained the country's transportation center and, though much tarnished by economic change, it is still the focus of goods productions.

After the World's Columbian Exposition in Chicago in 1893, business and civic promoters championed the idea that the planning and development achieved for the World's Fair could be applied on a larger scale to the entire city. The Commercial Club of Chicago, comprising Chicago's most prominent business leaders, enlisted Daniel Burnham in 1909 to draft the Chicago Plan for the city's economic and physical development. Charles H. Wacker, chairman of the Chicago Plan Commission, and his colleague, Walter D. Murphy, sold the development plan to politicians and then to the general public through the newspapers, movie theaters, lecture series, and eventually to the public schools, which introduced an eighth-grade textbook explaining the plan.

So successful was this public-private partnership that no public bond issue related to the plan was ever defeated at the polls. The Burnham plan provided Chicago with a shared vision that would guide its development for generations to come. Charles Merriam observed: "The full development of this design is undoubtedly one of the most striking events in municipal history."[15]

Could business again play a major role in guiding Chicago's future? If civic guidance no longer begins and ends with City Hall, could leadership emerge from those outside the political structure? These questions are now taken seriously.

Whether motivated by pride or economic self-interest, Chicago's business community rallied in the early 1980s, seeking to rekindle the commitment that had rebuilt the city after the 1871 Chicago fire, reversed the flow of the Chicago River, and planned two successful world's fairs. Rising to the challenge, the Commercial

Club of Chicago, sponsor of the Burnham plan seventy-five years earlier, brought together 300 business, government, and academic leaders in 1983 to examine a decade of economic decline in the Chicago metropolitan area. Once having analyzed the area's strengths and weaknesses, the Commercial Club prepared a public plan to guide strategies for reversal — *Make No Little Plans: Jobs for Metropolitan Chicago*.

In addition to business-led task forces formed to capitalize on economic-growth opportunities, the Commercial Club undertook specific activities and projects supportive of its recommendations. It established a Chicagoland Enterprise Center to enhance small-business access to managerial and financial resources, formed a Financial Planning Committee to develop a strategic plan for Chicago's fiscal stability, and developed an Information Industry Council to promote the area's information-telecommunications position. To bring these and other new partnership activities together, the club started a monthly newsletter, *Chicago Enterprise*, to link burgeoning economic-development efforts throughout the metropolitan area.

The Commercial Club's new ventures proved to be catalytic, redirecting often disparate and competitive efforts toward a common objective — jobs. Like fitting pieces into a mosaic, other civic and business organizations would better relate to a consensual, if not a tangible, goal. Chicago United, a coalition of black, white, and Hispanic business leaders, was created in response to the urban upheavals of the 1960s. It would also redirect its efforts during the post-Daley era to school stabilization, minority purchasing, summer-youth employment, and overall urban economic development. The Chicago Central Area Committee, whose efforts since the 1950s had centered largely on the well-being of the central business district, redefined its master plan to include adjacent neighborhood development.

Chicago's utilities responded to a more deregulated environment and emerging new order by forming partnerships throughout the city with housing and consumer groups to promote housing preservation and energy conservation. The Chicago Energy Savers Fund, one of Chicago's largest, most innovative urban partnerships, now operates through a community-based delivery system as a collaborative effort to preserve the city's housing stock. Illinois Bell helped start "Friends of Small Business" and, with local foundations, the Community Equity Corporation to provide equity for small businesses in Chicago's neighborhoods. Neighborhood development corporations, a key linkage in business-community partnerships, now exist in more than fifty Chicago neighborhoods and operate through a peak association known as CANDO, an acronym for Chicago Association of Neighborhood Development Organizations.

The transition of labor to the new order has been more problematic. The building-trade unions had been at the very heart of the old Chicago partnership, an alliance based on the Chicago government's paying its members the prevailing private-industry wage as a buffer against public unionization of the city's work force. Between 1980 and 1985, the city's police, fire, and white-collar work forces were unionized with the American Federation of State, County and Municipal

Employees (AFSCME), representing formerly patronage-based white-collar municipal workers. AFSCME, with forty-four trade unions, now constitutes a labor coalition that represents more than 20,000 city employees. Pay comparability, affirmative action, and collective bargaining had arrived in Chicago, but not without a struggle. The full force of new labor has yet to materialize either in the city's changing politics or new partnership formation. It is likely to grow in the near future.

The most demonstrable change in Chicago partnerships is the changing focus from the often horizontal linkage — political, government, private-interest group system — to a more unstable, if not volatile, vertical linkage among segments of the old system and neighbor-community groups. Like other older cities, Chicago sprang from neighborhoods that were developed as almost independent communities with local employment, commercial strips, and support systems. Neighborhood traditions, ethnic institutions, parishes, and ward boundaries have been altered by time. Chicago's legacy to the country's urban-neighborhood movement runs deep and continuously — for example, Jane Addam's settlement houses, labor's activism, Saul Alinsky's pioneer community-organization efforts, and Gail Cincotta's national battles to stem financial institution disinvestment from troubled neighborhood lending.

Although most neighborhood-community organizations operated independently of the ward-based political structure, the tensions and conflict between them heightened under conditions of racial and economic change. Federal programs aimed at job and community development often reinforced the political structure in Chicago, contrasted to the participation-power dispersion that occurred in other cities. Machine breakup provided an impetus to community activism, enabling new groups and organizations to become part of Mayor Harold Washington's political contituency, set against the remnants of the old machine and its supporters.

Moving rapidly from a quasi-centralized, almost hierarchical structure of governance to a more decentralized, fluid activism has not come easily to Chicago. Long-festering problems like housing abandonment, gangs, school dropouts, and the education system will require years to improve, while revival of the area's economic base will require decades.

Promising beginnings may be found, for example, in new housing partnerships among Chicago's financial institutions, city government, and neighborhood housing rehabilitation networks. The Community Investment Corporation, using private capital to obtain public funds to preserve housing stock and neighborhoods, has been a successful partnership as the city's leading rehabilitation lender. The South Shore Bank of Chicago and its holding company, the Illinois Neighborhood Development Corporation, is a nationally acclaimed model of a partnership across sectors that has rehabilitated more than 3,000 housing units, stemming decline in changing neighborhoods. In education, the United Neighborhood Organization of Chicago, Chicago Schools Advisory Panel, Save Our City/Save Our Neighborhoods, Chicago United, and others have focused on the public schools and human-resource development. Local philanthropic foundations have become active participants in promoting these new partnerships.

In an earlier period, civic groups often functioned as electoral watchdogs in a dominant one-party city, viewing their principal role as a check on City Hall power. Narrow in focus and limited in effectiveness, civic groups experienced a rebirth in the post-Daley period. Some of these groups were Metropolitan Planning Council, TRUST, Community Renewal Society, and the City Club. Although sometimes overlapping in agendas—housing, race relations, transit, infrastructure, regional planning, and economic development—Chicago has no end of solutions to its problems.

As a major social and cultural force in Chicago partnerships, the Roman Catholic Archdiocese, the largest in North America, has also undergone profound change under Joseph Cardinal Bernardin, who succeeded John Cardinal Cody in 1982. The transition from Cody, the authoritarian prelate troubled by finances, Vatican II reforms, and sweeping urban events, to the new prelate's consensual and open style could not be more striking. As a leader of fellow bishops on theology and social positions, Cardinal Bernardin has moved to decentralize the church, involving laity and clergy in its governance.

Responding to its own demographic and economic problems—declining church attendance and parish consolidation within Chicago—the church has redefined its mission in the changing partnership scene, especially in education. The Archdiocese operates the country's largest parochial school system, with 270 schools and 100,000 students, one-half of whom are black and Hispanic. As Nicholas Lemann wrote recently in the *Atlantic Monthly*: "In the Chicago ghetto today the only institution with a record of consistently getting people out of the underclass are the parochial schools."[16]

## Partnerships Reconsidered

With all of its excesses and adverse publicity, Chicago's transformation should be considered remarkable. The old political order—ward structure, patronage employment, and domination of local elections—continues to disintegrate. Neighborhood and community organizations function as competitors and possible successors to the political ward organizations. Municipal unions and civil-service protection have transformed the old bureaucratic–trade-union power base. The business community has proved to be surprisingly resilient to change, adapting to its own leadership turnover. Civic groups have become a major force in modifying, if not shaping, political agendas. New immigrants have replaced old ones in the ethnic order of succession. Television camera crews are proving to be more effective than precinct captains in reaching the city's electorate.

An inward-looking, seemingly parochial large city is making progress in reaching out to its suburbs for a partnership based on interdependency and mutual needs. And the goal of making Chicago an international service center for finance and commerce has not been lost in efforts to accommodate an emerging new order but gradually redefined to allow those most affected by change to have a greater stake in progress.

This is not to conclude that the old order was bad or the new order is good but that change is constant. Historical revisionism can be unkind. From the 1930s to the mid-1950s, no major office construction took place in downtown Chicago. This period was followed by an architectural and building renaissance that ensured Chicago's place among world-class cities.

Democracy and its instrument, participation, also bring their own set of problems, a kind of hyperpluralism that, in full force, can work against stability and governance. Harold Washington's election as Chicago's mayor in 1983 was followed by a bitter power struggle over control of Chicago's fifty-member City Council. Because of a court-imposed remap of ward boundaries and special aldermanic elections in 1986, Chicago's mayor operates with a fragile majority within the council going into the 1987 city elections. Political battles have extended beyond city boundaries to regional authorities and the state legislature, often reducing the city's ability to focus on its immediate problems. All public controversies, large and small, seemingly end in protracted court battles among rival factions.

Faced with declining Federal assistance and scarce city resources, newly invigorated neighborhood organizations have attempted to pressure downtown real estate developers and commercial and financial interests to put money and expertise into the city's neighborhoods. The downtown-neighborhood cleavages run along geographic and functional lines. Some are highly constructive and positive, generating new partnerships and accommodations. Others are seemingly destructive and confrontational; their agendas include taxes, exactions, or simple retributions upon business for alleged past sins.

The older order has not entirely passed from the Chicago scene, nor has the new order become so firmly established that it dominates. Once the chasm between the neighborhoods and the downtown erupted on the political scene, discussions and debates among the two worlds would become acrimonious — us versus them — in the context of downtown development being antithetical to neighborhood activity. Efforts aimed at using new political leverage to gain economic empowerment amply test business leaders, who sometimes find such experiences new or foreign to their operations. Turning zero-sum political contests into win-win situations challenges all leaders, old and new.

Unsuccessful in their efforts to redevelop Chicago through the 1992 World's Fair, the Commercial Club and civic leaders have found the challenges of embracing the vast, complex economy of the Chicago metropolitan area far greater than efforts generations before that resulted in the Burnham plan. Equally formidable is the task of getting business together with the neighborhoods and city government on a semblance of equality, shared risks, and mutual benefits.

In sum, Chicago is not so much a case of partnerships that do not work but of public-private partnerships that worked in a previous period, under a particular set of conditions. The transition to a new order of partnerships requires time, patience, trust, and reestablishment of civic foundations that permit such partnerships to prosper.

In the transition from the old to the new, large-scale developments or anything that smacks of public-resource diversion to the downtown may fall victim to the shifting alliances of veto groups. In the meantime, the hundreds of new, innovative, and smaller partnerships provide the hope and basis for Chicago's painful but inevitable transition. Other older, large cities survived economic change. Urban political machines have collapsed before. The rising expectations of community and neighborhood groups have also clashed with major economic and business interests. Most cities, in fact, experienced these phenomena decades earlier and may be further along than Chicago in sorting them out.

But no other large, old city has emerged as the ultimate partnership that bridges the gulf between rich and poor, neighborhoods and downtown, city and suburbs, black and white. Public-private partnerships moving in that direction represent Chicago's great challenge. If that occurs, Chicago may again be a leader in urban development and public-private partnerships.

Chicago is a study of contrasts—ethnic diversity and racial tensions, parochialism and internationalism, individualism and bold collective actions, old and new politics. Its transition has been noisier, livelier, and tougher than the transitions of other cities. Opportunities have been missed in Chicago, but more promising and perhaps durable foundations are emerging.

## Notes

1. Dan Rottenberg, "The Power Connection," *Chicago Magazine*, February 1982, 108.
2. "Facing The Truth About Chicago," *Chicago Tribune*, 3 May 1982.
3. See Eugene Kennedy, "Hard Times in Chicago," *New York Times Magazine*, 9 March 1980, 20-40; John Helyar and Robert Johnson, "Tale of Two Cities," *Wall Street Journal*, 19 May 1986; and idem, "Brawling City: Chicago Political Rift Deepens, Worsening City's Many Problems," 6 Aug. 1984.
4. R. Scott Fosler and Renée Berger, "Public-Private Partnership: An Overview," in *Public-Private Partnership in American Cities*, ed. R. Scott Fosler and Renée Berger (Lexington, Mass.: Lexington Books, 1982), 6.
5. Charles E. Merriman, *Chicago* (New York: MacMillan Co., 1929), 5.
6. Milton Rakove, *Don't Make No Waves: Don't Back No Losers* (Bloomington: Indiana University Press, 1975),1.
7. Ibid., 33.
8. William Grimshaw, "The Daley Legacy: A Declining Politics of Party, Race, and Public Unions," in *After Daley*, ed. Samuel Gove and Louis Masotti (Urbana: University of Illinois Press, 1982), 66.
9. Rakove, "Jane Byrne and the New Chicago Politics," in ibid., 222.
10. *Chicago Tribune*, 3 May 1982.
11. *Chicago Sun-Times*, 12 Mar. 1981.
12. *Chicago Tribune*, 10-14 May 1981.
13. Chicago World's Fair-1992 Authority, *Core Site and Satellite Concept Plan* (Chicago: World's Fair Authority, Feb. 1985), 7.
14. Rottenberg, 108.
15. Merriman, 111.
16. Nicholas Lemann, "The Origins of the Underclass," *Atlantic Monthly*, July 1986, 67.

# The Future of Public-Private Partnerships

WILLIAM S. WOODSIDE

Public-private partnerships have now developed across a wide range of activities. Some involve enormous, multiple-sponsored undertakings, such as the revitalization of an entire downtown area. Others involve much smaller, more time-limited projects with a one-to-one relationship between a private partner and a nonprofit organization. Examples of successful models abound.

"Jobs for Connecticut's Future" is a statewide public-private partnership that seeks to predict the impact of economic and technological change on Connecticut's employment opportunities. The results will help the state's education and training institutions develop programs to meet these projected job requirements.

The 219 community-based Neighborhood Housing Services agencies are another example of successful public-private partnerships. Launched in Pittsburgh in the early 1970s as a local initiative, this model program has been successfully replicated across the nation by the autonomous, federally funded parent, Neighborhood Reinvestment Corporation. Today, local NHSs combine Federal, state, and local government investments with those of the private sector to revitalize older and decaying neighborhoods.

The New York City Job and Career Center, which was created by the New York City Partnership, opened 6 June 1986. It draws together corporate leaders, the education community, community service organizations, and government leaders so that young people can explore job opportunities more vigorously and more directly.

In the field of public education, the growth of corporate involvement in all kinds of school-business partnerships is a strong indication of a change in how corporations see themselves in relationship to contemporary society. The rapid proliferation of these school-business partnerships suggests just how far the business world has come in recognizing that it cannot exist as an island, walled off from the community.

---

These remarks were presented at "Public Private Partnerships," a conference sponsored by New York City Partnership, Inc., and the Academy of Political Science, New York, New York, 13 June 1986.

Instead of defining institutional relationships in terms of the barriers and differences that keep them apart, more and more corporations seek to define their relationship to community institutions in terms of common goals and shared values. At last, the private sector is beginning to acknowledge that no community can prosper if its members, including corporations, local public institutions, and nonprofit organizations have no contact with one another or have no common ground on which to meet and work together. In that sense, all partnership programs are important. They provide the business community with a much-needed window on the world beyond its front doorstep. But I am concerned that we may overlook, downplay, or wish away some serious shortcomings of the partnership concept.

When we look at the constellation of complex domestic problems this nation must address—poverty, hunger, homelessness, unemployment, and public education—I think we must recognize that public-private partnerships will prove to be an inadequate vehicle on which to depend. These partnerships can help us find some innovative solutions to certain aspects of those problems. By drawing attention to problems, for example, they can help us set the agenda. But they cannot by themselves solve major social problems, and we must not act as if they can.

I do not want to minimize the contributions that hundreds—indeed, thousands—of successful partnerships have made to the resolution of local problems. Rather, I want us—the members of civic and business communities—to realize that even in their aggregate these successful partnerships will continue to fall far short of eliminating or even substantially reducing the problem areas on which they are focused.

I realize that no one has actually said public-private partnerships were intended to be the answer to any national domestic problem. However, many people do have the impression that we do not have to worry much about cutbacks in government funding and public responsibility because public-private partnerships will fill the void. Thus, my concern revolves around the ambiguity of definition and the lack of clarity regarding the roles and responsibilities of the public and private partners.

What is it we are trying to accomplish in a partnership? In pursuing these goals, who is responsible for what? More important, who should be responsible for what? As we consider these kinds of questions, we need to remember that the concept of public-private partnerships came into vogue at the same time that limits on government spending and limits on government involvement in social programs started to become popular. Proponents of cutbacks in government programs and services seized on the partnership concept as evidence that government programs could be reduced without causing much harm, dislocation, or hardship. On the other hand, people who opposed these reductions, beaten at the polls in various elections, grasped at the partnership concept as a way of preserving some services that otherwise might be lost.

There is no question that we all subscribed to a very good idea. The problem is that we overstated its potential. And the danger is that by focusing on what is happening in the private sector, we may ignore what is happening, or not happening, in the public sector.

I want partnership programs to grow and flourish. But I do not want declining public support for public purposes to be the price we pay for private-sector involvement. And it is up to us, as business and civic leaders, to use our influence and our energy to make sure this does not happen.

A brief analysis of the issue of domestic hunger will illustrate what I mean. Although this is not the most commonly cited example of a public-private partnership, it does serve to highlight the issues that must be considered.

In the late 1960s and early 1970s the Federal government mounted a sizable attack on the problems of hunger and malnutrition in the United States. Through a combination of programs — such as the Special Supplemental Food Program for Women, Infants and Children, food stamps, and school meals — considerable progress had been made in eliminating some of the tragic conditions that existed in the late 1960s. But in the past five years, the Federal food assistance programs have been subjected to budget and regulatory pressures that have limited their capabilities. During this same period, domestic hunger has once again become a very serious problem.

In response to these reemerging conditions, many major food companies have made magnificent contributions of food and assistance to Second Harvest and its member food banks around the country. From a strictly programmatic point of view, this partnership has been outstanding. It has developed an efficient and effective operation to collect and redistribute donated food products around the country. Over the past six years, corporate donations of food to the Second Harvest network of food banks have grown from 2.5 million pounds to 100 million pounds.

But we must consider the public-policy questions that are inherent in this example. Are we making a substantial impact on the overall problem? Can private-sector donations of food replace cutbacks in Federal food assistance programs? My answer is no, and I think it is wishful thinking to suggest otherwise.

In the field of public education a recent proposal by Secretary of Education William Bennett provides another example. He wants to provide $600 worth of vouchers per child so low-income children who are not doing well in public schools can attend private schools. The issue, however, is not how one feels about vouchers, although I think the voucher proposal is seriously misguided. The issue is that vouchers are being proposed as a way of dismantling Federal aid to education. They are being proposed as an alternative to the Chapter I program (formerly Title I) at a time when the need for this program may be greater than at any time in its twenty-year history.

What will happen to the public schools if such a proposal should be enacted? Are school-business partnership programs going to provide the New York City schools with the $300 million they receive each year from the Chapter I program? The answer, of course, is *no*!

When corporations first started developing partnership programs several years ago, many of us said we did not want to become involved simply to let government off the hook. We said we did not want government using our involvement as an excuse to ignore its own responsibility. We said we did not want our programs to become a screen of voluntarism behind which an entire generation of young people, many of them underprivileged, would be denied basic opportunity and justice.

The time has come for us to make good on that promise. It is time for all of us to combine the knowledge we have gained with the resources already at our disposal and become organized advocates for an increased and more defined public role in such fields as education, hunger, employment, job training, and community development; not a role that tries to recreate the approaches of the 1960s, but rather a role that prepares us for the remainder of the 1980s and 1990s.

That means doing more than telling our corporate lobbyists to put in a good word for domestic social programs every now and then. It means more than sending an executive on a symbolic goodwill visit to Capitol Hill or asking an executive to testify at a public hearing. It means organizing ourselves into a vigorous, active political force so that we can help this country complete its unfinished social agenda and develop strategies and programs to implement that agenda. It means supporting candidates for elective office who share our views about the need to move this agenda forward. It means forming broad-based coalitions with other groups and organizations to work in behalf of our long-range goals.

Dale Mann, a professor at Teachers College, Columbia University, pointed this out more than a year ago. Professor Mann studied school-business partnerships in twenty-three large cities. He found that the dollar value of the grants, goods, and services the private sector provided in all those cities was about $25 million a year. While that may sound like a lot of money, it is in fact only a minuscule fraction of the annual costs of operating these school systems.

Professor Mann concluded that school leaders had to be far more systematic and thoughtful in developing programs that could mobilize these marginal resources in order to achieve the widest possible results. Partnership programs as a whole, he said, could achieve maximum results only if they matured into long-term programs of political support. "The most helpful results of school-business partnerships," Professor Mann said, "are those political coalitions aimed at major and permanent increases in financial support for public schools."

Some notable examples of what Professor Mann had in mind are the Business Roundtables in California and Minnesota and the Boston Compact. In California and Minnesota, roundtables not only have made it possible for business leadership to focus on public problems; they have also succeeded in obtaining increased funding for public education from their state legislatures. In Boston, the Boston Compact, formed in the wake of that city's problems with school desegregation, has produced strong working ties between individual schools and area industries.

Although Professor Mann addressed his remarks to school superintendents, the business community needs to hear his message as well. And the message is not limited to school-business partnerships.

Many of us in the corporate world vigorously support public-private partnerships. But have we been as vigorous in opposing public-policy decisions that we knew would have an adverse impact on the institutions with which we are involved or associated? We have often said our partnership programs were more than public-relations gimmicks. But have we advocated public-policy actions that would substantially improve the lives of the people with whom we are working in our partnership programs?

In the long run, the success of our partnership programs will depend not so much on what happens within each individual program. It will depend on the extent to which we are able to translate our success in individual programs into support for major social initiatives.

In an article in the *Harvard Business Review*, Fred Hechinger, education editor of the *New York Times*, wrote about this issue and the particular challenge it poses to that part of the business community supporting the public schools. "In the end," he said," all these cooperative ventures will amount to little more than public relations unless the business community abandons this frequently schizophrenic posture; supporting the local schools while simultaneously instructing or at least permitting, its lobbyists to support cuts in state and Federal expenditures for public education and such legislation as tax credits for parents whose children attend private schools. . . . Common sense should show the futility of any corporate policy that gives to the local schools with one hand and yet takes away funds with the other."[1]

The points Hechinger made with respect to school-business partnerships should be applied to the whole spectrum of public-private partnerships. We cannot have one social agenda for our partnership activities and another for our business activities. We need, instead, a vision of ourselves and our society in which it is possible to be both responsible business people and responsible citizens.

In the final analysis, we are a society of interdependent institutions. Whether we accept it or not, the business community has a long-term stake in how we as a society handle the social problems of today. Public-private partnerships can be helpful. But if they are inadequate to the problems we have laid at their doorstep, we should not let ourselves be deluded by the glow of good press notices. Let us be hard-nosed in our appraisals and become advocates of consistent public policies that will help us develop the best possible society. For the nation's long-term success depends not so much on the business decisions we make today or tomorrow but on the social policy we develop during the next decade.

NOTE

1. Fred Hechinger, "Turnaround for the Public Schools?" *Harvard Business Review* 63 (Jan.-Feb. 1985): 136–44.

# Index

Action Forum, 106
Adopt-A-School program, 10, 26, 32, 62, 65, 68, 124
Advisory Council on Private Sector Initiatives, 26
Advocacy, public policy, 74–86, 128, 134
Allegheny Conference for Community Development, 1, 7, 35, 63
Allen, Ivan, Jr., 105–7
American Can Company, 65
American Federation of State, County and Municipal Employees (AFSCME), 40, 145–46
Armour, Philip, 142
Atlanta Chamber of Commerce, 104, 106
Atlanta Economic Development Corporation, 103
Atlanta, Georgia, 100–110; Midtown, 103; Midtown Business Association, 107; Peachtree Center, 139; Underground District, 102–3
Atlanta Regional Commission, 104

Baker, Howard, 16
Baker, James, 15–16
Baltimore, Maryland: Charles Center/Inner Harbor, 9, 11, 139; Harborplace, 10–11, 51, 102. *See also* Greater Baltimore Committee
Bankers Trust Company, 88
Bank of Boston, 63
Basic Industry Research Laboratory, 54, 58
Bennett, William, 152
Bernardin, Joseph Cardinal, 147
Block grants, 28

Booz, Allen & Hamilton, 124
Boston Compact, 46, 63, 153
Boston Housing Partnership, 46, 113
Boston, Massachusetts, 47–48, 51–52; Faneuil Hall, 51, 102; Quincy Market, 9, 10
Boyer, Ernest, 65
Brademas, John, 133
Bradley, Richard, 44
Bronx, New York, 117, 119
Brooklyn, New York, 87–99, 117, 119, 124; Atlantic Center, 87; ATURA (Atlantic Terminal Urban Renewal Area), 90–91
Brooklyn Union Gas Company, 90
*Brown* v. *Board of Education*, 104
Budget cuts. *See* Federal aid, cutbacks in
Building Trade's Carpenters Union, 119
Burnham, Daniel, 1, 144
Burnham plan. *See* Chicago Plan
Business Roundtable, 16, 153
Byrne, Jane, 141, 143

California, 27, 33, 52, 153. *See also* Proposition 13
California Business Roundtable, 64
Calthorpe, Peter, 93
CANDO (Chicago Association of Neighborhood Development Organizations), 145
*Capitalism, Socialism and Democracy*, 37
Carey, Hugh, 129
Carnegie Foundation, 39
Carter, Jimmy, 28, 113; administration of, 4–13, 27
Catherine's Stout Shoppe, 67

Central Area Study, I and II, 102
Central Atlanta Improvement Association, 101
Central Atlanta Progress, 100–110
CETA (Comprehensive Employment and Training Act), 16
Chauncey, Sam, 59
Chemetron Corp., 144
Chevron Oil Co., 27
Chicago Central Area Committee, 145
Chicago Energy Savers Fund, 145
*Chicago Enterprise*, 145
Chicago, Illinois, 137–49; Age of Discovery (1992), 143; Century of Progress (1933–34), 143; ethnic composition of, 141, 149; infrastructure of, 143, 147; ward system of, 141, 147; World's Columbian Exposition (1893), 143–44; World's Fair (1992), 142–43, 148
Chicagoland Enterprise Center, 145
*Chicago Magazine*, 137
Chicago Plan, 1, 144–45, 148
Chicago Plan Commission, 144
Chicago River, 144
Chicago Schools Advisory Panel, 146
*Chicago Sun Times*, 142
*Chicago Tribune*, 137, 142
Chicago 21/Dearborn Park Project, 138
Chicago United, 145–46
Chief executive officers, 127–36
Citizens Forum/National Municipal League, 44
City University of New York, 37
Cleveland, Ohio, 4, 36
Colorado, 45
Columbus, Ohio, 28
Commercial Club of Chicago, 1, 144–45, 148; Financial Planning Committee, 145; Information Industry Council, 145
Commercial Equity Corporation, 145
Commission of Black New Yorkers, 37
Committee for Economic Development, 8–9, 138; Research and Policy Committee, 8
Community Development Block Grants, 7, 113, 115
Communities in Schools program, 65
Community Investment Corporation, 146
*Community Power Structure*, 103–4

Community Reinvestment Act (1978), 121
Community Renewal Society, 147
Connecticut, 96, 150
Construction costs, 88
Continental Illinois Bank, 144
Council on Foundations, 29
Coyne, James, 25–26
Crime, 53, 96, 103. *See also* Crime Stoppers program; Youth gangs
Crime Stoppers program, 33, 128
*Critical Issues for National Urban Policy*, 9
Crown Zellerbach, 27
Cuomo, Mario, 82, 129, 133


Daley, Richard J., 137–38, 141–42
Dallas, Texas, 62–63
Day-care centers, 103
*Death of Cities*, 45
Deaver, Michael, 16, 21, 28
Denver, Colorado, 32–33, 35, 38–39, 42, 46; Larimer Square, 9
Detroit, Michigan, 4
Dole, Elizabeth, 16
Dorf & Stanton Communications, 67
Downtown Denver Partnership, 39
Downtown redevelopment, 5, 38–39, 51, 87–99
Drucker, Peter, 2


Economic Development Administration (EDA), 27
Economic Development Council, 123, 127, 131, 135
Economic-development projects, 78, 82, 128
Economic Opportunity Atlanta, 107
Education, public, 34, 36, 60–73, 82, 84, 146, 150, 152–53. *See also* School-business partnerships
Elitism, 39
Emmerich, Charles O., 107
Employment, youth, 10, 82, 128. *See also* CETA (Comprehensive Employment Training Act); Summer Jobs program; Youth Employment Program
Energy: costs, 78, 82, 88; preservation, 145

Energy, U.S. Department of, 54
Enterprise zones, 7, 78, 82
Environmentalists, 58
Evans, John, 49
Evanston, Illinois, 47, 49–51, 54–59
Evanston Inventure, 51, 54, 57
Executive volunteers, 116–17
Exxon Education Foundation, 64

Family Housing Assistance Fund, 113
Fansteel, Inc., 144
Fantus Company, 92
Federal aid, cutbacks in, 8, 18, 25, 29, 33, 50, 52, 61, 116, 148, 151
Federal Home Loan Bank, 113
Federal Housing Administration (FHA), 112
Filer, John, 20
First Federal Savings, 144
Fiscal reform, 82
Flaherty, Pete, 35–36
Food stamps, 152
Fosler, Scott, 44
France, 28
Friends of Small Business, 145
Fulton County [Georgia] Commission, 104

Gardner, John, 24, 39
Georgia, 40. *See also* Central Atlanta Progress
Georgia State University, 107
Goals of partnerships, 80–83
Golden, Howard, 89, 93
Government National Mortgage Corporation, 112
Gramm-Rudman-Hollings Act (1985), 133
Greater Baltimore Committee, 7
Grenada, 27
Grimshaw, William, 141

Hands Across America, 34
Harrington, Michael, 34
Harris, Sydney, 36
Hartsfield, William, 105

*Harvard Business Review*, 154
Health and Hospitals Corporation, 93–94
Health and Human Services, U.S. Department of, 26
Hechinger, Fred, 154
Hill, Jesse, 106
Hilton Hotels, 95
Homelessness, 4, 25. *See also* Housing
Homeport, 84
Housing, 10, 33, 45, 82, 84, 94, 111–21, 125, 133–34, 145–47. *See also* Boston Housing Partnership; Housing Partnership Development Corporation (HPDC); Jubilee Housing; Neighborhood Housing Services; New York City Housing Partnership
Housing and Urban Development, U.S. Department of, 27
Housing Partnership Development Corporation (HPDC), 116, 118–19
Housing Partnership Mortgage Corporation, 115
Houston, Texas, 23, 28, 63, 66
Hunger, 18, 152. *See also* Hands Across America; School lunch program
Hunter, Floyd, 103–4

Illinois General Assembly, 142
Illinois Neighborhood Development Corporation, 146
Income, per capita, 37
Indianapolis, Indiana, 42
Inflation, 4
Interest rates, 4, 111
International Business Machines (IBM), 62–63, 65, 67
Internal Revenue Code: section 501(c) (3), 76; section 501(c)(6), 76–77
International Downtown Association, 101
International Harvester, 144
*Investing in America*, 23
*Investing in Our Children*, 64

Jackson, Ira, 104
Jackson, Maynard, 103–5, 108–9

Jacobs, Jane, 45
Japan, 27, 48
Javits Civic Center, 139
Jersey City, New Jersey, 88
Jobs for Connecticut's Future, 150
Johnson, Lyndon B., 15, 29; administration of, 14
Join-A-School program, 78, 128, 133–34
Jubilee Housing, 10

Kean, Thomas H., 79
Kid's Place program, 46
King, Martin Luther, Jr., 105, 142
Kinley Enterprises, 102
Koch, Edward I., 88, 93–94, 129
Koppers Co., 38
Korea, 48
KTVI television station, 63, 67
Kucinich, Dennis J., 36

Labor unions, 32, 36, 40, 42, 119, 130, 137, 145–47. *See also* American Federation of State, County and Municipal Employees (AFSCME)
Lamm, Richard, 45
Lane, Mills B., 106
Leadership Atlanta, 106
Lederberg, Joshua, 124
Light Up Atlanta, 109
Lincoln Center, 139
Loans, long-term development, 8
Lobbying. *See* Advocacy, public policy
Lomax, Michael, 104
Longworth, R.C., 142
Los Angeles, California, 65, 66
Los Angeles Dodgers Corporation, 63
Lugar, Richard, 42
Luntey, Eugene, 89
Lyet, J. Paul, 77, 128
Lyman, Richard, 24

Macchiarola, Frank J., 46, 89, 93
McCormick, Cryus, 142

McKesson Corporation, 66, 71
McKinsey & Company, 123, 127
Maddox, Lester, 105
*Make No Little Plans for Chicago: Jobs for Metropolitan Chicago*, 145
Management and Budget, Office of (OMB), 24, 29
Manhattan, borough of, 77–78, 87
Manhattan Central Business District, 87–89
Mann, Dale, 70, 147, 153
Marshall Field & Co., 144
MARTA (Metropolitan Atlanta Rapid Transit Authority), 106, 109
Martin, Joe, 14
Massell, Sam, 107
Media, the 40–41, 45
Meese, Edwin III, 16
Memphis, Tennessee, 67–68
Merriam, Charles, 140
Metropolitan Planning Council, 147
Metrotech, 90, 95
Midwest, 51
Milwaukee, Wisconsin: Grand Avenue and Theatre District projects, 9
Minneapolis, Minnesota, 113
Minnesota, 153
Minorities, 43, 95, 139
Mississippi (state), 40, 64
Moderate Income Housing Program, 133
Monsanto Corporation, 67
Montgomery Ward & Co., 144
Moore, Donald, 88
Moorhead, Jay, 21, 24–25
Morgan Stanley & Company, 95
Mosbacher, Robert Jr., 15–16
Municipal Assistance Corporation, 77, 94, 132–33
Murphy, Walter D., 144

National Alliance of Business (NAB), 14
National Association of Manufacturers, 16
National Federation of Independent Businesses, 16
National Research Council, 5, 9
National School Volunteer Program, 65
*National Urban Policy*, 5–7, 12
National Urban Policy, Committee on, 5

National Year of Partnerships in Education (1984), 61
Neighborhood Housing Services, 150
Neighborhood Reinvestment Corporation, 113, 150
New England Telephone Company, 59
New Federalism, 15–16
New Haven, Connecticut, 47, 49–50, 53–55, 58–59
New Jersey, 78, 88
*Newsweek*, 25
New York Alliance for the Public Schools, 64
New York Chamber of Commerce and Industry, 123, 127, 131
New York City, 34, 37, 40–41, 44–46, 79, 87–99 passim, 113–19, 122–36; Battery Park, 139; Board of Education, 82, 135; Emergency Financial Control Board, 77, 132; fiscal crisis of 1975, 4, 36, 39, 77, 122, 127, 129; 132; public schools, 60, 64, 152; South Street Seaport, 102; Transit Authority, 135. *See also* New York City Partnership
New York City Community Preservation Corporation (CPC), 114, 116, 125
New York City Housing Partnership, 82; New Homes Program, 116–18, 125
New York City Job and Career Center, 150
New York City Partnership, 31, 33, 41, 45, 63, 74–86 passim, 89, 115–16, 127–36, 150; Business Labor Working Group, 130; Committeee on Public Issues, 86, 133; "Competing for Back Offices" report, 90; High Technology Committee, 124; Project Planning Review Committee, 130. *See also* Join-A-School program; Moderate Income Housing Program; New York City Housing Partnership; New York City Job and Career Center; New York City Community Preservation Corporation; State Affordable Homeownership Development Program; Youth Employment Program
*New York Daily News*, 94, 123
New York State, 34, 79, 81, 130; State Affordable Homeownership Development Program, 118

New York State Power Authority, 82
*New York Times*, 18, 154
Nonprofit Coordinating Committee of New York (NPCC-NY), 81
Northwest Industries, 144
Northwestern University, 49–57, 59
Not-for-profit organizations, 130

Occupational Safety and Health Administration (OSHA), 7
Office space, 88, 93–95
Ohio, 28
Olin Corporation, 49, 51, 53

Palmer, Potter, 142
*Partnership Blueprint, The: Strengthening New York as a World City*, 80
Partnership, definition of, 6, 31–33, 122, 139
Partnerships Data Net, 27
PATHS (Philadelphia Alliance for Teaching Humanities in the Schools), 64
Pennsylvania, 41
Phelan, John J., Jr., 28
Philadelphia City Science Center, 49
Philadelphia, Pennsylvania, 10, 41, 47, 49
Philanthropy, 29
Pittsburgh, Pennsylvania, 7, 35, 41–42, 45; Renaissance II, 139
Polytechnic Institute of New York, 90
Port Authority of New York and New Jersey, 78
Poverty, 37, 109
Presidential Board of Advisors on Private Sector Initiatives, 28
President's Task Force on Private Sector Initiatives, 14–30 passim
Private Sector Initiatives, Office of, 25–27
Proposition 2½, 4, 64
Proposition 13, 4, 64
Public-approval process, 94–96
Public-policy positions, 78
"Public-Private Partnership: An Opportunity for Urban Communities," 8–9
Public/Private Ventures, Inc. (P/PV), 10
Public-safety programs, 78

Pullman, George, 142

Race relations, 100, 103–10, 141, 147. See also Minorities
Rakove, Milt, 141
Reagan, Nancy, 21
Reagan, Ronald, 17, 61, 116, 122, 129; administration of, 12, 14–30, 33, 42
Real Estate Board of New York, 89
Regan, Donald, 28
Regan, Edward, 82
Regional Plan Association (RPA), 79, 88–89, 98
Research, funding for, 54–57
Research Triangle, 52
RiverWalk, 9
Robinson, James D. III, 86, 133
Rockefeller, David, 1, 31, 33, 42, 74, 77, 83, 89, 94, 114, 116, 127, 131
Rohatyn, Felix, 133
Rose Associates, 91–99 passim
Rosebush, James, 17, 21
Rose, Fred, 91–99 passim
Rose, Jonathan, 91–99 passim
Rosenwald, Julius, 74
Rouse Company, 102
Rouse, James, 1, 10
Rudin, Lewis, 83
Russell, Herman J. and Company, 102
Ryan, Frederick, 28

St. Louis, Missouri, 1, 61–63, 66–67, 72
St. Paul, Minnesota, 113; Galleria, 9
Salomon Brothers, 91
San Antonio, Texas: RiverWalk, 9
San Diego, California, 28
San Francisco, California, 23, 71; Corporate Action Committee, 66
San Francisco Chamber of Commerce, 27–28
Save Our Schools/Save Our Neighborhoods, 146
School-business partnerships, 60–73, 150, 152–54
School lunch program, 33, 154
Schools, public. See Education, public

Schumpeter, Joseph, 37
Science Park, 51, 53–54, 58
Science Park Development Corporation, 54
Seattle, Washington, 46
Second Harvest, 152
Security Pacific National Bank, 65
Seed-capital corporations, 58
Seed programs, 17
Shinn, Richard, 77
Skidmore, Owings, and Merrill, 93
Small Business Administration (SBA), 27
Small businesses, 28, 43, 57, 145
South Shore Bank of Chicago, 146
Southwestern Bell, 1, 61–62, 66, 72
Special Supplemental Food Program for Women, Infants and Children, 152
Stagflation, 4
Stamford, Connecticut, 28
Staten Island, New York, 117
Straus, Ellen Sulzberger, 123–24
Summer Jobs program, 128, 134
Supply-side economics, 16
Sweat, Dan, 107–8

Taiwan, 48
Targeted Jobs Tax Credits, 82, 84
Taxes, 81–84, 86, 88, 95, 134; property, 50–53, 140. See also Tax reform
Tax reform, 83–84, 133
Technological Institute, 57
Technological Commercialization Center, 57–58
Texas, 33, 65
Thornburgh, Richard, 41
Thrifty Corporation, 66
Tocqueville, Alexis de, 1, 138–39
Toledo, Ohio: Sea Gate, 9
Treasury, U.S. Department of, 28–29
Tuchman, Barbara, 39

UDAG (Urban Development Action Grant), 10–11, 27, 78, 82, 94, 117, 125; Assistance Fund, 113
Underground Festival Development Company, 102

Unemployment, 4, 14, 18, 25, 53, 129, 140
United Neighborhood Organization of Chicago, 146
Universities, 47–59, 130. *See also* City University of New York; Georgia State University; Northwestern University; Yale University
Urban fiscal crisis, 4, 50. *See also* New York City, fiscal crisis of
Urban infrastructure, 7, 58. *See also* Chicago, infrastructure of
Urban renewal, 5–7, 9, 11–12, 51, 53, 101–4

Van Gelder, Lindsy, 88
Verity, C. William, Jr., 17–20, 24–25
Voinovich, George, 36
VOLUNTEER (National Center for Citizen Involvement), 21, 26
Volunteer fire departments, 42

Volunteerism, 42

Wacker, Charles H., 144
Ward, Montgomery, 142
Washington, Harold, 141, 146, 148
Westway, 80–81, 84
Whitehead, John, 89–90, 93, 124
Williamson, Richard, 16
Wood, Robert E., 142

Yale University, 49–55, 58–59; Office of Sponsored Research, 58
Yates, Sidney, 54
Young, Andrew, 104, 108–10
Young and Rubicam, 117
Youth Employment Program, 133
Youth gangs, 109